Information Landscapes : A Scenario
(Dr. PSG Kumar Festchrift)

INFORMATION LANDSCAPES : A SCENARIO
(Dr. PSG Kumar Festchrift)

Editor
Dr. Shalini R. Lihitkar
Assistant Professor,
Department of Library and Information Science,
Rashtrasant Tukadoji Maharaj Nagpur University, Nagpur

Ess Ess Publications
New Delhi

INFORMATION LANDSCAPES : A SCENARIO
(Dr. PSG Kumar Festchrift)

ISBN : 978-81-933597-3-0

First Published 2017

Published by:
Ess Ess Publications
4831/24, Ansari Road,
Darya Ganj,
New Delhi-110 002.
INDIA
Phones: 23260807, 41563444
Fax: 41563334
E-mail: info@essessreference.com
www.essessreference.com

Cover Design by *Patch Creative Unit*

Printed and bound in India

Contents

Dr. PSG Kumar : The Subject

Preface

AUTOMATION SOFTWARE

1 Implementation of Libsys Automation Software in the Madras School of Economics Library, Chennai: Issue, Challenges, Problems and Prospects 1
K. Baskar
S K Asok Kumar

CONSORTIA

2 Consortia Based Approach for Resource Sharing in Library & Information Network: Some Experiences from the ICMR 20
K V Ratnakar
Sunil Kumar Bisht
K Satyanarayana

3 Current Trends of Library Consortia in India 27
S. M. Nikose

CONTENT ANALYSIS

4 Content Analysis of Open Access LIS Journal "Webology" (2005 -2009) 38
Rahul S Lokhande
A N Chikate

CONTENT CREATION

5 Content Curation : Quality of Information for Knowledge Based Research 54
M Natarajan

CYBER SOCIETY

6 Role of Library Professionals in Cyber Society 72
D.R.Gabhane

DATABASE CORRECTION

7 VTLS-VIRTUA - Books Database Correction: A Case Study of Indira Gandhi Memorial Library, University of Hyderabad 77
R Pommal Rao
A Panikkar
B Isthari

DIGITAL LIBRARIES

8 Open Source for Library Systems and Digital Libraries 86
G. Sujatha

9 Digital and Virtual Library Resources for Veterinary Science Education: An Overview 98
K.Veeranjaneyulu
G. Rathinasabapathy

10 Open Access and Digital Repositories in Scholarly Communication : An Institutional Experience 110
Y M Patil
Girija Srinivasa

E-RESOURCES

11 A Catalogue of E-Resources in Social Sciences with a Special Reference to Sociology 137
Jivesh Bansal
Vinod Kumar

E-GOVERNANCE etc.

12 Excelling Communications Through E-Governance and E-Learning 145
Bibha Prasad Panda
Dilip K Swain

INFORMATION, KNOWLEDGE AND WISDOM

13 Information, Knowledge, Wisdom : A Value Added Pyramid 159
M P Satija

INSTITUTIONAL REPOSITORIES

14 Contributors, Users and Benefits of Institutional Repositories of Delhi and NCR : A Case Study 176
Nazrul Islam Azmi

KNOWLEDGE AUDIT

15 Knowledge Audit of Social Mobile Applications 185
P.B.Jain

ONLINE REFERENCE MANAGEMENT

16 Online Reference Management Software: An Overview 192
Shalini Lihitkar
Archana More

OPEN ACCESS

17 Emerging Open Access Environment Vis-à-vis Copyright 204
Amitabha Chatterjee

18 Publishing an Open Access Journal : An Introduction 215
M.R.Murali Prasad

OPEN SOURCE SOFTWARE

19 KOHA : An Open Source Library Management Software 223
Khaiser Nikam
M Nandish Kumar

PUBLIC LIBRARIES

20 Post Independence Childrens and Other Public Libraries in Delhi 229
Prof C P Vashishth

21 Use of 24/7 Hours Reading Room Facility in Prof. S.S. Basavanal Library: A Study 249
Gururaj S. Hadagali
Satishkumar Naikar
M.M. Bachalapur
Satish V. Totar

RESEARCH PUBLICATIONS

22 Research Publication Trends Among College Librarians In North Maharashtra University, Jalgaon 258
Rahul B. Khandare
Shashank S. Sonwane
B. G. Mukhyadal

SCHOLARLY COMMUNICATION

23 Scholarly Communication and Evaluation through Metrics: From Librametrics to Altmetrics 277
Prof. B Ramesh Babu

SOCIAL NETWORKING

24 Social Networking in Libraries: Making Awareness Among the Library Professionals 300
Giriraj Halkar

25 Social Networking Sites (SNS) and Library Services 316
P. Phani Bhargavi

TOTAL QUALITY MANAGEMENT

26 Quality Management (TQM): Requisite for Libraries to Succeed and Survive in Digital Environment 330
J Lohia

VIRTUAL REFERENCE SERVICE

27 Virtual Reference Service in IISC/IISER Libraries : User Awareness 349
Amol D. Khobragade
Shalini R. Lihitkar

WEB BASED SERVICES

28 Web Based Library and Information Services 359
Sandeep S. Pradhan

29 Changing Mode of Libraries Towards Web-Based Services 379
Rajwant Kaur
Balkar Singh

WEB 2.0, WEB 3.0 etc.

30 Web 2.0, 3.0, Cloud Computing 388
Sunil H. Urkudkar

WRITING MATERIAL

31 Alphabets, Writing Materials and their Preservation: A Historical Perspective 403
Sukhdev Singh

Dr. PSG Kumar : The Subject

ACADEMIC CAREER

Born on 9 June 1946 at Bapatla (Andhra Pradesh), he has his schooling at Board/Municipal High School, Bapatla. He was a student of the first batch of the Bapatla College of Arts and Science doing Pre-University course. He did B.Sc. (Agri) from the Agricultural College, Bapatla. Thereafter, we developed interest in the field of librarianship and obtained B.Lib.Sc. from Andhra University and M.Lib.Sc. from Hindu University, Banaras. He had a brilliant academic record with a first division from B.Sc. (Agri) to M.Lib. Sc. He topped all the successful candidates at M.Lib.Sc. at B.H.U. He did course on 'Advanced Courses in Information Work' at shaffiord in 1978; and doctorate in library and information sciences from Gulbarga University in 1985.

PROFESSIONAL RECORD

He started his career as Lecturer in Library Science at IT Collage, Lucknow and within four months shifted to BHU, Varanasi. He moves to Nagpur University in 1973 and served there till retirement in various capacities. He devoted all his energies for teaching, research, librarianship, library associations, library structure, etc. and carved a notch for himself in the mind of professionals in India and abroad.

He served for 28 years as a teacher of Library and Information Science; 10 years as University Librarian; and 24 years as Head of the University Department of Library and Information Science. He was/is associated with 86 universities in India in various capacities. He was a member/secretary/chairman of 51 academic bodies all over India.

Apart from teaching research and administration, he organised about a dozen national conferences, seminars, workshops, etc. He attended around 140 national and international conferences.

A PROLIFIC WRITER

He has to his credit 58 books on diverse branches of library and information science. Important series published by him includes : 1 Kumar's Curriculum Series (16 Volumes); Library Movement and Library Development in India (15 Volumes); Indian Encyclopedia of Library and Information Science (28 Volumes) currently in Press.

He wrote more than 160 technical papers; 75 reviews, 9 forewords, etc. Besides he has been associated with 17 professional journals as editor or member of the Editorial Board.

RESEARCH GUIDANCE

So far 32 students have obtained Ph. D. under his guidance. He served as examiner of more than 30 doctoral studies. He also guided 52 M Lib Sc dissertations.

MATCHLESS ORGANISOR

His activities as President of Vidarbha Academic Libraries Association (VALA) (1983 - 86), As General Secretory, Vice-President and President of Indian Association of Teachers of Library and Information Science (IATLIC) (for 10 years); As chairman of the Central Sectional Committee on Education and Training (ET), as

Vice-President (two terms) and finally as President of Indian Libraries Association (ILA) (for another 10 years); As Council Member of Indian Association of Special Libraries and Information Centres (IASLIC) (4 years); As President of Library Association of SAARC Countries (LA SAARC), Good Offices Committee (GOC), President, Joint Council of Library Associations in India (JOCLAI), and as Founder Chairman of Indian Foundation for Library and Information Services he made women service to the cause of library profession in India. He is a life member of 8 professional bodies.

He is a first person to get elected as President of Indian Library Association outside of Delhi and first from South including Maharashtra to occupy the Presidentship. He got 91% of votes polled through a nation-wide postal ballet which is a record in the annals of the association.

At nagpur University, he worked as Secretary and President of the Heads Forum; Vice-President and President of Association of University Teachers (AUT) and Registrar of the University.

WIDER CONTACTS

He had been to UK, USA, Mauritius and France on invitation and participated in the conferences of IFLA (International Federation of Library Associations and Institutions); FID (International Federation for Documentation); COMLA (Commonwealth Library Association); ALA (American Library Association); International Conference on Francoridian Relations (La Reunion) enhanced his international contacts. He had been to almost all corners of the country and has delivered 25 keynote addresses at National Seminars and even 200 lectures at various institutions. He gave 6 radio talks and 2 TV interviews.

His biography has been included in more than 16 international and national biographical dictionaries. A biopic (video) on autobiography were released recently.

FELLOWSHIP / HONOURS

He received UNESCO/FID/IFLA Fellowship in 1975; USIA Fulbright Fellowship in 1988 and was selected for International Man of the Year (UK) (1998), Man of the year (USA) (1998), Secular India Award (2000); Panjab Librarian Award (2001), P S Telugu University Honour (2003); Ranganathan - Kaula Gold Medal (2005); etc. which speak of his international and national recognition.

He was felicitated at different places in India and was decorated with the title "*Granthalaya Sastra Ratna*" in 2006 by the Vidarbha Library Association.

RECOGNITION

Recognising his matchless contribution in the field of library and information science he was felicitated by an International Festschrift Committee at the time of his retirement and presented the Festschrift titled "Library and Information Profession in India : Reflections and Redemptions" (in 3 volumes). In his honour :

1. Dr. PSG Kumar Oration on Library and Information Science (at RTM Nagpur University);
2. ILA — Dr. PSG Kumar Life-time Achievement Award (Indian Library Association); and
3. Dr. PSG Kumar Library Foundation (Nagpur) were instituted.

Dr. PSG Kumar Library Foundation is publishing *Mahitiyug* (Marathi); and *Information Age* (English) since 2006 and 2007 respectively.

Preface

It will not be an exaggeration if we say that there may be no one in the library profession in India we have not heard about Dr. Kumar nor read his books.

He was contributed humanely to library literature provided outstanding leadership through various library associations in India. He was president of Indian Association of Teachers of Library and Information Science (IATLIS); Indian Library Association (ILA), etc.

He provided excellent leadership as Head of the Department of Library and Information Science; as University Librarian; as Registrar; as President of Heads Forum; President of Association of University Teachers; and through various academic bodies of Nagpur University.

In view of his multifarious contribution to his library profession and particularly to RTM Nagpur University, we, some of the students of Dr. Kumar decided to bring-out a Festschrift in his honour on his 71st birthday.

Though the time given for contribution was short there has been a good response. The Festschrift committee take this opportunity to thank every one who sent their papers for inclusion in the volume.

Thanks also to M/s Ess Ess Publications, New Delhi for coming forward to publish this volume.

I hope the contents provide a good reading to library professionals.

Shalini R. Lihitkar

1

Implementation of LIBSYS Automation Software in the Madras School of Economics Library, Chennai: Issues, Challenges, Problems and Prospects

K. Baskar
Librarian, Madras School of Economics
Gandhi Mandapam Road, Behind Government
Data Center, Kotturpuram, Chennai 600 025
S K Asok Kumar
University Librarian i/c
Tamil Nadu Dr Ambedkar Law University
Chennai 600 028

INTRODUCTION

An automated library is one where a computer system is used to manage one or several of the library's key functions such as acquisition, circulation, cataloguing, serial control and Online Public Access catalogue (OPAC). Library automation refers to the processing of certain routine works of the library, with the help of computers and other allied machineries. In other words, mechanization of library housekeeping operations, predominately by computerization is known as Library Automation.

PLANNING FOR LIBRARY AUTOMATION

Computerisation of any library operations involves three basic factors; the hardware, the software and the user. These are not independent factors. The hardware requirement will depend to some extent upon the specific software that is being used. There are two main types of software; the system software and the application software. It is the system software that controls the functioning of the computer and its peripherals. It may contain the operating system, the compilers, the utilities etc. each of which is a programme. Application software is designed for a specific task and they are platform dependent. Planning is the process by which we make decisions about what to do and how we will do it. (Bhardwaj and Shukla, 2000).

MADRAS SCHOOL OF ECONOMICS (MSE): A BRIEF NOTE

The Madras School of Economics came into existence in 1995, thanks to the vision and efforts of some leading academicians, industrialists and financial institutions in India. The primary objective was to create a centre that would nurture quality teaching and research programs in economics. Within a short span of time it has realized this objective and is today counted among the premier institutes for higher education and research in economics in India. The MSE library is rapidly building up to be one of the leading professional research and reference libraries in Chennai. All bibliographic details of books, journals, reports and CD-ROM databases are accessible through the campus-wide Ethernet network from a dedicated OPAC server. The library of the Institute aims to be a leading research library in the fields of Economics, Econometrics, Mathematical Economics,

Macroeconomics, Microeconomics, International economics, Financial economics, Capital Markets, Environmental Economics, Energy Economics and Agricultural Economics. MSE library has over 26426 volumes, which includes 11713 Books, 5883 Reports, 746 Theses, 3337 Working Papers, 134 Occasional Papers, 807 Discussion Papers and it subscribes to over 50 national and international journals. The card catalogue is computerized using the LIBSYS software. MSE library has been included in the IMF Depository Library Programme. Bibliographic details of books, journals, reports, and CD-ROM databases are accessible through a campus-wide network. Online Public Access Catalogue has been installed in the journal section for the general users. The library provides access to the resources through UGC Infonet consortia.

LIBSYS

Library software has become the most powerful tool for changing the scenario of libraries from traditional to automated, from automated to electronic, from electronic to digital, and from digital to virtual. Software has become increasingly more sophisticated and the introduction of new applications has increased. LIBSYS is one of the very highly demanded Library management software across the India and offers solution such as Library automated system.

LIBSYS, a software company, is engaged in providing software solution since 1984. LIBSYS is an integrated library management software package designed and developed by LIBSYS Corporation has made LIBSYS the most trusted brand for libraries in India for almost three decades. Its wide acceptance in market strengthens its population as the most field proven library system with unmatched depth in functionality and features. Libsys is a complete and a comprehensive library system that manage all aspects of all kind of libraries(Public, National, higher Education and Research library) Libsys modules include Acquisition, Cataloguing, Circulation, Serials Control, Acquisition, Web OPAC, Inventory management and System management. Libsys is a fully integrated Information management system which uses a shared database eliminating the need for redundant data entry. Transaction takes place in real time, which ensure that whatever information is displayed is accurate and up to date . It runs all modules concurrently and allows the user to move quickly and easily between modules . .

DESIGN AND IMPLEMENTATION OF THE LIBSYS IN MADRAS SCHOOL OF ECONOMICS, CHENNAI

LIBSYS is best used for Library automation in most of the libraries. Therefore, this software has high priority on the basis of cost and efficiency. The implementation of the LIBSYS has been demonstrated in the Madras School of Economics Library, Chennai by presenting the screen shots of the out puts of various modules and provisions. Screen shots of the LIBSYS software in Madras School of Economics Library

Figure 1 depicts the snapshot of the LibSys opening page with Login and Password option for Madras School of Economics Library Operations as such.

Fig. 1. Snapshot of the Libsys Opening page with Login and Password options

Figure 2 exhibits the snapshot of various modules together with the options there of for Libsys software which is used by the Madras School of Economics Library.

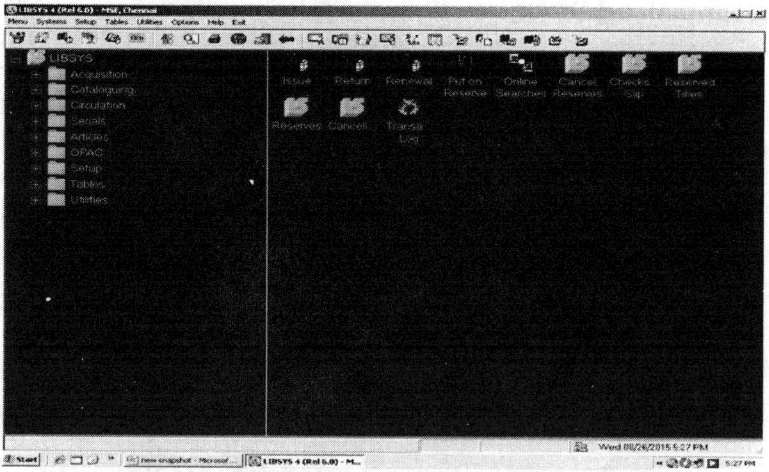

Fig. 2. Snapshot of Libsys with its modules and options

Figure 3 shows the snapshot of Acquisition module in LibSys software that is being used in Madras School of Economics Library with various options that are being covered within the said module.

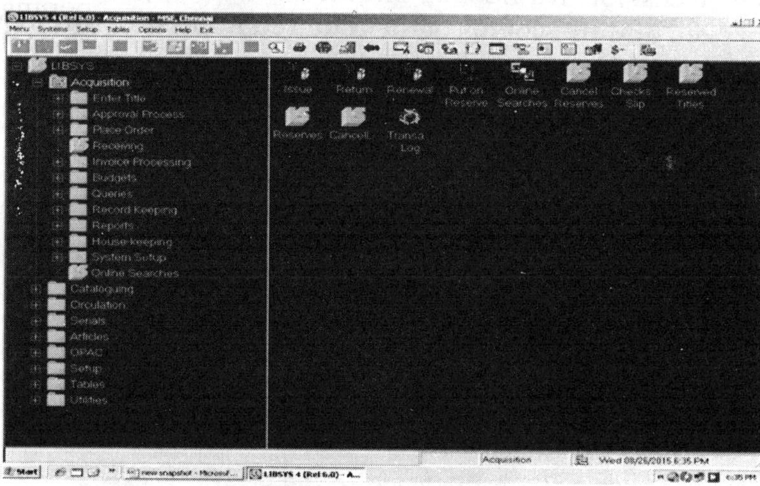

Fig. 3. Snapshot of Acquisition module

Figure 4 portrays the snapshot of various options in cataloguing module that is available in the Libsys software that is being used in the Madras School of Economics Library.

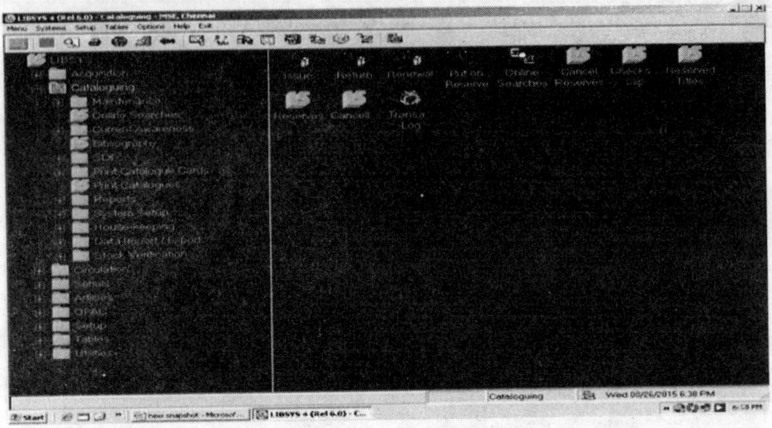

Fig. 4. Snapshot of Cataloguing module

Figure 5 gives an outline of the snapshot of the maintenance option available in the cataloguing module of the Libsys software that is being operational in the Madras School of Economics Library. In figure 5 Titles by Accession Number is shown with sub option being clicked and the details of the required Accession Number is retrieved and shown.

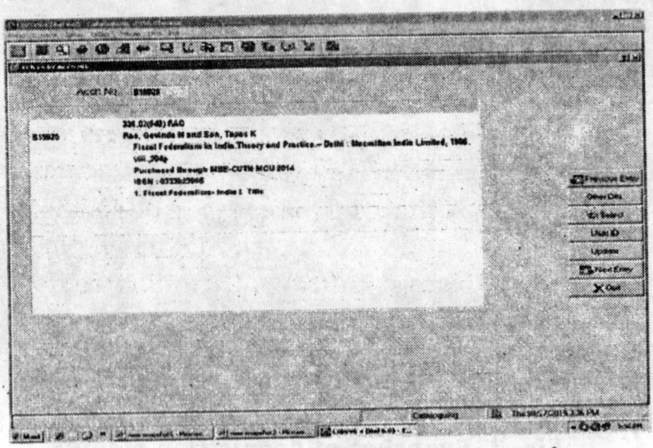

Fig. 5. Snapshot of Maintenance option in cataloguing module

Figure 6 presents the snapshot of the entry of the option in cataloguing module which initiates the process of cataloguing of books.

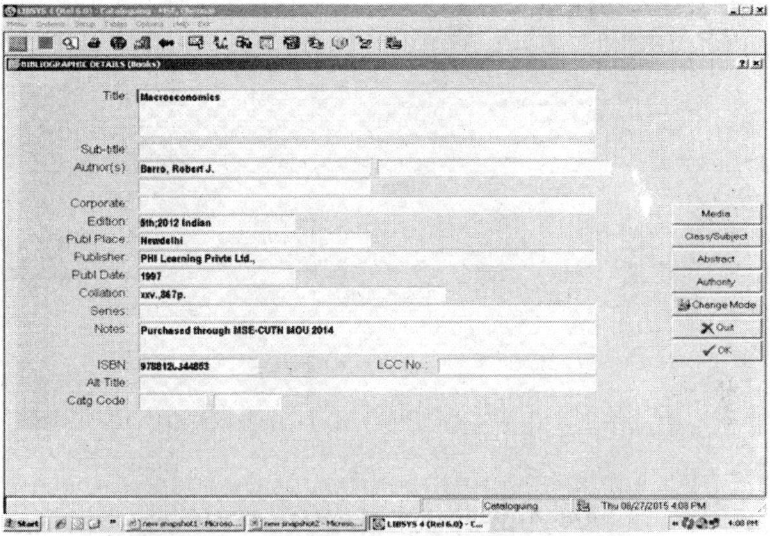

Fig. 6. Snapshot of entry of bibliographic details through the cataloguing module

Figure 7 depicts the snapshot of the entry of class number and subjects/keywords through bibliographic details option in the cataloguing module.

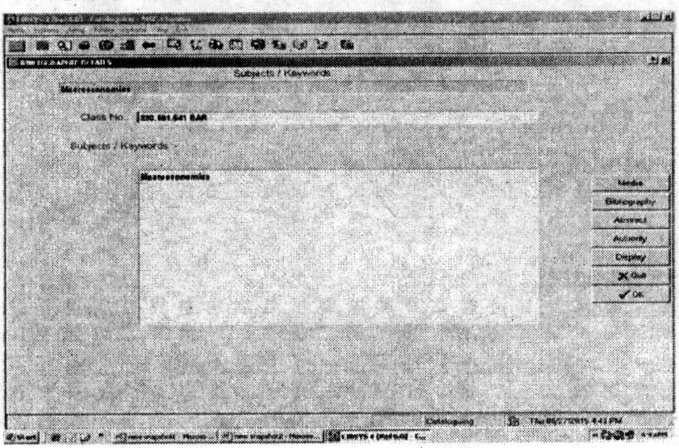

Fig. 7. Snapshot of entry of Class number and key words through the cataloguing module

Figure 8 shows the snapshot of the options through which bibliographic details for the titles according to their respective accession number is being retrieved.

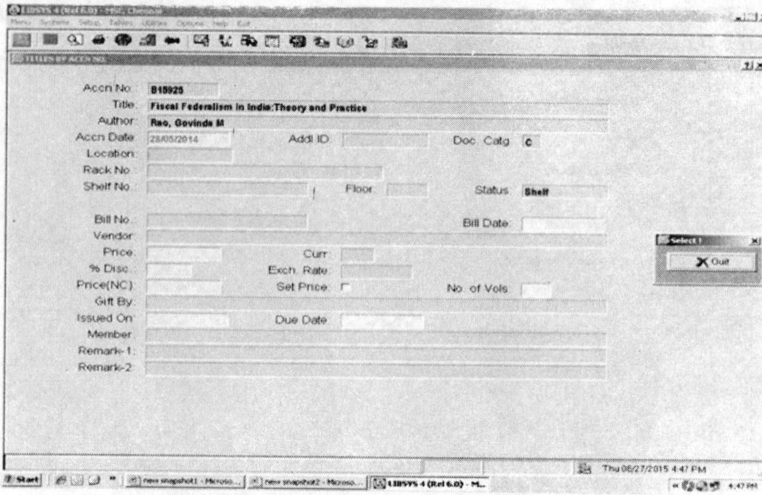

Fig. 8. Snapshot of option "Titles by Accession Number" in Cataloguing module

Figure 9 displays the snapshot of various options of circulation module.

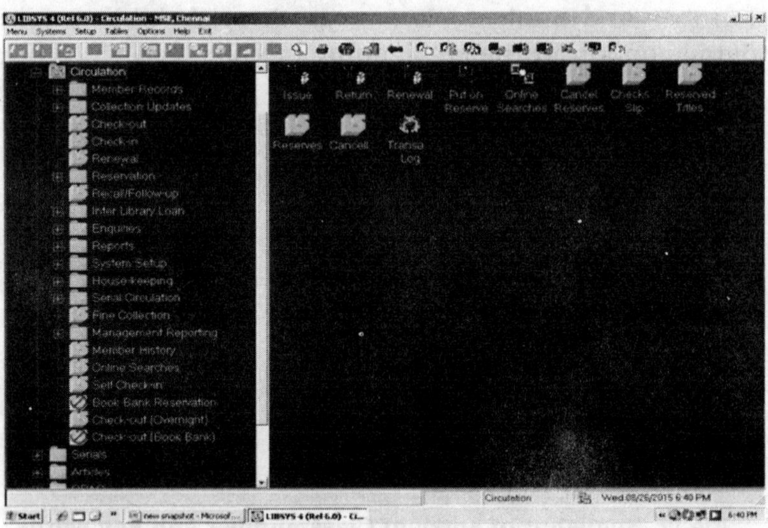

Fig. 9. Snapshot of Circulation module with its options

Figure 10 displays the snapshot of a membership record that is being modified through the option of member records in the circulation module.

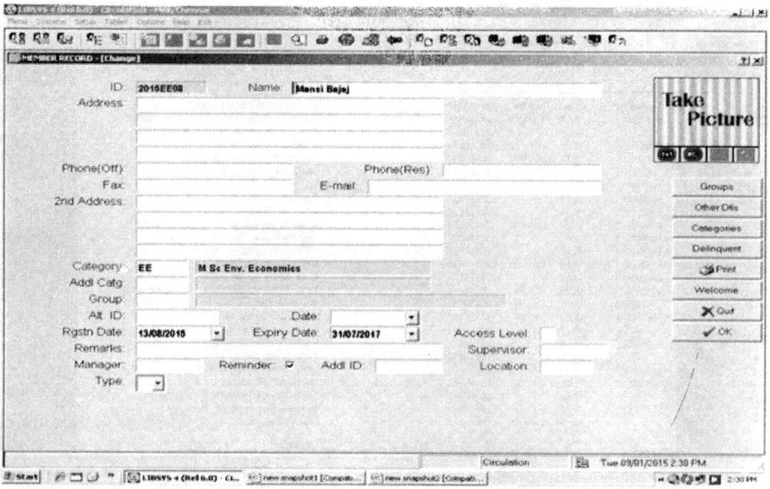

Fig. 10. Snapshot of modification of a Membership record

Figure 11 elucidates the snapshot of option for Find/ Search in the membership directory in the circulation module.

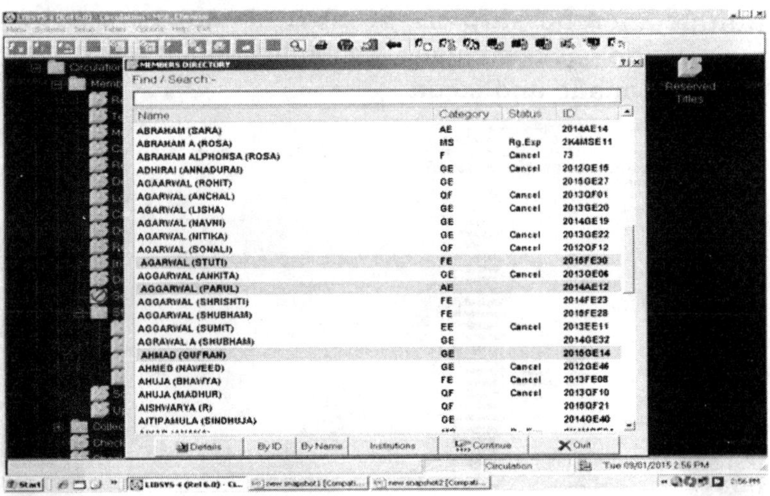

Fig. 11. Snapshot depicting Member Directory alphabetically arranged

Figure 12 protrays the details of the book that have been put on reserve or cancellation of such reservation of books subequently opted by the user.

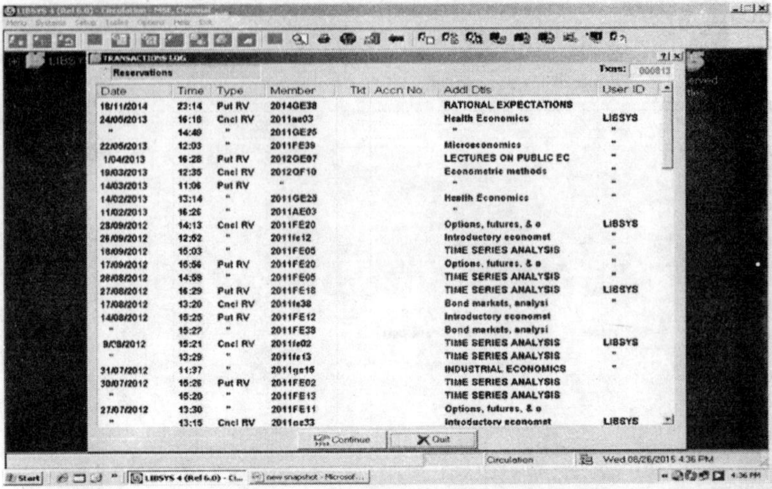

Fig. 12. Snapshot of transaction log option of circulation module for reservation of a book

Figure 13 exhibits the details of membership records such as the date and time of registration together with unique membership ID number. It shows whether registration has been made or modification in registration has been made and so on.

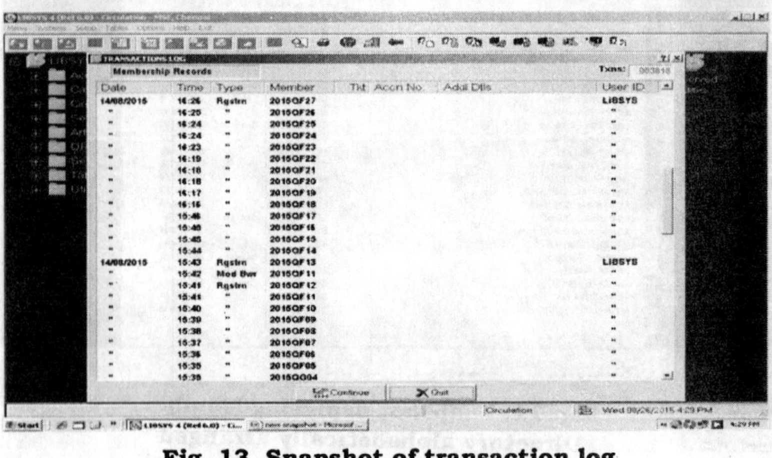

Fig. 13. Snapshot of transaction log option of membership option

Figure 14 reveals the options available in serial module such as subscription, issues management, article indexing, record keeping, enquiries, reports, system setup, system options, housekeeping, stock verification, circulation, union catalogue and online searches.

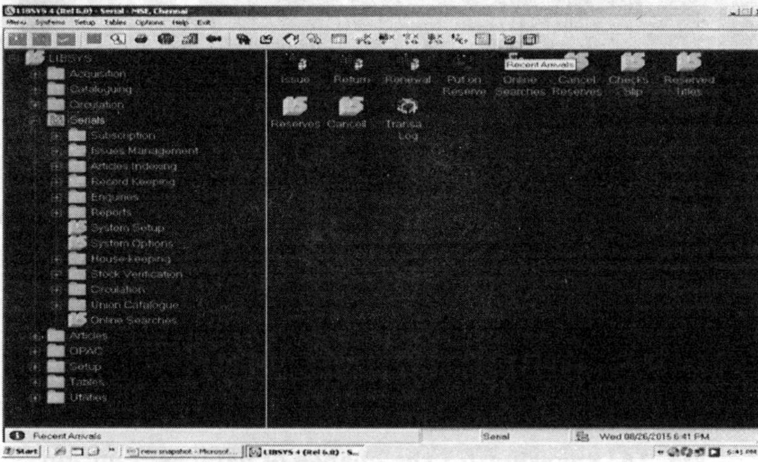

Fig. 14. Snapshot of Serials module

Figure 15 outlines the options available in the articles module such as maintenance, retrivals, miscellaneous and selective dissemination of information.

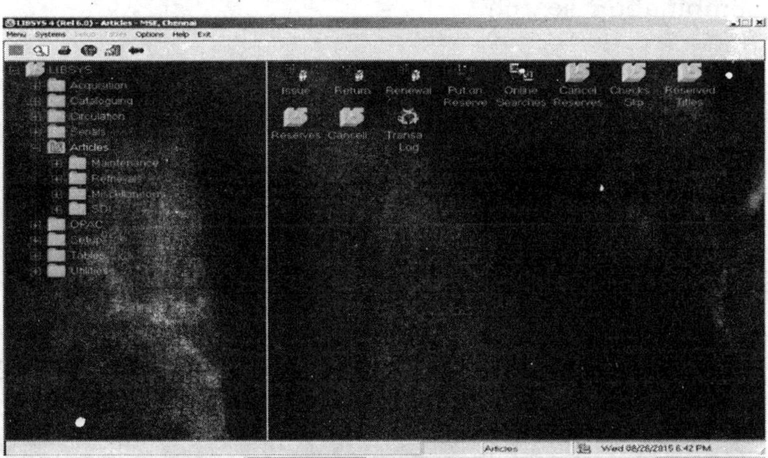

Fig. 15. Snapshot of Articles module

Figure 16 exhibits the option available in the OPAC module 'Change Database' which gives the choice of databases to be chosen from books, reports, theses, working papers, occassional papers, discussion papers, e-resources and monographs.

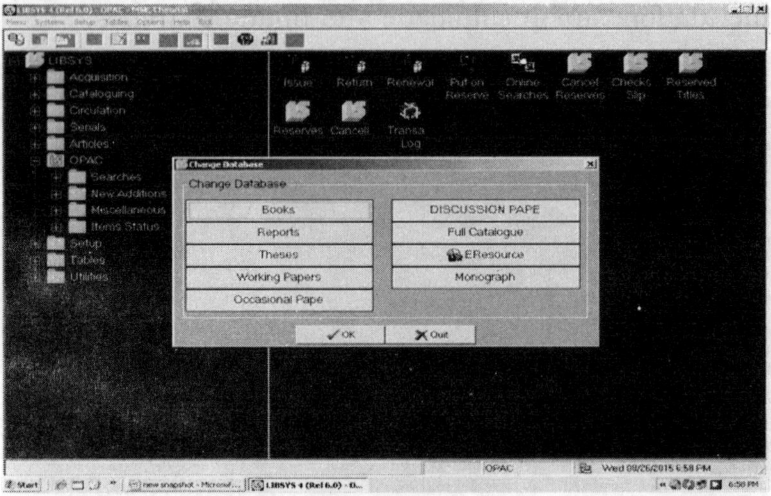

Fig. 16. Snapshot for the change of databases option available in OPAC module

Figure 17 illustrates the database in OPAC module 'books' option with suboptions such as author, title, classified, subject, place, publisher, words in title and combination search.

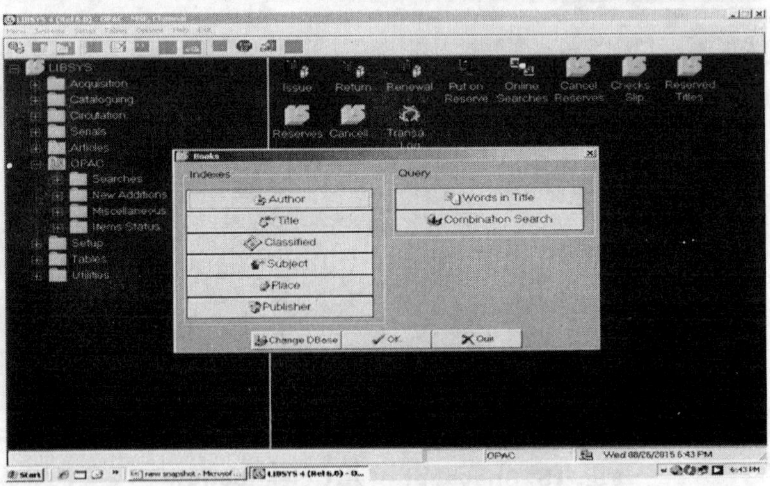

Fig.17. Snapshot of books database option in OPAC module

Figure 18 portrays the new additions options available in OPAC module with sub options books and documents and journals and the other two options namely miscellaneous and items status for the effective and efficient operation of the OPAC Module.

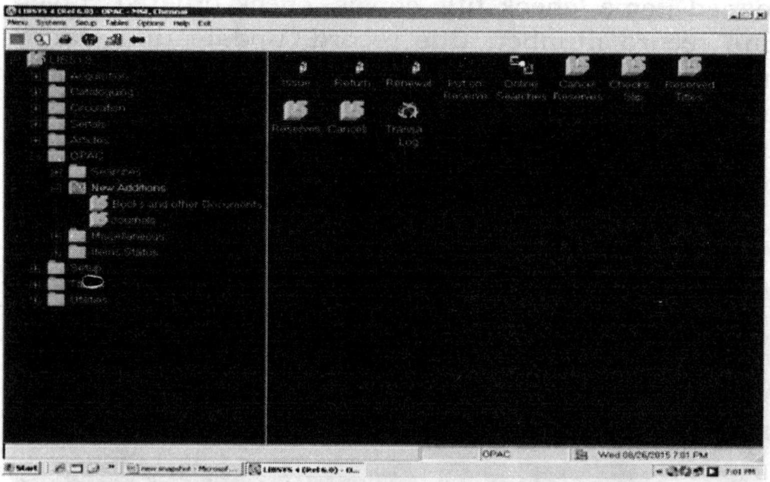

Fig. 18. Snapshot for new additions options in OPAC Module

Figure 19 retrieves the alphabetical wise latest additions in the library collections by using new additions option in the OPAC Module.

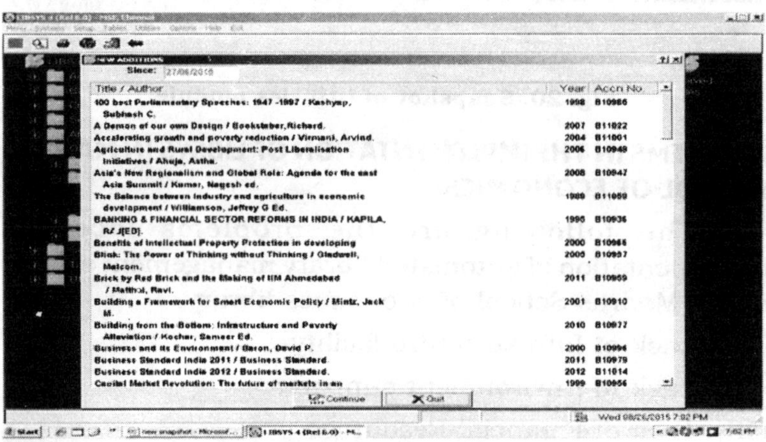

Fig. 19. Snapshot of retrieving latest additions in the Library

Figure 20 portrays the various options available in the utility module such as define security, print files path, check accession numbers, reservation links, check-out links (books), check-out links(back volumes), check-out links (journal volumes), check-out links (loans), check loaned items, check title copies, check ordered copies, find record number, title record, update title status, missing accession numbers, news bulletins and extended utilities. These options help in the maintenance and upkeep of the Libsys software together with the options of the setup module independently.

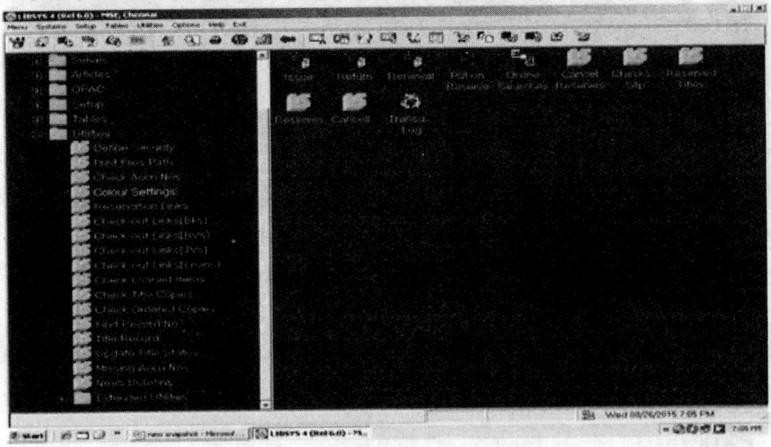

Fig. 20. Snapshot of Utilities module

PROBLEMS IN THE IMPLEMENTATION OF LIBSYS IN MADRAS SCHOOL OF ECONOMICS

The following are the problems faced in implementation of automated library management system in the Madras School of Economics library.

I. Lack of Infrastructure facility

II. Lack of Environment support

III. Lack of Financial Resources

I. Lack of Infrastructure facility

The Problems relating to infrastructure could be studied from the following angles: Lack of Hardware; Lack of Software and Lack of Network facility. Only computers have been purchased. In accordance with the same the bandwidth and such other capacity have not been increased.

II. Lack of Environment support

To environment problem are to be taken seriously by School of Economics Library. This problem can be divided in to two categories namely External and internal. Internal problem can be solved by the institution, but it may difficult to solve the external problem. The problem can be identified related to environmental are Power and lighting.

III. Lack of Financial Resources

The financial support is allocated only for books and racks and computers only, but not for upgradation of the existing Libsys Automation software package. Due to financial paucity and sudden growth in the terms of the infrastructure only in buildings have resulted in the reduction of budget towards all possible recurring expenditure. It is found that LIBSYS enable in systematic designing and examination of all library operations in an automated environment. All the documents details and the member details of the School of Economics have been completed to enable to have a full fledged automation of the library and also there by easy to integrate the School of Economics Library.

RECOMMENDATIONS

i. More generous financial support should be made available to provide the basic ICT infrastructural facilities, The Libsys software should be upgraded with the latest version so as to keep pace with the advancement in the ICT evolution and to cater to the needs of the increased number of users of the Library over the number of years.

ii. Since Information and Communication Technology (ICT) has come to stay, library staff those are not computer literate should take positive steps to remedy their deficiencies so as to flow along with the reforms. By this, library and information services will become enabled through the acquisition of adequate ICT knowledge/skill and its full application or else they will become irrelevant in this era of ICT.

iii. Effective and efficient power supply supplemented with standby generators should be provided to check the menace of the frequent electricity power failure. In the same vein, the government should address the problem of erratic power supply more seriously not through military order but through research and development. The Madras School of Economics should have better step-up electricity facility to help the better functioning of the ICT facilities of the school as such.

iv. Every division of the academic libraries should be automated in order to facilitate and create an avenue for effective services.

v. Short computer training and retraining programs should be organized from time-to-time to assist Librarians who do not have knowledge and computer skills. This will also aid awareness of computer potentials and capabilities.

vi. Orientation programs on the use of computer for information retrieval should be conducted and made compulsory for new entrants into the profession.

vii. Imported ICT equipments should be tax free.

- Institutions having without qualified librarians

should recruit qualified librarians to understand the user's needs and render better and improved services to the clientele.

- Few college libraries are fully automated. The libraries in which automation has been initiated should try to become fully automated
- Retrospective conversion of the documents as well as the other jobs related to automation may be outsourced to complete the automation of the library.
- Technical experts may be employed in automation related activities.
- Staff of the library should be sent for training courses to upgrade their IT skills by which efficiency of the existing system may be enhanced.

TOP ISSUES AND CHALLENGES FOR LIBRARIES IN THE THIRD MILLENNIUM

The future of academic scenario in India in general and Chennai in particular faces many challenges. For libraries in Chennai, the management concerns are becoming as crucial as technical processes and technology adoption and assimilation issues. The management of change is itself is a great challenge. There is a need for special management to ensure greater flow of information, requirement for fund allocation, more staff recruitment and support for technological up gradation. Librarians must continuously upgrade their skills and competencies and shall perceive how users are satisfied with the provision of services and information products. The major issues are as follows:

1. Recruitment, education, and retention of librarians.
2. Role of library in academic enterprise.
3. Impact of information technology on library services.

4. Creation, control, and preservation of digital resources.
5. Chaos in scholarly communication.
6. Support of new users.
7. Higher education funding (Hisle, 2002)

CONCLUSION

The inevitable conclusion that the researcher has arrived at in this study is that ICT has fulfilled its promise in academic libraries, there is remarkable rise in the use of ICT, many of the libraries activities are now ICT driven. This has led to the speed on acquisition, processing, storage, retrieval and dissemination operations. ICT has also help to curb the problem of information explosion in this information era.

With the invention of Information and Communication Technology, libraries now use various types of technologies to aid the services they render. Everyday new technological advances affect the way information is handled in libraries and information centers. The impacts of new technologies are felt by libraries in every aspect. Computing technology, communication technology and mass storage technology are some of the areas of continuous development that reshape the way that libraries access, retrieve, store, manipulate and disseminate information to users. The academic library has been from its inception an integral part of institutions of higher learning, rather than an appendix or adjunct. The librarian with the administrators has to set up the priorities after analyzing the current status and future requirements. Selection of the suitable integrated library management package according to the needs of the users and the library is important. Therefore, for the successful implementation of an integrated library system all key factors like support from administration/ authorities, staff competence, consideration of user requirements, presence of the infrastructure (hardware, software, network), available data, excellent managerial skills among the librarians, fund raising ability, etc. must be in place. Then only, the purpose of successful implementation of library automation can be achieved. Librarian shall be confident enough while selecting the library automation software depending on its need, budget, manpower, technical expertise and the future goals.

REFERENCES

- Husain and Other's (2008). Library automation software packages in India: a study of cataloguing modules of Alice for windows, Libsys, virtue. *DESIDOC Journal of Library & Information Technology,28(6), 34-38.*
- Jayaprakash M & Balasubramani R (2011) 'Status of automation in university libraries of Tamilnadu: a study'. *Euro Journals Publishing,* Vol.53 No.1, pp.17-24.
- Hisle, W Lee (2002). Top issues facing academic libraries : A report of the focus on the future Task Force, *College and Research Libraries News,* 63 (10).
- Kochar & Sudarshan (2007). Library Automation: Issues and Systems. New Delhi : APH Publishing Corporation.
- LIBSYS Ltd: Library Management, Automation Software. (n.d.). Retrieved from http://www.libsys.co.in/
- Neelakandan et.al. 2010, 'Implementation of automation library management system in the School of Chemistry Bharathidasan University using KOHA open source software'. *International Journal of Applied Engineering Research,* Vol. 1, No.1.
- Niranjan Singh (2006). Plan for Library automation: Problems and Prospects. IN: Vistas for Information Management (Professor H R Chopra Felicitation Volume), edited by P. Venkata Rao. Ambala Cantt: Wisdom House Academic Publishers Pvt. Ltd, pp. 377- 382.
- Ramesh Babu B (1995) Automation of Public Libraries in India : Myth or reality. IN: *'Preparing Libraries for the 21st century* / edited by C.V.Subba Rao, A.P.Gakhar and O.P.Sharma, 40th All India Library Conference, Goa University,Goa,pp.229 234.

2

Consortia Based Approach for Resource Sharing in Library & Information Network: Some Experiences from the ICMR

K V Ratnakar
Sunil Kumar Bisht
K Satyanarayana
Division of Publication Information
Indian Council of Medical Research
Ansari Nagar, New Delhi - 110029

INTRODUCTION

Information as we all know that is something on which the socio-economic growth of a country largely depends. Information plays an important role not only in the initial stages but throughout a research process. Mainly the nascent information is required for the research purpose. Journal being the main source for nascent information is always looked for journal article by the researcher. But due to financial constraint and publication of large number of journals it is almost impossible to have all those in the library. The only possible solution is the library cooperation, in the form of Resource sharing. Resource sharing can be achieved by forming a consortium. Consortia in context of library and information science can be defined as an association of libraries having a common interest and which comes together usually for the purpose of resource sharing. But even after forming such consortia it is difficult to locate a journal or the article in a journal by manual process. Realizing this problem ICMR with the help of Informatics India pvt. Ltd. formed e-consortia of ICMR libraries to facilitate the process of resource sharing among them using the latest tool of Information Communication and Technology. The present initiative of the Indian Council of Medical Research (ICMR), the JCCC@ICMR (http://www.jccc- icmr.informindia.co.in) is one such initiative in the field of biomedical science.

About ICMR

The Indian Council of Medical Research (ICMR) is the apex body in India in the field of biomedicine. Since, its inception in 1911, it is involved in formulation, coordination and promotion of biomedical research. As early as in 1911, the government of India set up the Indian Research Fund Association (IRFA) with the objectives of supporting and coordinating the various medical researches in India. It was renamed as Indian Council of Medical Research (ICMR) in 1949. ICMR is getting monetary support for its various activities from Ministry of Health & Family welfare.

The governing Body of the council is presided over by the Union Health Minister. The Council is supporting research activities in various branches of biomedicine. The Council is promoting various biomedical researches in the country through intramural as well as extramural research.

Intramural research is carried out by the council's various institutes which includes (i) 21 Permanent Research Institutes/Centres which are devoted to the research in specific discipline of biomedicine and (ii) 6

Regional Medical research Centres which take regional health problems into consideration.

Extramural research is promoted by ICMR through (i) Establishing Centres for Advanced Research in different research areas around existing expertise and infrastructure in selected medical colleges, Universities and research institutes, (ii) Task forces which are target oriented, time specified, standardized and follows certain specific methodology, (iii) Open ended research on the basis of application for grants-in-aid received from scientists in non-ICMR Research Institutes, Medical colleges, Universities etc.

In addition to all the above activities ICMR is also running some short term programmes for the human resource development like Short Term Visiting Fellowships, Research Fellowships/ Associate ships, Ad-hoc Research Schemes, Emeritus Medical Scientist Scheme, Junior Research Fellowships and Short Term Research Studentship.

NEED OF JCCC@ICMR

Although libraries and Information centres of ICMR's network subscribe a large number of journal but due to lack of a common pool earlier it was difficult to know about the availability of journals. To solve the problem and to have an efficient resource sharing and for optimum utilization of subscribed literature the JCCC@ICMR was initiated. Some of the major barrier for smooth information flow which leads to the formation of JCCC@ICMR are mainly availability and accessibility of article.

Availability Gap : While the country as a whole subscribe to significant number of journals, what is available at individual institutional level is a very small number. Resource sharing through library cooperation could have bridged this availability gap. But it did not take off in an organized manner for many reasons. The electronic availability of union catalog of journals could change the thing for us.

Access Gap : To help their users to find out the contents of these journals, libraries subscribe to bibliographic database (indexing and abstracting journals). Without these databases, there is simply no way by which a user can search for the contents in the journals are physically available. Here also the solution is to have an electronic database.

JCCC@ICMR is the cost effective option that can do the trick for the member libraries of the consortia.

JCCC@ICMR http://www.jccc-icmr.infonnindia.co.in

Before discussing the JCCC@ICMR consortia, JCC and JCCC are described:

What is JCC? : J-Gate Custom Content (JCC) acts as a bibliographic database and provides single access point for searching the locally subscribed journals - both print and electronic. This is based on Ranganathan's local documentation list. The major advantage of JCC is its ability to maximize the usage of the journals subscribed by the library. It brings all the print and electronic journals before the users under a single platform.

What is JCCC? : JCCC is an extension for library consortia. It is the J-Gate Custom Content for Consortia (JCCC). It is a sharable bibliographic database between the member institute which allows the members of the consortia to access the full text and the incorporated union catalog of the journals which is managed by the Informatics India Pvt. Ltd.

JCCC@ICMR : As we know that it is always a daunting task to locate an article or journal from the collection of more than one library. For the faster retrieval of details regarding a particular journal or the article, it is difficult to rely on manual technique. ICMR with the help of Informatics India Pvt. Ltd. took the initiative to provide a common access point to its different libraries and Information centres, so that they can know what the other libraries of the council are subscribing and at the same time also increases the usage of these sources among the council's library. All the 28 ICMR's libraries and Information centres are the members of JCCC@ICMR and are taking the benefit of it. JCCC@ICMR was launched on 27th of July 2004, since then it is catering the need of ICMR's library and information network. Presently JCCC@ICMR is providing a single point access to around 788 journals, out of which 523 journals are subscribed by 28 ICMR's network of library and Information centres and 265 open access (Free) biomedical journals. The consortium provides access to journals of around 467 publishers under one roof.

The scientists can access the full text and the abstract of all the journals available free on that platform. The scientists can easily locate the journal of their interest from the journals subscribed by the member library and if they find any article then by using the same platform they can send an e-mail request to the designated library of the consortia.

JCCC@ICMR is a bibliographic database of print and electronic journals that the member libraries are subscribing. It provides a common platform for all the members to have an access of detail regarding the availability of journals.

After locating the article, one needs, request can be made by clicking the "hardcopy" button. A window will appear, after filling up the particulars, send it to the designating library having that article. One can easily know through JCCC about the subscription of a particular journal, like how many libraries are subscribing it.

Significant features of JCCC@ICMR

JCCC although have various significant features through which the optimum use of the journals subscribed can be achieved but few of them need to be explained, these are:

- Scientist can get full text articles from 265 online open access journals.
- The JCCC@ICMR provides a facility of searching the database either through the Title/Keyword or Author they can narrow down their search by limiting it to free journals if required. At the same time they can mention the period to make it much more specific. Search can be made for both free and library subscription.
- There is a common access to Table of Content.
- It has provided a facility of giving feedback also.
- For optimum use of available resources and faster information access the JCCC@ICMR provide e- mail facility request for full text to designated library who is subscribing the journals.
- It also provides information regarding the latest update i.e. about the new journals that are added in the database.

Usage statistics : As far as usage of the JCCC@ ICMR is concerned it has recorded a number of hits in the past year. It has served the need of many users. If we take the last year statistics, the JCCC@ICMR was used for database search about 710 times, around 273 abstracts were browsed through this consortium and around 1513 full text articles were seen using this consortium. The above statistics indicates that ICMR & its institutes are rapidly switching over to consortia approach for journal literature.

CONCLUSION

Libraries are facing significant challenges in new digital publishing environment. Due to tremendous explosion of information, financial constraints, information in different forms etc., the resource sharing and networking have emerged as important alternative. The JCCC@ICMR is one such initiative which not only maximizes the use of available resources scattered in different library and Information Centres of ICMR but also help the scientists to get their information quickly. Now in the digital era we do have technology like web technology which paved the way for effective resource sharing. JCCC@ICMR is very useful for optimum utilization of the available resources. But on the ground level it need some involvement on the part of Library staff, as it is necessary that all the library staff should be well aware with the facility that JCCC@ICMR is providing, so that they would able to provide better services. To make the user independent and fulfill their needs, library must run some users training programme to impart the knowledge about the functioning and the services that are offered by the consortium.

REFERENCES

1. JCCC@ICMR (http://www.jccc-icmr.infomiindia.co.in).
2. Pinelli T E. The information seeking habits and practices of engineers. Science & Technology Libraries' 1991; 11 (3): 5-25.
3. Rajshekhar T.B. "J-Gate : an Indian e-journal portal initiative for international journals. Information Today and Tommorrow" 2002; 21 (3&4): p.3-10.
4. Mallik S.K., Saxena Shyamala and Roy P.K. "Online Journal Usage Pattern: a case study of CDRI, Lucknow As a member of CSIR E- journals consortium" Library and Information Network- NACLIN 2006, DELNET, New Delhi,2006, p.243-254.

3

Current Trends of Library Consortia in India

S. M. Nikose
Assistant Professor
Department of Library and Information Science
RTM Nagpur University, Nagpur

A library consortium is a group of libraries whos partner to coordinate activities, share resources, and combine expertise. Library consortia offer significant advantages to increasingly strapped libraries. The sharing of electronic information resources and collaboration on shared goals often enable libraries to deliver higher quality services than they would be able to deliver on their own.

The term consortia may be defined as "A cooperative arrangement of purchasing electronic recourses among a group of institutions, which will provide collective purchasing power and enable them to avail best possible bargaining facility to ensure highest discount price for electronic journals". Library Consortia is an association or a partnership has long being a principle of librarianship. It refers to cooperation, coordination and collaboration between libraries for the purpose of sharing information resources and services.

Rajgoli, Birdie & Karisiddappa, (2005) stated that a

consortium is a co-operative arrangement among groups or institutions or an association or society. Consortia are commonly formed to increase the purchasing capacity of the collaborating institutions, to expand the resource availability and to offer automated services. In other words, it is described as a group of organizations whose purpose is to collectively facilitate and support the work of a service.

Program in the ways that ad material and human resources beyond those available to each organization individual. Pathak and Deshpande, (2004) discuss the importance of consortia and their impact on society especially in developing countries like India. The present scenario of consortia among university libraries, special libraries and different technical institute libraries in India is elaborated. Francis (2005) depicted that the new model of library consortia in which all academic intuitions and government research organizations could participate. The formation of such a unique library consortia under the direction and full support by the government of India are stressed.

BENEFITS TO CONSORTIA USERS

- Space and time –invariant
- Helps save time for users
- Provides value addition such as search ability, alerting services, links from one article to another, forward links like citing articles etc.
- Accelerates publications.
- Articles cannot be mutilated, stolen or lost.

BENEFITS TO LIBRARIANS

- Speedup resources delivery.
- Reduced shelving, binding, maintenance, clamming, etc.

- Cost saving.
- Time saving at work.
- Improved services
- Public relation opportunities
- Greater visibility of products.

LIBRARY CONSORTIA SERVICES IN INDIA:

There are some major library consortia are serving in the higher education and research system in India.

S. N.	*Name of Consortia*	*Members*	*No. of Resources*	*Publishers*	*URL (User Resource Locator)*
1.	UGC INFO-NET 2.0 (INFLIBNET)	422	7500	26	http://www.inflibnet.ac.in/infonet
2.	CeRA	134	3000	15	http://www.cera.jccc.in
3.	ERMED	98	1812	10	http://www.nmlermed.in
4.	INDEST	82	6500	17	http://www.paniit.iitd.ac.in/indest
5.	NKRC	68	4500	23	http://ejournal.niscair.res.in/index.php
6	DeLCON DBT e-Library Consortium	33	917	19	http://delcon.gov.in
7.	FORSA	11	25	10	http://www.ncra.tifr.res.in/library/forsaweb/index.htm

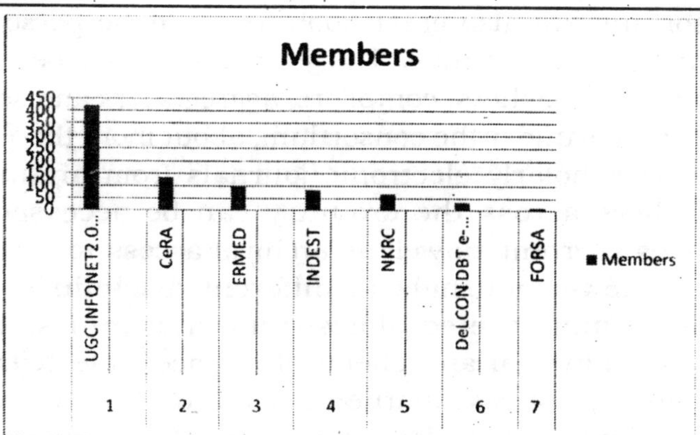

Fig. 1. Showing members of each consortia.

With increases in prices of journals, shrinking library budgets and cuts in subscriptions to journals over the years, there has been a big challenge facing Indian library professionals to cope with the proliferation of electronic information resources. There have been sporadic efforts have been taken by different groups of libraries in forming consortia at different level. The online information access system in India is had been past around two decades with the establishment of the Information and Library Network (INFLIBNET) Center. This one is a national Institute established by the University Grants Commission (UGC) of India in 1991. Now various subject-oriented consortia are established to improve the quality and status of research and educational development.

1. UGC-Infonet Digital Library Consortium (INFONET)

The UGC-Infonet Digital Library Consortium was formally launched in December 2003. In this consourtium 419 universities libraries are utilising to provide online digital information services to their users. More than 7500 full text e resources are available from more than 20 international publishers to members universities and more than 5 types of bibliographical databases are availabe under the subcription. UGC-INFONET: e-journal consortium are also great boon to academic persons in the Indian universities. The journals subscribed from renouned publishers, compilers, aggregrators and society publications under the consortium, about more than 4000 full text scholarly electronic journals from around 25 publishers across the crountry can be accessed. Its provides currrent as well as archival access to core and peer-reviewed journals in different disciplines. This sconsourtium covered almost arts, humanities, social sciences, physical and chemical sciences, life sciences, computer sciences, mathematics and statistics other subjects areas are added time to time. This consourtium are sponsored by UGC and monitored by INFLIBNET (Information Library Network Centre) Ahmedabad.

2. CeRA e-journal consortium

The Consortium for e Resources in Agriculture is a targeted programme initiated by Indian Council of Agricultural Research in sub-project of NAIP, funded by World Bank. CeRA is an e-Consortium for Agricultural Libraries under National Agricultural Research System (NARS), established for facilitating accessibility of select scientific journals related to agriculture and allied fields, to all researchers in the (NARS). The subscriptions to journals by Libraries of ICAR Institutions and State Agricultural Universities (SAU) have been difficult due to financial crunch. To fulfill the requisition of the researchers and students the CeRA providing equal agricultural information access system facilities to all the agricultural university of states and CAU. The activities in CeRA are governed by Steering monitoring and negotiation and working committees and well supported by the Project Implementation Unit, NAIP. Its covered Deemed Agricultural Universities, ICAR Institutions, National Bureaus, Project Directorates, National Research Canter, SAU and CAUs. CeRA aims to develop the existing research and development information resource base of ICAR institutes / universities comparable to leading institutes/organizations in the world, to subscribe e-journals and create e-access culture among scientists/ teachers under the ICAR institutes/agricultural universities, and to study the impact of the consortium on the level of research publications measured through Science Citation Index (SCI) and NAAS Rating. CeRA members have access to on-line journals through only IP authentication. It's provide completely full-proof system of security and also no need to memorizing user ID, password, and publishers User Resource Locator (URL).

3. Electronic Resources in Medicine in India (ERMED-India) Consortium

National Medical Library's Electronic Resources in Medicine Consortium is an initiative taken by Director General of Health Service & MOHFW to develop nation wide electronic information resources in the field of medicine for delivering effective health care. 39 centrally funded Government Institutions including 10 DGHS libraries + 28 ICMR Libraries and AIIMS library are selected at the initial stage as its core members. The MOHFW aims to provide fund required for the purchase of electronic journals under the NML-ERMED consortium project. The consortium will be coordinated through its headquarter set up at the NML. The nomenclature of the consortium is provisional; the same will be finalized after the approval of the competent authority. NML is already providing over 3380 print journal articles/ months across the country through postal service. Now efficiency of the same may be enhanced through electronic options are available to NML. 2068 print journals will be available for cross sharing. Package of 1350 online e-journals will be available from 12 leading publishers in the field of medical sciences. Free of charge 80 titles of Immunology & Microbiology + CIP will access complete 102 neuroscience collection + MEDLINE + Current Content database will be directly available to members. About 300 open access free journals will also be available.

The Consortium will purchase online e-journal from 12 different publishers. Users of e-journals have to visit website of different publishers to make use of full text. It may be time consuming and frustrating.

4. INDEST (Indian National Digital Library in Engineering Science & Technology)

The "Indian National Digital Library in Engineering Sciences and Technology (INDEST) Consortium" was set up in 2003 by the Ministry of Human Resource

Development (MHRD) on the recommendation of an Expert Group appointed by the Ministry. The IIT Delhi has been designated as the Consortium Headquarters to coordinate its activities. The Consortium was re-named as INDEST-AICTE Consortium in December 2005 with the AICTE playing a pivotal role in enrolling its approved engineering colleges and institutions as members of the Consortium for selected e-resources at much lower rates of subscription. The Consortium enrols engineering and technological institutions as its members and subscribes to electronic resources for them at discounted rates of subscription and favourable terms and conditions. The Ministry provides funds required for subscription to electronic resources for 62 centrally funded Government institutions including IITs, IISc Bangalore, NITs, ISM, IIITs, IIMs, NITTTR's and few other institutions that are considered as core members of the Consortium. The benefit of consortia-based subscription to electronic resources is not confined to its core members but is also extended to all educational institutions under its open-ended proposition. 60 Govt./Govt.-aided engineering colleges are provided access to selected electronic resources with financial support from the AICTE and 102 universities/institutions have joined the Consortium under its self-supported category in 2012. The total number of members in the Consortium has now grown to 1235. The INDEST-AICTE Consortium is the most ambitious initiative taken so far in India. It is the biggest Consortium in terms of number of member institutions in Asia. The Consortium attracts the best possible price and terms of agreement from the publishers on the basis of strength of its present and prospective member institutions. The Consortium subscribes to over 12,000 electronic journals from a number of publishers and aggregators. The consortium website at *http://paniit.iitd.ac.in/indest* hosts searchable databases of journals and member institutions to locate journals subscribed by the Consortium, their URLs and details of member institutions.

5. NKRC (CSIR-DST)

National Knowledge Resource Consortium (NKRC), established in year 2009, is a network of libraries and information centres of 39 CSIR and 24 DST institutes. NKRC's origin goes back to the year 2001, when the CSIR set up the Electronic Journals Consortium to provide access to 1200 odd journals of Elsevier Science to all its users. Over a period of time, the Consortium not only grew in terms of the number of resources but also in terms of the number of users as more like-minded institutes evinced interest to join the Consortium. Today, NKRC facilitates access to 5,000+ e-journals of all major publishers, patents, standards, citation and bibliographic databases. Apart from licensed resources, NKRC is also a single point entity that provides its users with access to a multitude of open access resources. The Consortium envisions emerging as a leader to serve the R&D sector with much needed information to strengthen the research and development system in the country.

6. DeLCON DBT e-Library Consortium

Department of Bio-technology e-Library Consortium (DeLCON) is a unique Electronic Journal Consortium, which is operational since January 2009. Currently the Consortium includes 16 DBT Institutions including ICGEB, New Delhi and 18 North Eastern Region (NER) Institutions. The Biotechnology Industry Research Assistance Council (BIRAC), New Delhi is also part of DeLCON. Now, the total 'DeLCON Members' are 34. A total of 926 selective Journals and a Database (SCOPUS) are covered under DeLCON. These all are accessible by the DeLCON Consortium Members through the DeLCON Portal (http://delcon.gov.in). Others can also view and access abstracts of papers as free of costs. DBT e-Library

Consortium (DeLCON) is a unique Electronic Journal Consortium, which is operational since January 2009. Currently the Consortium includes 16 DBT Institutions including ICGEB, New Delhi and 18 North Eastern Region (NER) Institutions. The Biotechnology Industry Research Assistance Council (BIRAC), New Delhi is also part of DeLCON. Now, the total 'DeLCON Members' are 34. A total of 926 selective Journals and a Database (SCOPUS) are covered under DeLCON. These all are accessible by the DeLCON Consortium Members through the DeLCON Portal (http://delcon.gov.in). Others can also view and access abstracts of papers as free of costs.

7. FORSA (Forum for Resource Sharing in Astronomy and Astrophysics)

The oldest Library Consortium in India is the Forum for Resource Sharing in Astronomy and Astrophysics (FORSA) in subject of Physics was established in 1982. The types of consortia identified are generally based on various models evolved in India in a variety of forms depending upon the participants' affiliations and funding sources. Indian astronomy library professionals have formed a group called Forum for Resource Sharing in Astronomy and Astrophysics (FORSA), which falls under 'Open Consortia', wherein participants are affiliated to different government departments. This is a model where professionals willingly come forward and actively support consortia formation; thereby everyone benefits. As such, FORSA has realized four consortia, viz. Nature Online Consortium; Indian Astrophysics Consortium for physics/ astronomy journals of Springer/Kluwer; Consortium for Scientific American Online Archive (EBSCO); and Open Consortium for Lecture Notes in Physics (Springer), which are discussed briefly.

CONCLUSION

Besides of the above many other consortium are also running in the country as per need like ISRO,

HELINET, ICMR, ICICI Knowledge Park, IIM Consortium etc. The online access through Internet system the consortia are playing a very crucial role in the higher education and research work. This creation has control the physical maintenance work of library professionals. The accessibilities of the research literature and their availabities as 24x7 have been increased. The time of the student and academic persons in searching of needful information save and directly took as soft copy in their devices to any time use. The different areas of subjects are created different portal of particular discipline information access. So there is no problem of interlinking of other subjects in each other. The benefits to procure more electronic resources in the library in limited library budget. And this is what the libraries required in the present scenario. The libraries are preparing their own archives of soft copies collection of literature for future use. Now in this way the libraries are becoming very reach as their own repositories of knowledge, information. Only needful the any particular peace of information can be taken printout.

There are some difficulties are seen against the print paradigm, the e-journal subscription and access models permit only licensing of the content or product for a period of stipulated time. Now the Soft copy cost is more in comparison to printed one. Now the online information access is an attractive information access and dissemination system for library and information services. The library consortia are full filling the main role of the libraries. Its require more promotion and enhancement in the country.

REFERENCES

- Chandrashekharan, H.; Patle. Sarita; Pandey, P.S. et al (2012). CeRA- the e-Journal Consortium for National Agricultural Research System. Current Science102(6), 847-851.

- Chakravarti, R. and Singh, S. (2005). e-Resources for Indian universities: new initiatives. SRELS J.inf.Manage.,(42), 57-73.
- Evans, G.E. and Margaret Zarnosky Saponaro. (2012). Collection Management Basics: Sixth Edition. Library and Information Science Text Series, Libraries Unlimited. Oxford, England. (161-177).
- Francis, A.T. (2005). Library consortia model for country wide access of electronic journals and databases. In TAV Murthy et.al (Ed.s) Proceedings of International Conference on Multilingual Computing and Information Management in Networked Digital Environment, Cochin.
- Mark, T. (2007). National and international library collaboration: Necessity, advantages. Liber Quarterly: The Journal of European Research Libraries, 17(3/4), 1–7.
- Pathak, Sandeep. & Neela Deshpande. (2004). Importance of consortia in developing countries an Indian scenario. The International Information & Library Review, 36(3),227-231.
- Rajgoli, Iqbalahmad, U., Birdie, Christina, & Karisaddappa, C.R. (2005). Use of resources through consortia made in Indian Library & Information centers: A case study of FORSA Consortium. IASLIC Bulletin, 50(2), 74-82.
- Sridhar, M.S. (2002) Resource sharing among ISRO libraries: A case study of consortia approach. SRELS Journal of Information management.39(1),41-58.
- Thompson, T. L. (2004). Library consortia in the 21st century: Beyond the buying club. Trends in Law Library Management & Technology, 15(2), 1–4.
- *http://ugcinfonet.jccc.in/about/about.asp*
- *http://www.inflibnet.ac.in/publication/annualreport/AR-2009-2010.pdf*
- http://www.nmlermed.in
- http://paniit.iitd.ac.in/indest
- http://ejournal.niscair.res.in/index.phphttp://ejournal.niscair.res.in/index.php
- *http://delcon.gov.in*
- http://www.ncra.tifr.res.in/library/forsaweb/index.htm

4

Content Analysis of Open Access LIS Journal "Webology" (2005 -2009)

Rahul S Lokhande

(Librarian), Librarian, Arts, Science & Commerce College, Manmad (Dist-Nashik) (M.S.),India

A N Chikate

(Deputy Librarian), North Maharashtra University, Jalgaon (M.S.), India

ABSTRACT

The present study investigated the trends of LIS open access Journal "WEBOLOGY" by analysing articles, authors and LIS subjects covered in the articles. Quantitative content analysis was carried out for which the data were analysed in order to project literature growth, authorship pattern and related bibliometric phenomena. The analysis indicates that there were 62 articles published during 2005 to 2009. The authorship pattern indicates that the majority of articles published with multi-authorship. Authors from teaching faculty were paid more interest in "WEBOLOGY". The subject coverage of this journal is mostly towards bibliometric and scientometric study, covering other LIS subjects in the articles. The analysis of data clearly indicates that OA ejournal "WEBOLOGY"rapidly establishing themselves as a most viable media for scholarly communication.

Keywords : Content analysis, Bibliometric study, Scientometrics and Informetrics.

1. INTRODUCTION

About the journal: Webology

Bibliographic Information:

Webology is an international peer-reviewed journal in English devoted to the field of the *World Wide Web* and serves as a forum for discussion and experimentation. It serves as a forum for new research in information dissemination and communication processes in general, and in the context of the *World Wide Web* in particular. Concerns include the production, gathering, recording, processing, storing, representing, sharing, transmitting, retrieving, distribution, and dissemination of information, as well as its social and cultural impacts. There is a strong emphasis on the Web and new information technologies. Special topic issues are also often seen.

Bibliographic Information

Title of the Journal	*Webology*
ISSN	1735-188X
Subject	World Wide Web—Periodicals Web science—Periodicals Information science—Periodicals Library science—Periodicals
Language	English
Start Year	2004 - Vol. 1, No. 1 (August) -
Frequency	Biannual, since 2009 - Quarterly (2004-2008)
Editor-in-Chief	Alireza Noruzi, Ph.D.
Place of Publication	Iran
Publisher	Regional Information Center for Science and Technology (RICeST)
Status	Active
Refereed	Yes
LC No.	ZA4226.W42
DDC No.	020
OCLC No.	57390951
URL	http://www.webology.org/
Type of Access	Open Access (OA)
Type of Publication	Free of charge
Type of Material	Serial (Periodical)

2. CONTENT ANALYSIS

"Content analysis is any research technique for making inferences by systematically and objectively identifying specified characteristics within text" (*Stone, Dunphy, Smith & Ogilvie*, 1996, with credit given to Holsti, p. 5).

Content analysis, a method which can be used qualitatively or quantitatively for systematically analyzing written, verbal, or visual documentation, goes back to the 1950s and the study of mass communication (*White & Marsh*, 2006, p. 22).

This article accepts a broad-based definition in a recent content analysis textbook by *Krippendorff* (2004).For the purpose of this article, content analysis is "*a research technique for matter to the contexts of their use*" (Krippendorff, 2004, p. 18). The notion of inference is especially important in content analysis. The researcher uses *analytical constructs,* or rules of inference, to move from the text to the answers to the research questions. The two domains, the texts and the context, are logically independent, and the researcher draws conclusions from one independent domain (the texts) to the other (the context). In LIS studies the analytical constructs are not always explicit.

Content analysis involves specialized procedures that, at least in quantitative content analysis, allow for replication. The findings of a good study using quantitative content analysis, therefore, do not rely solely on the authority of the researchers doing the content analysis for their acceptability.

3. LITERATURE REVIEW

A review of related literature reveals that a number of authors have presented the results of the analysis of library and information science literature in different countries.

Rochester M. K. and Vakkari, P. (2003) reviewed national and inter-national trends in LIS research based on research articles in a core collection of journals in studies comparing distribu-tion of topics, subtopics, approaches and methods in Australia, China, Finland, Spain, Turkey and the United Kingdom.

Koufogiannakis et al. (2004) conducted a content analysis of LIS research articles published in 91 journals in 2001. The theme of access and retrieval had the highest number of research articles, followed by collections, man-agement, education and reference.

Tigga, Usha P., Lihitkar Shalini and Rajyalakshmi D. (2005) conducted content analysis of 33 issues of 'DESIDOC Bulletin of Information Technology' published during January 1997 to July 2002.

Blessinger, K. and Frasier, M. (2007) analyzed trends in publication and citation in LIS journals over a decade (1994–2004), concluding that librar-ians are still writing about practical issues that face the pro-fession and, moreover, that the Internet has had a tremendous impact on the LIS community.

Liu, Zao and Wan, Gang (2007) analyze the publication trends of scholarly journal articles on open access in the library and information science literature from 2000 to 2005. The authors used the method of content analysis to systematically analyze the selected scholarly articles. A total of 227 articles were selected from the relevant databases and a comprehensive bibliography on open access. They were subject to a content analysis according to a classification scheme developed by the authors.

Mukherjee, Bhaskar (2009) in his study, quantitative content analysis was carried out using 17 fully open access electronic journals published uninterruptedly during 2000–2004 in the field of Library and Information Science. In this study he investigated the trend of LIS Open Access e-journals' literature by analysing articles, authors, institutions, countries, subjects & references.

Aharony, Nao (2011) describe and analyze journal research publications in the top 10 Library and Information Science journals from 2007–08. The paper presents a statistical descriptive analysis of authorship patterns (geographical distribution and affiliation) and keywords. Furthermore, it displays a thorough content analysis of keywords and abstracts extracted from 10 leading Information Science journals in 2007–08, using Zins' (2007) classification scheme of Information Science.

4. METHODOLOGY

Since this study has been designed to analyse the content of the articles published in LIS OA ejournal "Webology", the use of survey method has been found suitable. The survey method is an acceptable device for collecting data or factual information on certain decided characteristics or items of a universe of population. For the analysis of the study, five volumes (Vol. 9 to 13) containing 5 issues of "*Webology*" published during the year 2005 to 2009 have been taken up for evaluation.The details with regard to each published article such as number of articles in each issue of the journal, number of authors, name of authors, place of authors, country of the author and subject of the article etc., were recorded and analyzed for making observations. The data were collected; organised and analysed using MS-Excel spreadsheets.

5. OBJECTIVES OF THE STUDY

The objectives of this study, covering the period 2005-2009, were:

5.1 To know the publication output of WEBOLOGY.

5.2 To examine authorship characteristics of LIS literature published in WEBOLOGY.

5.3 To know the length of the articles.

5.4 To know the most prolific author contributing to WEBOLOGY.

5.5 To know the geographical distribution of articles (countrywise and statewise) published in WEBOLOGY.

5.6 To know the institutional involvement of publication in WEBOLOGY.

5.7 To analyze LIS literature published in WEBOLOGY so that areas of interest for LIS researchers and current trends may be explored.

6. ANALYSIS AND FINDINGS

6.1. Yearwise distribution of issues and articles

Table 6.1

Year	*Vol.Nos.*	*No.of Issues*	*No. of articles*	*Percentage*
2005	2	4	12	19.35
2006	3	4	13	20.96
2007	4	4	14	22.58
2008	5	4	16	25.80
2009	6	2	07	11.29
	Total	18	62	100.00

Table 6.1 gives details regarding the distribution of total 62 articles published in WEB during the period 2005-2009. Maximum number of articles i.e., 16 (25.80%) has been published in 2008 and minimum number of articles i.e., 7 (11.29%) in 2009. From the above table it is clear that WEB published 4 issues annually upto 2008 and 2 issues annually from 2009.

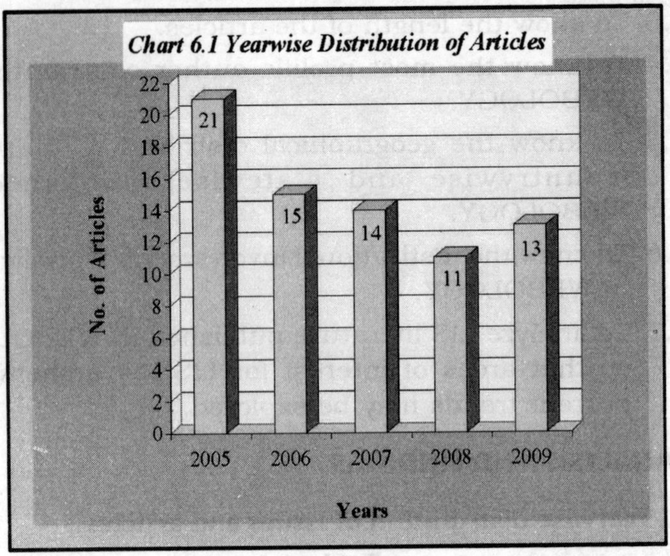

6.2. Authorship pattern of articles (Volumewise)

Table 6.2

Year	*Vol. Nos.*	*Articles contributed by the Authors* Single	Two	More than two	*Total articles*
2005	2	5	6	1	12
2006	3	7	4	2	13
2007	4	11	1	2	14
2008	5	9	6	1	16
2009	6	3	4	0	07
	Total	35	21	6	62

Table 6.2 gives the details about the authorship pattern of the journal WEB. Out of total 62 articles, 35 articles have been contributed by single author, 21 articles by two authors and 6 articles by more than two authors.

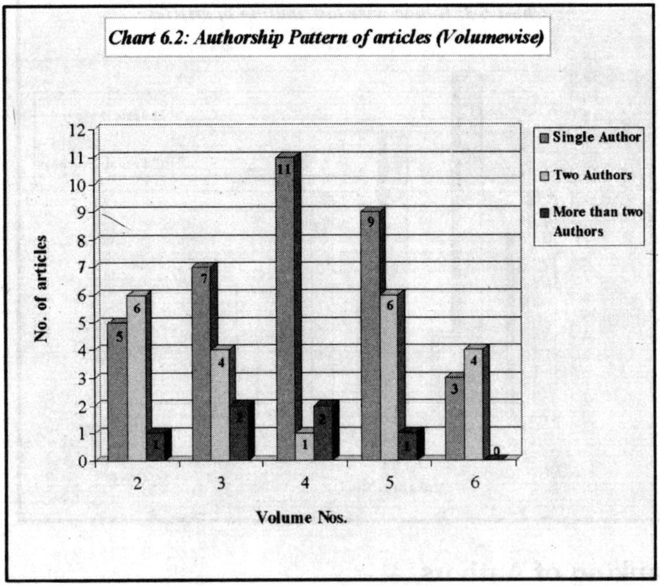

6.3. Genderwise distribution of articles

Table 6.3

Vol. No.	*Male Authors*	*Female Authors*	*Total Authors*
2	11	9	20
3	17	4	21
4	14	6	20
5	11	13	24
6	4	7	11
Total	57	39	96

Table 6.3 shows that in WEB, out of total 96 authors, 57 authors are male authors and 39 authors are female authors. From the table it is clear that in WEB, male authors contribution is more than that of female authors.

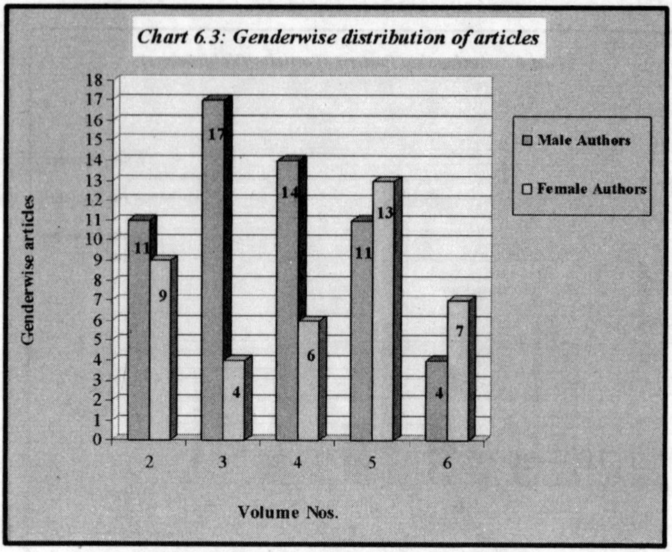

6.4. Ranking of Authors

Table 6.4

Sr.No.	*Rank*	*Author(s) contributed articles*	*No. of articles*
1	1	Neelameghan A.	3
2	2	6 authors	2
3	3	81 authors	1

Table 6.4 depicts the ranking of authors in the journal WEB during the period 2005 to 2009. From the above table it is clear that out of total 96 authors, 3 articles are contributed by the author *Neelameghan A.* securing *first* rank. Whereas 6 authors contributed *two* article each securing *second* rank and 81 authors contributed 1 article each securing third rank.

6.5. Types of institutions and their involvement in publication

Table 6.5

Types of institution	*No. of authors from the institution*
Academic	80
Organization	13
Commercial	02
Individual	01
Not Identified	00
Total	96

Table 6.5 depicts the types of institutions and their involvement in the journal WEB. From the table it is clear that total out of 96 authors, maximum of 80 authors are from Academic institutions, 13 authors are from Organizations and 2 authors are from Commercial institutions. Whereas 1 authors is an individual author.

6.6. Prolific institutions and their involvement in publication (Institutions contributing 5 or more than 5 articles)

Table 6.6

Name of the institution	*No. of authors from the institution*
University of Tasmania, Australia	6

Table 6.6 depicts the prolific institutions and their involvement in the journal WEB during the study period 2005-2009. From the table it is clear that *University of Tasmania, Australia* is the most prolific institution contributing 10 authors in WEB.

6.7. Number of articles under specific subject headings

Table 6.7

Specific Subject Heading		*Number of articles*
1.1	Librarianship	01
3.16	Electronic Resources	02
3.17	Resources by Subject	01
5.0	User Services	01
6.0	Use & Users Studies	01
6.1	Bibliometrics, Scientometrics, Infometrics & Webology	12
6.2	Information Seeking Behaviour	04
7.0	Information Storage & Retrieval	10
7.2	Thesaurus	01
8.0	Library & ICT	05
8.2	Digital Library & Digitization	05
8.3	Library Resource Sharing & Networks	01
8.4	Issue related to Web 2.0 & Semantic web	10
9.1	Publishing	02
9.4	Other Aspects	06
	Total	62

Table 6.7 shows the articles under the subject heading during the study period (2005-2009) in the journal WEB. From the above table it is clear that 62 articles in the journal WEB are distributed in 15 different subject headings. Out of total 62 articles, maximum of 12 articles are under the subject heading *6.1 Bibliometrics, Scientometrics, Infometrics & Webology,* 10 articles are under the subject headings *7.0 Information Storage & Retrieval* and *8.4 Issue related to Web 2.0 & Semantic web* each.

6.8. Geographical Distribution of articles (country wise)

Table 6.8

Sr. No.	*Country*	*No. of author contributions*	*% of contribution*
1	India	27	28.12
2	USA	16	16.66
3	Australia	12	12.50
4	Iran	09	9.37
5	UK	08	8.33
6	Canada	07	7.29
7	Bahrain	02	2.08
8	Finland	02	2.08
9	Germany	02	2.08
10	Nigeria	02	2.08
11	Pakistan	02	2.08
12	Brazil	01	1.04
13	France	01	1.04
14	Korea	01	1.04
15	Malaysia	01	1.04
16	Norway	01	1.04
17	Taiwan	01	1.04
18	Thailand	01	1.04
	Total	96	100

From Table 6.8 it is clear that in WEB, there are total 96 authors representing 18 different countries. Out of 96 authors, the highest number, i.e., 27 (28.12%) authors has been contributed from India and lowest number i.e., 1 (1.04%) author has been contributed from Brazil, France, Korea, Malaysia, Norway, Taiwan and Thailand each. From the table it is clear that most of the articles are from Indian authors though the publication of the WEB takes place at Iran.

CONCLUSION

The analysis indicates that there were 62 articles published in the journal "Webology" during 2005 to 2009.

The authorship pattern indicates that the majority of articles published by single authors. *Neelameghan A* is the most productive author during the study period. Authors from academic institutions were paid more interest in "Webology". The subject coverage of this journal is mostly towards Librarianship, covering other LIS subjects in the articles. The analysis of data clearly indicates that OA ejournal "Webology" rapidly establishing themselves as a most viable media for scholarly communication.

REFERENCES

- Aharony, Nao (2011). Library and Information Science research areas: A content analysis of articles from the top 10 journals (2007-08). *Journal of Librarianship and Information Science, 44*(1), 27-35, retrieved Jan 27, 2013, from http://lis.sagepub.com/content/44/1/27.
- Atinmo,M.I., Jimba, S. W. (2002). Gender and authorship pattern in an African librarianship journal(1991–1997). *Library Review,* 51(9), 458–463.
- Bates, M. (1999). A tour of information science through the pages of JASIS. *Journal of the American Society for Information Science,* 50, 975–993.
- Blessinger, K. and Frasier, M. (2007). Analysis of a decade in library literature (1994-2004). *College & Research Libraries,* 68(2), 155-170.
- Cano, V. (1999). Bibliometric overview of library and information science research in Spain. *Journal of the American Society for Information Science,* 50, 675–680.
- Cline, G. S. (1982). College and research libraries: Its first forty years. *College and Research Libraries,* 43, 209–232.
- Harsanyi, M. A. (1993). Multiple authors, multiple problems – bibliometrics and the study of scholarly collaboration: A literature review. *Library and Information Science Research,* 15 (Fall), 325–154.
- Hawkins, D. T. (1978). Bibliometrics of the online information retrieval literature. *Online Review,* 2, 345–351.
- Hawkins, D. T. (2001). Bibliometrics of electronic journals in information science. *Information Research,* 7(1), Available

at http://InformationR.net/ir/7-1/paper120.html. [Access on 04th January 2012].

- Hawkins, D. T. (2001).Information Science Abstracts: tracking the literature of information science. part 1: definition and map. *Journal of the American Society for Information Science and Technology, 52(1),* 44-53.
- He, S. Y., Spink, A. (2002). A comparison of foreign authorship distribution in JASIST and the Journal of Documentation. Journal of the American Society for Information Science and Technology, 53(11), 953–959.
- Hussain, Akhtar., Fatima, Nishat. (2011). A bibliometric analysis of the 'Chinese Librarianship: an International electronic journal,(2006-2010)'. *Chinese Librarianship: an International electronic journal,*31, Available at http://www.iclc.us/cliej/cl31HF.pdf. [Access on 14th January 2012].
- Jarvelin, K., Vakkari, P. (1990). Content-analysis of research articles in library and information-science. Library and Information Science Research, 12, 395–421.
- Jarvelin, K., Vakkari, P. (1993). The evolution of library and information science 1965–1985: A contentanalysis of journal articles. Information Processing and Management, 29, 129–144.
- Jena, Lochan Kamal; Swain, Dillip K. and Sahoo, K. C.(2012). Annals of Library and Information Studies, 2002–2010: A Bibliometric Study. Library Philosophy and Practice (e-journal), 716.
- Korytnyk, C. A.(1988). Comparison of the publishing patterns between men and women Ph.D.s in Librarianship. Library Quarterly, 58 (1), 52–65.
- Koufogiannakis, Denise, Slater, Linda and Crumley, Ellen. (2004). A content analysis of librarianship research. *Journal of Information Science,* 30(3), 227-239.
- Krippendorff, K. (2004). *Content analysis: An introduction to its methodology* (2nd ed.). Thousand Oaks, CA: Sage.
- Liu, Zao and Wan, Gang. (2007). Scholarly journal articles on open access in LIS literature: a content analysis. *Chinese Librarianship,* 23, 4-14, Retrieved April 19, 2013, from: http://web.ebscohost.com/ehost/detail?vid=10&hid=104&sid=3bfbb3973154-463d-9ddc- d24651029c12%40sessionmgr108 .

- Lokhande, Rahul. (2013). Content Analysis of Open Access LIS Journal 'ALIS' (2002-2011). IJORS in Social Sciences, 1(1), 2-13.
- Lokhande, Rahul. (2013). Content Analysis of Open Access LIS Journal 'D-lib Magzine' (2005-2009). IJORS in Social Sciences, 1(3), 2-12.
- Mahapatra, G. (1994). Indian library and information science journals: A bibliometric analysis of the rate of citations and their characteristics. Library Review, 43 (3), 41–46.
- Mittal, Rekha (2011). Library and information science research trends in India. Annals of Library and Information Studies, 58,319-325.
- Mukherjee, Bhaskar. (2009). Scholarly research in LIS open access electronic journals : A bibliometric study. Scientometrics, 80(1), 167-194.
- Naseer, Mirza Muhammad and Mahmood, Khalid (2009). LIS Research in Pakistan: An Analysis of Pakistan Library and Information Science Journal 1998-2007. Library Philosophy and Practice, 1-10.
- Neuendorf, K. A. (2002). *The content analysis guidebook.* Thousand Oaks, CA: Sage.
- Nisonger, T. E. (1999). JASIS and library and information science journal ranking: A review and analysis of the last half century. Journal of the American Society for Information Science and Technology, 50, 1004–1019.
- Rochester, M. K. and Vakkari, P. (2003). International Library and Information Science research: A comparison of national trends. *IFLA Professional Reports*, 82, 1-40.
- Schloegl, C., Stock, W. G. (2004). Impact and relevance of LIS journals: A scientometric analysis of international and German-language LIS journals-citation analysis versus reader survey. Journal of the American Society for Information Science and Technology, 55 (13), 1155–1168.
- Terry, J. L. (1996). Authorship in college & research libraries revisited: Gender, institutional affiliation, collaboration. College and Research Libraries, 58, 377–383.
- Tigga, Usha P., Lihitkar, Shalini and Rajyalakshmi, D. (2005). Content analysis of DESIDOC bulletin of information technology (1997-2002). *DESIDOC Bulletin of Information Technology,* 25(4), 5-18.

- Verma, Niraj; Tamrakar, Rajnish and Sharma, Priyanka (2007). Analysis of contributions in 'Annals of Library and Information Studies'. Annals of Library and Information Studies, 54,106-111.
- Voorbij, H. (1999). Searching scientific information on the Internet: A Dutch academic user survey. Journal of the American Society of Information Science, 50 (7), 598–615.
- White, M.D., & Marsh, E.E. (2006). Content analysis: A flexible methodology. *Library Trends 55*(1), 22-45 doi: 10.1353/lib.2006.0053
- Zhang, Y. (1998). The impact of Internet based electronic resources on formal scholarly communication in the area of library and information science: A citation analysis. Journal of Information Science, 24, 241–254.

5

Content Curation : Quality of Information for Knowledge Based Research

M Natarajan

Senior Principal Scientist (Retd), Ex-Head,
Education & Training, Editor – JSIR
NISCAIR, Dr K S Krishnan Marg
New Delhi – 110012

ABSTRACT

The purpose of the article is to provide an overview of the development and recent focus on content curation (CC) and the need for it for doing the knowledge based research. It provides the different definitions of CC with the need for the same. The concept of information obesity has been given to follow the CC. The need for CC centres for developing a reliable data, for future use with need for developing tools and techniques. The major aspects of CC like different types of CC, Five laws of CC, Different models of content curation are discussed. The variety of CC tools as per the curation activity, available are discussed with the important considerations for CC. The role of content curators / authors, data scientists and data managers are discussed in detail. Major role played by the library professionals for content curation activities are discussed. The competencies required for CC activity are given in detail. The advantages and disadvantages of doing the content curation activity has been enumerated with the conclusion stating that LIS professionals are already carrying out the CC activity in other manner and try to be better content curators in future.

Keywords : Content curation, curation tools, information obesity, information overload, social media.

INTRODUCTION

Collecting, preserving, and distributing intellectual works has always been an important mission of libraries. The digital age has presented new challenges and new opportunities. It is important that the enormous amount of information being produced in electronic format not be lost if the format in which it resides is replaced with the next latest and greatest technical advance. The dissemination of these works via the web provides access to otherwise hidden materials and enhances information sharing across the scientific community. Relevant and decision ready information is becoming a valuable commodity in its own right, and many organizations are beginning to appreciate the roles and skills of people who understand the specific information needs of their information consumers and can provide it in a timely and effective manner. The answer to these needs lies in the disciplines, competencies and skills of content curation. Effective curation requires technology and tools to find, filter and validate content at the speed of the real-time Web. It requires knowledge domain experts who can interpret and add insight to the content they are harvesting. It needs people who can utilize the power of networks and networking to source relevant and reliable information.

Content curation community's aggregate, validate, and annotate *existing* content with its associated intellectual property claims into a comprehensive repository, while content creation communities avoid intellectual property concerns by *creating* their own content from scratch. Both content creation and content curation communities share some aspects with organizational repositories, mainly the need to "shape" knowledge—whether created or curated—into a more useful format that will create a "dynamic memory system" (Yates, Wagner, & Majchrzak, 2010) that will serve the community members. As such, both communities fill important niches in the information landscape and have already proven their worth. Although content creation communities, particularly Wikipedia, have been examined extensively to uncover the principles that have led to their successes and failures (c.f. Forte & Bruckman, 2005; Kittur, Chi, Pendleton, Suh, & Mytkowicz, 2007; Kriplean, Beschastnikh, & McDonald, 2008; Nov, 2007), there have not been comparable studies of content curation communities. To realize the ambitious goals of such communities, we must understand how to effectively design the technologies, information standards, processes, and social practices that support them.

The goal of this article is to characterize content curation communities and their increasing prominence in the information landscape, and then to use the formative years of the Encyclopedia of Life (EOL) as a case study for providing insights into the design of such communities. Our key research questions are as follows:

- What are the unique informational and social challenges experienced by EOL, as an example of a content curation community?
- What are the key information and social design choices available to designers of content curation communities?

DEFINITIONS

Curation connotes the activities of identifying, selecting, validating, organizing, describing, maintaining, and preserving existing artifacts. This term follows the term "content" because the artifacts being curated by the community are content, not necessarily the objects themselves.

Content curation is a term that describes the act of finding, grouping, organizing or sharing the best and most relevant content on a specific issue. It is such a powerful idea because curation does NOT focus on adding more content / noise to the chaotic information overload of social media, and instead focuses on helping any one of us to make sense of this information by bringing together what is most important.

"Content curation is the act of continually identifying, selecting and sharing the best and most relevant online content and other online resources (and by that I mean articles, blog posts, videos, photos, tools, tweets or whatever) on a specific subject to match the needs of a specific audience." - Ann Handley, *TopRank Online Marketing Blog* (2011).

Content curation is the process of sorting through the vast amounts of content on the web and presenting it in a meaningful and organized way around a specific theme. The work involves sifting, sorting, arranging and publishing information. A content curator cherry picks the best content that is important and relevant to share with their community. (Beth's blog). Content curators provide a customized, vetted selection of the best and most relevant resources on a very specific topic or theme.

Social media sharing has enabled anyone to share anything with the world. Technology has enabled anyone with an Internet connection to become a curator. Now the waves of the web are just too big. Curation is the new magic that makes the web work. Bringing the web back to human scale with human filters you trust and love. A powerful mix of passion and context turns noise back into signal.

INFORMATION OBESITY

Information obesity is a failure to turn information into knowledge, and thus use it to sustain our minds, bodies, lives and communities. But just as physical obesity is not simply the result of too much food, so information obesity is caused by more than just 'information overload'. Also responsible are:

- reductions in the quality of information
- problems with mental 'fitness', that is, a lack of skills, training, etc. in the consumer of information
- external pressures, whether from 'information industries', peers, or organizations within which we work, to consume information before we have properly judged its worth. (Whitworth, 2009)

Information overload is a part of the phenomenon of information obesity. In the case of information obesity, the result is, essentially, the inability to make sense of or act effectively on information – as Whitworth states, the inability to turn information into knowledge. We become increasingly powerless and unable to make sense of things.

LITERATURE REVIEW

There is no shortage of articles and reports that describe potential roles for libraries in managing and curating research data, and the skills that librarians may need to acquire to do so. In the middle of the last decade, the Association for Research Libraries (ARL) produced two reports that set the stage for discussing potential roles for libraries, as organizations, in supporting the emerging research paradigm of e-Science. Both reports advocated for libraries to develop infrastructure and services for the curation and preservation of research data, and to develop partnerships with faculty, research communities, and other entities to develop and maintain these services (Friedlander and Adler, 2006; ARL, 2007). At the same time, Anna Gold surveyed data librarianship and recommended that libraries expand into new roles. She suggested that libraries continue to build on efforts to develop roles in the post-publication or "downstream" side of the research cycle which would include crafting services towards supporting data publication as well as building collections of published data sets. There are now multiple libraries that are offering services and support for data management and curation, and many other libraries are taking actions to explore how data services could be incorporated at their respective organizations. Many of these libraries have written up and published their approaches and experiences in developing data services, including the Georgia Institute of Technology (Walters, 2009), Purdue University (Brandt, 2007) and Cornell University (Steinhart, Saylor, et.al, 2008). However, what tends to be documented in these publications are the nature of the services and the needs that they are intended to address.

WHY CONTENT CURATION?

It is a truism that the volume of information now available to researchers on almost any topic is staggering and often overwhelming. Rohit Bhargava (2009), a social media strategist and adjunct professor at Georgetown University, posits that the amount of content on the web is doubling every seventy-two hours. In response, Bhargava contends that this new environment calls for a new profession, that of a "Content Curator... who continually finds, groups, organizes and shares the best and most relevant content on a specific issue online." Many of us are already using tools like Libguides (www.libguides.com) to organize online tools and resources by topic and subject, or for creating course-specific web pages. We also use content management systems (CMS) to organize and manage information and for building our web sites.

People and organizations are now making and sharing media and content all over the social web. A content curator offers high value to anyone looking for quality content because finding that information (and making sense of it) requires more and more time, attention and focus. For some staff members, content curation can be professional of learning. Professional development used to be about getting trained or acquiring a specific skill. But, with so much information available and coming at us from many sources, we often don't know if it's the right information or if it's current. In today's world of content abundance, the skill of how to find, make sense and share content that we need to be effective in our work is critical. Simply put, being a content curator is a method to help you stay informed about your field and be more effective at your job (Beth's blog). Information overload is disorienting our lives and making it increasingly difficult for us to find the right information when needed. Many employees are feeling overwhelmed on a daily basis by documents, discussions on social tools, images and videos. Clearly the content burden is an issue that needs to be fixed. We need to separate the signal from the noise. We want to be able to take actionable decisions based on good quality information. Taking a drink from the raw, unfiltered, context-free Internet fire hose is no longer a viable option for any of us. Content curation provides a structure, a process, a system and a discipline to help us find (and use) more relevant information. The real benefit of it is dependent on the skills, knowledge and competencies of the human content curator. Social media has given us the tools to find and filter raw content, but it can't tell us what is right or what is useful. We have to utilize our own knowledge and experience of the world to apply critical thinking and 'sense' what is useful and relevant. We have to use our brains to make the connections between non-linear and asynchronous articles, stories and events. Already we are all doing the content curation one way or other known as "Personal knowledge management" (PKM) or "self-directed learning".

The content is curated depending upon the user

community. This might typically be an online community, a department in an organization, your managers or leaders, your blog followers and so on. The important thing about sharing is that the content curator has added some value to what is being shared, that is, it's not merely a regurgitation of content that has been found. This includes some insight to the content, even personal opinion. The more consummate content curators will use storytelling techniques to join up the dots between what might have been several disparate content sources. It is quite clear that relevant and decision-ready information is becoming a valuable commodity in its own right, and many organizations are beginning to appreciate the roles and skills of people who understand the specific information needs of their information consumers and can provide it in a timely and effective manner.

TYPES OF CONTENT CURATION

Beth Kanter (2012a) provides an understandable explanation of curation, which incorporates the idea of sense-making into the process like i) Actively manage your attention ii) Turn off some good stuff for good iii) Utilize personal management tools iv) Capture less, scan more v) Curate content yourself by adding value vi) Let yourself make sense of things and vii) Share your insights and be willing to have conversation.

THE FIVE LAWS OF THE CURATION ECONOMY

The first law : People don't want more content, they want less. We're overwhelmed in raw, unfiltered, context-free data. Humans want it to stop.

The second law : Curators come in three shapes. There are curation experts – people whose background and depth of understanding makes their curatorial choices valid. If you're looking for medical advice, you want your video viewing curated by a doctor, not a patient.

The third law : Curation isn't a hobby; it's both a

profession and a calling. Curators need to be paid to be part of the emerging ecosystem. What's a fair fee will depend on how critical the curator's output is in the category. But an economic basis is essential and inevitable.

The fourth law : Curation requires technology and tools to find, filter and validate content at the speed of the real-time web. Curation can't simply be a human with a web browser – the mix of man and machine is essential here.

The fifth law : Curation within narrow, focused, high quality categories will emerge to compete with the mass media copycats who are filling the curation space with lists, cat videos and meme links. The simple fact is this, the Web used to be a relatively. (Stephen Dale, 2014)

The cure for information overload is coherent curation, data-driven discovery managed by skilled, thoughtful and in some cases, expert curators. Curate or be curated – that's the new face of digital content in the always-on world.

MODELS OF CONTENT CURATION

Curation has many layers, from the simple to the complex. The five Models of Content Curation by Rohit Bhargava are i) Aggregation – is the act of curtain the most relevant information about a particular topic into a single location. ii) Distillation – is the act of curating information into a more simplistic format where only the most important or relevant ideas are shared. iii) Elevation – refers to curation with a mission of identifying a larger trend or insight from smaller daily musings posted online. iv) Mashup – are unique curated justapositions where merging existing content is used to create a new point of view and v) Chronology – is a form of curation that brings together historical information organsied based on time to show an evolving understanding of a particular topic. Content curation is finding and assembling useful and relevant information artefacts for 'sense making' and engaging with online communities is all part of this journey. Organizations that have recognized the benefits of self-directed learning over more traditional classroom training are more likely to approach content curation as a skill that needs to be developed in their workforce and (probably) more willing to allocate resources to this activity.

CONTENT CURATION TOOLS

There is a wide variety of content curation tools, platforms and services that can be used to curate digital content. These tools vary in many ways, including what data sources they can pull from, where they can share and who has access to them. Some of them are given below with their functions:

FINDING, AGGREGATING AND ORGANIZING TOOLS

- Feedly has become well known as the RSS aggregator successor to Google Reader. It is a content curation tool that has specialized on the collection of content for the user to evaluate. Besides doing a good job of keeping track of RSS feeds you wish to follow, Feedly also offers a search engine that allows users to search for additional sources of information on a topic.
- Hootsuite and Tweetdeck are examples of social media aggregation tools. They help keep track and manage many social network channels. They can monitor what people are saying about you, your topics or your brand.
- Evernote is one of the most well-known online note taking applications, alongside Google Keep and Microsoft's OneNote service. With Evernote, you can use as few or as many of the advanced note management tools as you like. A wide variety of Evernote's advanced tools are available free to users,

but the real power come from the paid for Premium service.

- Diigo is a powerful information capturing, storing, recalling and sharing tool. Features include saving important website URLs; categorising websites by titles, notes, keyword tags, lists and groups; searching through bookmarks to quickly find desired information; saving a screenshot of a website to see how it has changed over time; annotating websites with highlighting or virtual 'sticky notes'; viewing any annotations made by others on any website visited; sharing websites with groups or the entire Diigo social network; and commenting on the bookmarks of others or soliciting comments on shared bookmarks.
- Prismatic is an app that provides a home for all of a user's interests where they can follow all people and topics of importance to them and create a personalized news feed.
- Newsle sends news updates to users about connections in their social networks. Whenever a friend or contact is mentioned in a news article, Newsle will send an email about it in near real time.

NEWS CURATION AND NEWSLETTER TOOLS

- **Paper :** It combines entries from Twitter hashtags, photos, blog and newsline articles and Facebook into a magazine style layout.
- **Scoop :** it fills the need that a growing number of people and businesses have to publish content in an efficient and impacting way using big data semantic technology that helps them quickly find relevant content.

VISUAL CURATION BOARDS

- Pearltrees are the visual and collaborative curation tools that allow users to collect, organize and share any URL they find online as well as to upload personal images and notes I manage a curated Pearltree on content curation.

- Pinterest offers the ability to easily add both photos and graphics to topical pinboards. It also provides a search facility for other boards that have new items fitting your topics.
- Keeeb is a visual bookmarking tool and community.

SOCIAL PUBLISHING HUBS

- Rebelmouse allows users to create a blog, website or social page in seconds by connecting their social networks such as Twitter, Facebook, Instagram, Google+ and LinkedIn. (Stephen Dale, 2014) and many more are available for social publishing.

Essentially, librarians, students, and other educators gather resources from the web and organize them in user-friendly and in web-based formats. Curation tools can include online social-bookmarking services like Diigo, Delicious, Digg, Reddit, and more visually oriented bookmarking services like Pinterest and Symbaloo. Then there are hybrid curation tools that not only allow bookmarking but also enable creating stories (Storify) and customized magazines or newspapers (Scoop.it and Paper.li).

CONTENT CURATION COMPETENCIES

There are five fundamental skills or competencies required for effective content curation:

1. use of tools (social media, search, syndicated feeds etc.) to find and filter relevant information;
2. organizing information – categorization, tagging, scheduling and so on;
3. networking – participating in personal and professional networks to enhance and improve learning;

4. critical thinking and sense making; and
5. adding insight and value through storytelling techniques.

It is no accident that all of these competencies align very closely with those of the knowledge or information professional, and consequently why these professions are particularly suited to that of a content curator. Figure 1, overleaf, illustrates the activities that contribute to the core competencies for content curation.

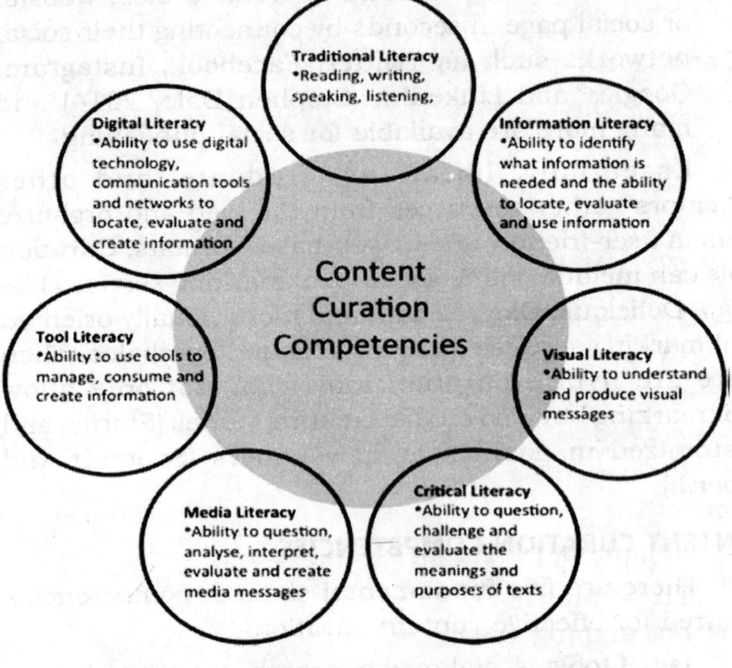

Fig. 1. Content curation competencies (concept by Dr Daniel Churchill)

From that simple observation of curation or creation there is a logic which helps shape a future of: new strategies, new sources, new tools, new companies and blogs every day. Content curation, when taken seriously, requires you to watch over the quality over the content you curate.

ADVANTAGES AND DISADVANTAGES

Some of the general factors and effects of content curation (CC) are as follows:

CC pro·'ides context and convenience

- CC does not overwhelm
- CC can build authority
- CC - disconnected, connected and hybrid

CC and search engine optimization

- CC, when well done, can positively impact search engine optimization.
- CC also increases industry knowledge
- CC establishes credibility and trust
- CC builds brand loyalty
- CC improves brand voice
- CC inspires and delights
- CC increases brand awareness (accessed from *http://relevance.com/embrace-content-curation-and-enjoy-these-6-benefits/*)

Some of the disadvantages are:

- Validity of CC produced information
- Time factor is something to consider when researching good content
- May be costly affair
- How to use the cc product – sometimes not available

It has been to provide fresh and quality content, many blog owners use content curation. To acquire the best results from utilizing content curation marketing, it's important to know how to use it and also what to avoid. Some of the Do's and Don't s are as follows:

Do's

1. Have a focus topic on what you want to write about.
2. Ensure this is in line with the focus of your blog or expertise or niche.
3. Source from a variety of sources (google blogs, amazon books, pictures, videos, etc.)
4. Build the ability to "know" which links are clicked by which customers/readers. That way you can then segment them according their preferences.
5. Keep tweaking the focus keyword as you look for material from different sources. This will help you finalize your keyword, and give you ideas for an attention-gripping title.
6. Don't just collect content and throw it out there. Weave a story or an insight around all the content you collected. If you have an opinion, or a conclusion, state it FIRMLY.
7. KNOW your reader. And provide what is in their best interest and what they would look favorably to.

Don'ts

1. Don't make all your posts "curated" only. Mix those up with interviews, surveys, news and some original content. Provide variety to your readers.
2. Always proof-read. Use the drag and drop feature. Don't delete any part of the final "curated" post (you may inadvertently delete original credits).
3. For photographs, ensure that you understand the license/royalty associated with the image.
4. Keep an eye out for the authors whose posts you end up (frequently) curating. Don't ignore them, but try to build a relationship with them.
5. Don't use curated content for guest-posting. Original content is looked upon more favorably by sites that

approve guest posts. (from *http://curationsoft.com/dos-donts-content-curation/*) by Raj Subramanyam.

CONCLUSION

Curation comes in many forms, from crowd sourced lists and aggregated collections to authored stories that provide new and insightful perspectives on previously published material. Content curation can be used as a personal competency to help us develop our understanding of this information rich, time poor world we live in. Relevant and decision-ready information is becoming a valuable commodity in its own right, and many organizations are beginning to appreciate the roles and skills of people who understand the specific information needs of their information consumers and can provide it in a timely and effective manner. It is still early days for curation in our world. Whilst the practices are old, the technologies are often new and as we get to grips with the possibilities that new technologies bring us, it's easy to see that more opportunities for storing, transforming and sharing resources will become available. Curation, as a skill, is on the verge of becoming a key differentiator for employees; knowledge workers could well be expected to bring their curated insights with them to their next job role. Developing successful librarians and library organizations are not separate paths of consideration, although they are often treated as such. The opportunities and barriers librarians encounter when engaging in data management and curation issues stem from both their own abilities and the environment in which they work.

REFERENCES

- Bhargava, R. (2009). Manifesto for the Content Curator: the new big social media job of the future? Retrieved from http://www.rohitbhargava.com/2009/09/manifestofor-the-content-curator-the-next-big-social-media-job-of-the-future.html (accessed 29 February 2016).

- Brandt, D. Scott. (2007). "Librarians as partners in e-research: Purdue University Libraries promote collaboration." *College & Research Libraries News* 68(6), 365-367, 396.
- Buzzfeed: http://www.buzzfeed.com/
- Content Curation Flipboard: *https://flipboard.com/section/content-curation-bU9AMh*
- Content Curation Tools, Platforms and Services: https://contentcuration.zeef.com/robin.good#block_3022
- Diigo: www.diigo.com/
- Evernote: http://www.evernote.com
- Feedly: http://feedly.com/index.html#welcome
- Flipboard: https://flipboard.com/
- Friedlander, Amy. and Adler, Prudence (2006). "To Stand the Test of Time: Long-term Stewardship of Digital Data Sets in Science and Engineering." *Association of Research Libraries (ARL).* http://www.eric.ed.gov/PDFS/ED528649.pdf
- Gold, Anna. (2007). "Cyberinfrastructure, Data, and Libraries, Part 2: Libraries and the Data Challenge: Roles and Actions for Libraries." *DLib Magazine* 13(9/10): 10.
- Goodbits: https://goodbits.io/
- Harold Jarche "Seek-Sense-Share": http://jarche.com/
- Hootsuite: https://hootsuite.com/dashboard
- Kanter B (2012a) Content Curation Primer. In: Beth's Blog. Available at: http://www.bethkanter.org/content-curation-101 (accessed Jan 2016).
- Keeb: http://keeeb.com/
- List.ly: http://list.ly/
- Mashable: http://mashable.com/
- Newsle: http://newsle.com/
- Paper.li: http://paper.li/
- Pinterest: http://www.pinterest.com/
- Prismatic: http://getprismatic.com/
- Rebelmouse: https://www.rebelmouse.com/
- Rohit Barghava's 5 Models of Content Curation: http://www.rohitbhargava.com/2011/03/the-5-models-of-content-curation.html

- Scoop.it: http://www.scoop.it
- Steinhart, Gail, John Saylor, Paul Albert, Kristine Alpi, Pam Baxter, Eli Brown, Kathy Chiang, Jon Corson-Rikert, Peter Hirtle, Keith Jenkins, Brian Lowe, Janet McCue, David Ruddy, Rick Silterra, Leah Solla, Zoe Stewart-Marshall and Elaine L. Westbrooks. (2008). "Digital Research Data Curation: Overview of Issues, Current Activities, and Opportunities for the Cornell University Library." *e-Commons @ Cornell* http://hdl.handle.net/1813/10903.
- Stephen Dale, (2014). Content Curation: the future of relevance. *Business Information Review*, 31(4), 199-205.
- Storify: https://storify.com/
- Storyful: http://storyful.com/
- The Guardian #smartakes: http://www.theguardian.com/commentisfree/series/smarttakes
- Tweetdeck: http://tweetdeck.en.softonic.com
- Videolink: http://www.thevideoink.com/features/voices/the-coming-age-of-the-curation-economy-building-contextaround-content/#.VEp5qZPF9Xo
- Walters, Tyler O. (2009). "Data Curation Program Development in U.S. Universities: The Georgia Institute of Technology Example." *The International Journal of Digital Curation* 4(3), 83-92,
- Whitworth A (2009) Information Obesity: Summary and Abstracts. Available at: http://personalpages. manchester. ac.uk/staff/drew.whitworth/information obesity/summary. html (accessed Jan 2016).

6

Role of Library Professionals in Cyber Society

D.R.Gabhane

Librarian, Samarth Mahavidyalaya,

Lakhani, Bhandra

ABSTRACT

In the fast changing world of information technology Libraries and Library Professionals have to cope with all tools and techniques of information technology. Due to introduction of modern tools and techniques today's society changed into cyber society. Students, Teachers and researchers Businessman Industrialists and other general public are the stakeholders of these tools and techniques. The services of the Libraries should be user oriented, but there is need to take care of user need and their satisfaction.

Library professionals have great responsibility to identify needs of these stake holders and update themeshelves accordingly. The paper discusses some innovative practices which helps them to motivate the users towards the use of library services and inculcate the the reading habits and skills to aware with the modern tools and techniques of cyber world.

INTRODUCTION

In this fast changing environment of information technology, library services ought to change with the par of library users. With the introduction of various tools of information technology to excel and accelerate the services of the library there is a need of user education to orient them with these tools and techniques. Due to introduction of modern tools and techniques today's society changed into cyber society. Students, Teachers and researchers Businessman Industrialists and other general public are the stakeholders of these tools and techniques. The services of the Libraries should be user oriented, but there is need to take care of user need and their satisfaction.

Library professionals now- a- days should have the keys to identify the needs of users. Traditional services of the libraries get changed due to the introduction advanced information technological tools, but it can not be finalized that the traditional services do not able to satisfy the needs of users. With the perfect amalgamation of traditional services, library professionals satisfy the needs of the users. Now-a- days, perfect managerial skill and with the help of soft skill management, library professionals do to satisfy the users.

Libraries are now information learning centers. There is great impact of information technology on library and library services. The services of the library should be users oriented. To deal with the different types of users according to their demand with the hard skills, soft skills are also essential to flourish the Personality of library profession. Following are some of aspects which explain the role of Library professionals in cyber society.

a) As a good leader

It is very essential to librarian to have good leadership quality, because library work and to deliver the library services effectively and promptly is not individual work, but it is a team work with spirit. So, it is a need to develop leadership quality. This skill create confidence amongst library staff.

b) As a good communicator

This skill mainly includes writing and speaking skill.

A good communication skill always has great impact while making a good rapport with the users. It is also helpful in making the library reports and correspondence. For good communication library professionals should have sound knowledge about mother tongue, language of the particular locality and have good command over English language.

c) As a Teacher of teachers

Librarian should be a good teacher. To orient the users with the library service, library professionals should have good teaching skill. This will be helpful to inculcate good reading habits amongst the users.

d) As a good listener

Listening skill is very useful to interact with the users of different age groups. With users of different age group, their requirement varies. By careful listening to users, one can exactly identify the demand of them. It helps in the betterment of library services.

e) Be the doorsteps of the user

In library field the users are considered as the customers of library. Current Awareness Service (CAS) and Selective Dissemination of Information (SDI) and other specialized services must be user oriented. These services should satisfy the users and assures and guarantee that users will always come back to library.

f) A man who molds with time

Now a day's information technology has great impact in library and information services. Library professional should have sound knowledge about e-based library services, and for that he/she must develops IT skill or E-skills. Library professionals should have the knowledge of computer network, E-books, copyright, Cyber Law, E-publishing, Internet resources, Scanning Downloading software purposes. So one has to change with time.

g) Be Less informative and more knowledgeable :-

Information about any thing will not mark so much. Domain knowledge or subject knowledge is very essential in every profession. Library professional have to deal with different type of users with their varying needs. A sound subject knowledge help them to make good communication with the users. Convert year library is a Knowledge Resource Center.

h) As a good Time Manager

In this age of fast life, one has to act according to time table. In ever fields of life time management is important so being library professionals we have to save the time of users. So plan your work and work your plan. So we will be unable to satisfy one of library laws of Dr. S.R. Rangnathan.

i) Sharpening of carrier

With the speed of information and technology, every library professional has to update his knowledge. So try to attend more and more workshop and conferences of your subject and also of peripheral subject. Updation of knowledge helps to shape your carrierin cyber world.

j) As a man of Positive Attitude

Negative attitude always demorals you. Library Profession also a noble profession like teaching So be positive and always keep ready to help the users and information seekers. Prejudice thinking always harms to your personality. So be positive and act according to it.

k) As a man of to say 'No'

Library profession is a multifaceted profession. All types of were come to library. Their needs may be different. Be positive but do not demolish the rules of the library. Try to say 'No' such unwanted practices which will ruin the image of library and library profession.

l) As a source of Teamwork spirit

To give effective library services to users is not a job of librarian alone . It is a team work. To inculcate team work spirit amongst library staff, it is very essential to nurture team work skill amongst library professional themselves.

The list and discussion on soft skills is unending, because soft skills are not limited to a particular profession.

These skills can be developed according to the environment and requirement of particular profession.

m) Application of soft Skills

Soft skills improves your professional excellence and also personality, attitude and interpersonal relation. Soft skill exhibits you real potential. Soft skills are collection of several skills and abilities such as interpersonal skills, communication skill, motivation skill, listening skills, leadership skills, decision making power, presentation skills, negotiation skills, reading and writing skills, stress management. Soft skills are polite presentation of hard skills.

At last it can be conclude that library professional have great responsibility on their shoulders to handle various issues regarding professional excellence in cyber society.

7

VTLS-VIRTUA - Books Database Correction: A Case Study of Indira Gandhi Memorial Library, University of Hyderabad

R Pommal Rao
A Panikkar
B Isthari
Indira Gandhi Memorial Library
University of Hyderabad, Hyderabad

INTRODUCTION

Any correction needs a technician and the technician has to apply various techniques and tools for the correction under the able guidance of a Manager. Various issues are to be verified and examined before conducting such correction.

In a Library where the books database has been computerized and the records were added over the years, there may be several affecting factors in building an erroneous database. Database maintenance is very important in library automation. In a University library, the size of collection may normally big according to various departments and courses run by the University.

The books database correction work requires a senior level manager and a good team of skilled professionals to attend various operations. The manager and the technicians are to involve themselves and should dedicate their services and expertise in building the perfect database. Every effort and ability has to apply while attempting the rectification. On the whole, the user's satisfaction while retrieving and locating the required data is very important.

Selection of a Manager and Professionals

The influence of the below mentioned issues affects the selection of a Manager and the team of professionals.

1. Knowledge of Library Application Software
2. Information on the existing collection
3. Understanding the genesis of misappropriation
4. Control on rectification procedures
5. Undertaking the operations and assessment
6. Coordinating with the Acquisition, Technical and Circulation Sections
7. Full-fledged involvement

There will be no fruitful results in a situation of lapse of any item listed above.

Verification of Relevant Issues

Verification is necessary prior to starting the correction work. The manager has to verify the existing system, the origin of mistakes, misappropriation, etc. and to analyze the existing procedures and practices, system support, software functions, etc. The personal strengths and involvement of staff are to be estimated. The manager has to check the suitable work place, which is convenient to carryout the therapeutic measures.

1. It should be nearer to circulation section
2. All the old accession registers are to be shifted from the acquisition section

General Issues

At the beginning stage of carrying out the operations, the manager has to inquire in to the below mentioned items thoroughly.

1. The collection, which has not undergone the re-accession, may be preferred in the initial stage.
2. The prefixes to the Accession Numbers should be continued? Or discontinued? {If the Librarian wishes to discontinue in this level itself, a suitable re-accession procedure may be coined or discontinuation of such prefixes may be undertaken in the next phase after completion of data correction work.
3. Staff members working at the circulation counters should be instructed not to attempt any changes to prefixes in the database.
4. If the circulation section staff found the data is missing for any book, they may be instructed to send the book to the Technical Section/Data Updation Project section. In an exigency, they may be going through cir-on-fly for the temporary cataloguing. Such information may be pass on to the Manager, Data Updation project.

Points of Misappropriation

1. Problems traced at the time of converting the records from the earlier used software
2. Non-availability of uniform data for the multi volume sets and serial publications
3. Prefixes to accession numbers
4. Erroneous data input

5. Incomplete records entered via "Cir-on-fly" function at the Circulation Section (temporary cataloguing)
6. Assignment of different Call Numbers for the multiple copies received in different intervals
7. Data pertaining to duplicate entries with plain and prefixed Accession numbers.
8. Approaching different tools for the derivation of Subject Headings.

Security Measures

In addition to the executives, few staff members working in the computer maintenance section have been given the access to all the modules of VTLS-Virtua to undertake various operations. Such members may be instructed to not to conduct any type of data corrections without informing the concerned manager.

If any user found the incomplete or imperfect data, they may be instructed to take in to notice of the concerned manager.

For the above, instructions may be incorporated in the OPAC first screen or a circular may be issued.

System Support

The following issues are interrelated pertaining to the Library application software. Understanding the system support is very much essential to undertake the database corrections. These issues can be enquired with the database administrator/manager.

1. Additional Ids. support {Volume Nos. and copy statement} is not available for the multi volume sets and serial publications. Additional Ids. provides the volume based searching and retrieves the specific entry. Serial publications like:
   - Lecture Notes in Mathematics
   - Methods in Enzymology
   - Census of India

2. Some sets have been entered under the individual titles. This should be transferred to 'series title' to maintain the uniformity
3. Whether VTLS supports the print generation of the accession register? Accession no. wise by selecting a string of accession nos. {a sample print out may be verified}
   - Whether VTLS supports the 'Bibcheck'? To find an incorrect record like LIBSYS?
   - Whether VTLS supports catalog card printing? If the Librarian wishes to restore the library catalog.
   - Whether it supports global changes with minimum keystrokes. For example, to remove the prefix 'C which used for science books earlier.

Requirements

1. Personal Computers
2. VTLS - Virtua Software connection
3. File edit permissions (available in VTLS-Profiler-Global Settings)
4. Data Entry Work Sheets
5. Dewey Decimal Classification Schedule
6. Cutter Table Book
7. VTLS-Virtua Users Manual - Technical Module

CHANNELS FOR DATA CORRECTION MAIN

Channels

1. Updating the data on par with the Accession Registers as main source record
2. Updating the data on par with the Shelf List Cards (Classified Catalogue)

To reach the goal of building perfect books database,

one should not depend on the main channel, but various side channels may be undertaken simultaneously for effective results.

In I.G.M. Library, only the online catalogue is in use. Card Catalogue has been discontinued since 1997 and the Shelf List became outdated. Hence the above first method is applicable to this library.

Sub-Channels

The sub-channels normally depend on the users and staff working at the circulation counters, etc.

Channel-1 : Updating the data pertaining to "Returned Books"

Channel-2 : Alphabetical Order of Title Catalog through the OPAC

Channel-3 : Data merging for the multiple copies found with different call nos. in the stack area

Channel-4 : Whenever finding the missed data at the issues counter

Channel-5 : As and when a user rushes with a complaint

THERAPEUTICS / DATA UPDATION PROCESS

In the main channel, the Accession Registers are source records. Call numbers will not be available in this method. The work involved in the database updation is sub-divided in to three stages:

1. Data Checking,
2. Filling Data Work Sheets for the Missing Titles,
3. Data Entry through MARC 21.

Stage-1: Data Checking

The books (catalogue) database may be checked on par with the Accession Registers.

a) If the data found against item bar code, the perfection may be verified.

b) For the incomplete records which do not have full bibliographic fields may be noted and data entry work sheet may be filled with an indication 'incomplete data'

c) If no entry found in the database, the data entry work sheet may be filled with an indication ' data missing'

Stage-2: Filling Data Work Sheets for the Missing Titles

Data entry work sheets are to be prepared for the incomplete entries and missing entries. The above two types (either 'b' or 'c' should be reflected on top of the work sheet. Printed Data entry work sheet should be similar to the data entry work sheet available in the software as it is more convenient while entering data by the operators. Data entry work sheet has been prepared according to MARC 21 format.

Supply of Call Nos. for the Untraceable Records

The work sheets pertaining to the missing and incomplete entries in the database require full bibliographic details. Primary data, which is available in the accession register, may be entered and for further details, the card catalogue may be consulted. The call no. of concerned book is an important bibliographic field.

Stage-3: Data Entry

After collecting the details pertaining to miss and incomplete entries in the database, the data is to be entered through MARC. The scattered entries pertaining to the multiple copies may be merged and the call nos. in the books duly corrected.

Data Entry Work Sheet: Marc 21
incomplete entry / missing entry

Field	*Tag No.*	*Details*
Bar Code/Accn. No.		
ISBN No.	020	
Class No.	082 a	
Cutter No.	082 b	
Author	100	
Corporate Author	110	
Title	245 a	
Sub-Title	245 b	
Statement of Responsibility	245 c	
Edition No.	250	
Place	260 a	
Publisher	260 b	
Year	260 c	
Pagination	300	
Series	440	
Note	500	
Subject Heading	650	
Author Added Entry	700	

Prepared by   Checked by   Data Entry by   Asst. Librarian

Transcription Standards

The manager has to verify the existing standards, which were applied for the data pertaining to Language Books other than the English. No manual has been prepared and followed by the staff or executives worked in the section. This is the suitable period to prepare a manual for data transcription. According to the manual the staff has to enter the data of Telugu, Hindi & Urdu language books.

CONCLUSION

There is a lot of affecting factors involved in routing a database to imperfectness. These factors whichever may be, should not repeat in future after attending the correction work once. Every precaution may be undertaken at the stage of data entry itself from the Acquisition Section where a primary bibliographic record is created (with minimum fields) and at the subsequent stage the same entry is to be carried forward by Technical Processing Section.

The database correction work is very much essential to any library to present a perfect error-free database to the users.

REFERENCE

Rama Reddy, E.; Pommal Rao, R. & Srinivasulu, P. *Database creation and maintenance operations; a case study of Indira Gandhi Memorial Library.* 1997. CALIBER' 97. p.63-67.

8

Open Source for Library Systems and Digital Libraries

G. Sujatha
University Librarian (Retd.)
Dr. B.R. Ambedkar Open University, Hyderabad

INTRODUCTION

Open source is a concept that has been gaining rapid momentum in the recent past. Open source has become synonymous with the Open Source Software (OSS), the source code of which is freely available to the users. This enables the users to improve the code, fix bugs and share the changes freely within the community. The open source movement has become a boon to the libraries. Through the open source, libraries can offer better services, improve their functionality and also share resources and information with other libraries. A wide range of open source software is being developed towards making efficient and paperless libraries as dreamt by Lancaster in the 20th century.

OPEN SOURCE: CONCEPT AND DEFINITION

The term open source is used to describe the process in which the services of the end product of a system can be accessed, used and improved. Open source systems are software created, the source code of which is freely available so that the users can read, modify, circulate and redistribute it. The open source software is typically created and maintained by a team of developers that surpasses institutional, regional and national boundaries. The rationale behind this concept is that a larger group of people not concerned with financial gain or proprietary ownership will produce a better product for everyone to use. In open source, any user can modify, improve, fix bugs, circulate and share his efforts with others. As the software is continuously worked upon, it rapidly and constantly improves and evolves.

According to the Open Source Initiative (OSI), a non-profit co-operation dedicated to promoting and managing the open source, "Open source promotes software reliability and quality by supporting independent peer review and rapid evolution of source code. To be certified as open source, the license of a program must guarantee the right to read, redistribute, modify and use it freely."

For software to be called an open source:

1. Its license should be free and should enable free redistribution,
2. Its program must include source code and allow distribution in source code as well as in the changed and compiled form,
3. Its license should allow modifications and derived works and should allow for their distribution under the same terms as the original,
4. Its license may require that the derived works carry a different name or version number from the original software,
5. Its license must not discriminate against any person or a group of persons,
6. Its license must not restrict anyone from making use of the program in a specific field of endeavour,

7. Its license must not be specific to a product,
8. Its license must not place restrictions on other software that is distributed along with it, and
9. Its license must be technology neutral.

BENEFITS AND CHALLENGES

Due to the free availability of the source code, open source software has quite a few advantages over any proprietary software. Open source software can be made to fulfill individual needs as the source code can be modified and adopted to specific applications. As the distribution terms of open source software allow for free distribution and redistribution of the software, initial costs are reduced. It generally has lower implementation and support cost as well. However the cost may escalate if a development team needs to be maintained to meet the local needs. An open source software also tends to be more secure and stable and less vulnerable to viruses. It provides more support options and the amount of vendor lock-in is also reduced.

Though largely beneficial, open source software raises a few challenges in the form of unanticipated costs, limited technical support and chaotic progress. Also open source software may not be as scalable and as fast as commercial software.

OPEN SOURCE SOFTWARE FOR LIBRARIES

Implementation and use of open source software in libraries facilitates improved services and access to more information. Some of the OSS currently available for library systems are Avanti Micro LCS, Emilda, Evergreen, Firefly, GNUTeca, Koha, Learning Access ILS, Open Biblio, Php Mylibrary, PMB, PYTHEAS and WEBLIS. A few of the OSS are discussed below:

(a) AVANTI : Peter Schlumpf essentially develops The Avanti LCS project, which began in 1998. Written in Java, it is a simple, scalable, networkable client server that is deployed in small to medium scale libraries. The Avanti LCS includes its own database management system.

(b) EMILDA : Emilda OSS is developed and maintained by the Real Mode Ltd and SDU is released under the GNU General Public License. It is a complete ILS that features.

1. Web OPAC, allowing comprehensive system management.
2. Template based layout (enabling alteration of visual appearance Emilda)
3. 100% MARC compatibility using zebra server.
4. Extensive configuration.

Emilda is currently used in some schools in Finland.

(c) EVERGREEN : It was developed by a group of librarians at the Georgia Public Library Service (GPLS). Evergreen is an ILS that manages, catalogs and tracks the circulation of library holdings. Written in C, Java Script and Perl it uses a post gre SQL database and runs on Linux with Apache. Evergreen powers PINES (Public Information Network for Electronic Services) and is highly scalable.

(d) FIREFLY : It was developed in Python, Perl and XML. Firefly is an integrated open source library system for public libraries. It is GNU general public licensed.

(e) KOHA : Koha is the first open source software for public library system. It was developed by Katipo Communications, and first deployed in January 2000 at the Horowhenua Library Trust In New Zealand. Koha which means 'gift' in the Maori language of New Zealand, is an enterprise class Integrated Library System (ILS) with comprehensive functionality including basic and advanced options. Its core features include a library catalogue front end /OPAC, library system intranet, a circulation tracking system and a document acquisition

/ budgeting system. It is a dual database design built using the library standards and protocols ensuring interoperability between the Koha and other open source systems and technologies.

(f) LEARNING ACCESS ILS : The Learning Access ILS is a standard based, fully integrated open source library system offered by the Learning Access Institute in Seattle. It was previously known as 'Open Book.' The system consists of web OPAC, cataloging, circulation and administrative modules. MARC, Z39.50 and UNICODE are supported. It uses SQL as the database management system and the programming languages are Perl and Php. The Learning Access ILS is specifically positioned to offer smaller libraries the opportunity to gain access to state-of-the-art library automation.

(g) OPEN BIBLIO : Open Biblio is an easy to use, automated library system written in PHP. It provides OPAC, cataloging and staff administration functionalities. The Open Biblio 0.5.2 is written in an interpreted language, which makes its operating system independent. It uses the MySQL database.

OPEN SOURCE SOFTWARE FOR DIGITAL LIBRARIES

Open source software is ideal for digital libraries whose objective is to enhance the utility of a digital collection, as well as integrate and aggregate the existing collections and services with an outstanding client interface. Greenstone Digital library software, Eprints, Dspace, Ganesha digital library, Keystone Digital Library suite, Fedora, Post Nuke, Refbase, WordPress, Drupal, Bricks are some commonly used open source digital library software.

(a) GREENSTONE DIGITAL LIBRARY SOFTWARE: The Greenstone is produced by the New Zealand Digital Library Project at the University of Waikato and developed and distributed in co-operation with UNESCO and the Human Info NGO. It is a suite of software for building and distributing digital library collections. It runs on all versions of Windows, Unix, MAC OS-Y and Apache. The Greenstone digital library system has two separate interactive interfaces: the reader interface and the librarian interface. The reader interface, which can be accessed by end users, operates within a web server while the librarian interface is a Java based Graphical User Interface (GUI) which makes material gathering, adding meta data, designing the searching and browsing facilities that collection will offer the user and build and serve the collection easier.

Using Greenstone, collections in libraries can be created from standard file formats such as HTML files, e-mail messages, PDF documents, JPEG and GIF images, Word documents as well as Plain text files. Its unique strength is the multilingual nature of its reader interface.

(b) EPRINTS : Eprints is an open source software package for building open access repositories that are compliant with the Open Archives Initiative Protocol for Metadata Harvesting. It shares many of the features commonly seen in Document Management systems, but is primarily used for institutional repositories and scientific journals. Eprints has been developed at the University of Southampton and released under a GPL license.

It is a Web and command-line application based on the LAMP architecture (but is written in Perl rather than PHP). It has been successfully run under Linux, Solaris and Mac OS X [2]. A version for Microsoft Windows is being developed but will be released under a non-GPL license.

Version 3 of the software introduced a (Perl-based) plugin architecture for importing and exporting data, converting objects (for search engine indexing) and user interface widgets.

Configuring an Eprints repository involves modifying

configuration files written in Perl or XML. Web based configuration tools are in development. The appearance of a repository is controlled by HTML templates, style sheets and inline images. While Eprints is shipped with an English translation it has been translated to other languages through (redistributable) language- specific XML phrase files. Existing translations include Bulgarian, French, German, Hungarian, Italian. Japanese, Russian, Spanish and Ukranian.

(c) DSPACE : The Dspace OSS is jointly developed by the Massachusetts Institute of Technology (MIT) and the Hewlett - Packard (HP) Labs, It is a digital repository system that captures, stores, indexes, preserves and redistributes an organizations' search data. The Dspace OSS makes submission easy and supports the long-term preservation of the digital material stored in its repository. It accepts all forms of digital materials including text such as articles preprints, technical reports, working papers, conference papers, e-thesis, datasets, images, audio files, video files, learning objects and reformatted digital library collections.

The Dspace OSS is available under the BSD open source license for research institutions. It runs on UNIX or LINUX operating system. As the Dspace OSS is an open source application designed so that institutions and organizations could run with relatively few resources, it is generally used by an increasing number of institutions, libraries, archives, cultural heritage institutions, government agencies and corporations.

(d) GANESHA DIGITAL LIBRARY : The Ganesha Digital Library OSS enables institutions and users to share their knowledge as well as simultaneously access and utilize knowledge. It is the first web- based digital software in Indonesia. The GDL OSS supports fast information searching and detail to all managed meta data. The latest version 4.0 was released in June, 2004.

(e) KEYSTONE DIGITAL LIBRARY SUITE (DLS) :

The keystone DLS is a family of open source digital content management, portal management and information discovery software packaged together to provide libraries, museums and archives with state-of- thc-art digital library services. Keystone OSS supports:

1. Portal creation and management,
2. Federated search services,
3. Harvesting meta data from remote repositories, and
4. Link resolver services.

Keystone system supports the Firefox, Internet Explorer, Konqueror, Mozilla, Netscape, Opera and Safari Web browser for accessing its functionality.

(f) FEDORA : The Fedora OSS is developed by the Cornell University and the University of Virginia. The Fedora open source digital library software runs on Linux, Windows and Tonot 2.4. The Fedora supports Word, PDF, HTML and GIF file formats.

(g) POSTNUKE : PostNuke is software that creates an impressive, dynamic web site and provides the webmaster with a site they can administer with a minimal amount of HTML knowledge through a web browser.

But, installing modules, blocks and themes can increase PostNuke's functionality. For example, you can add a forum, a gallery and contact form. You can also change how your entire site looks by changing themes. All of this can be done with just a few clicks in the administration panel saving you hours of time, both in the initial creation of the website and in its day-to-day maintenance.

PostNuke can do anything from traditional blog websites, to a community members' only website with hundreds of users. PostNuke can scale to thousands of uses but is just as easy to create a small website for friends and family.

(h) REFBASE : Refbase is web-based institutional

repository and reference management software, which is often used for self-archiving, refbase is licensed under the GPL and written in PHP and uses a MySQL backend.

It can import and export a variety of standard bibliographic formats, including BibTeX, Endnote, RIS, ISI, MODS XML, PubMed, Medline, RefWorks, and Copac. It can generate formatted bibliographies and citations in LaTeX. RTF, HTML, and PDF. refbase also has advanced search features and can generate RSS feeds from searches. Links using DOIs and URLs can be added, as can links to files. COinS and unAPI metadata are supported.

A Refbase package have been put in the official Gentoo Linux and Mandriva Linux repositories and has been used by the United States Geological Survey.

(i) WORDPRESS : WordPress is a state-of-the-art semantic personal publishing platform with a focus on aesthetics, web standards, and usability. It has been designed for blogging, but it is flexible enough to create all kinds of web sites. It's written in PHP, a web programming language that mixes with HTML to produce dynamic web pages, and it has a host of template functions and plugins that make it easy to customize. The Western Springs History Project uses WordPress to present historical photographs of buildings in Western Springs, IL. Visitors can leave comments about the buildings; these often come from current or former residents with stories about the houses. It's a great example of using a tool from outside the usual software to build an engaging digital library from a public library.

(j) DRUPAL : Drupal is a free software package that allows an individual or a community of users to easily publish, manage and organize a wide variety of content on a website.

The built-in functionality, combined with dozens of freely available add-on modules, will enable features such as: Content Management Systems, Blogs, Collaborative authoring environments, Forums, Peer-to-peer networking, Newsletters, Podcasting, Picture galleries, etc.

It is open source software licensed under the GPL, and is maintained and developed by a community of thousands of users and developers. Drupal is free to download and use.

(k) BRICKS : (Building Resources for Integrated Cultural Knowledge Services) is an open-source software framework for the management of distributed digital assets. BRICKS has been deployed on a number of cultural institutions under the umbrella of the BRICKS Cultural Heritage Network, a community of cultural heritage, scientific and industrial organizations across Europe. The software itself is shared under the LGPL license.

CONCLUSIONS

The applications and software discussed above all require some expertise in management of web servers, writing and styling HTML, a general notion of how a database works, and a basic understanding of programming (variables, if/then statements, and so on). Most of all, they require a willingness to experiment, to see what works and what doesn't.

Most of the open source applications have sufficient online documentation and active user groups, forums, and other resources. Other users are often willing to give you a hand. For additional help, one may look to the community for assistance. The help obtained could be surprising as some of the existing users are highly skilled.

Open source movement has gained popularity with the fast development of Internet as information resource connectivity. The OSS provides a platform for exchange of ideas from other systems and individuals through out the world. It allows access to large amount of information, which is not available within the four walls of institutional libraries. OSS enables resource sharing internationally, without any hindrance. It is developed, changed and improved continuously and collectively. Free How of information enables everyone to access it and derive benefit without copyright, and other intellectual property restrictions, and hence reduces the gap between generation of ideas and use by the end user. The inherent advantages make the open source software (OSS) the preferred option for making libraries user friendly and enable them to function effectively and efficiently.

The OSS is an effective system in the hands of intelligent librarians to satisfy their users to a great extent as Melvil Dewey once said about the ALA: 'Ask Library Anything.' The OSS makes the libraries more information rich and less burned with paper resources and hence ideal for digital libraries. The consortia and the library networks can use the nascent information at the generation stage itself in scientific labs and research institutions.

The value of information and the consciousness of recency of information will increase and its cost will decrease. This may be essential for the dawn of Information Society or Knowledge Society. The information wealth or resource should be used to maximum extent by maximum number of people to make the global life better and to meet the future challenges effectively by the mankind.

REFERENCES

1. Sreekumar M.G. and P. Sreejaya. "Digital Library Initiatives and Issues in India: Efforts on scholarly knowledge management." In *Digital Libraries in Knowledge Management* by M.G. Srikumar ... [et al.]. 2006, ESS ESS Publications, New Delhi p 17-37.
2. Naik, Umesha and D. Shivalingaiah. "Digital Library Open Source Software: A Comparative Study." In 4th *International Convention CALIBER - 2006 on Dynamic Interoperable Web*

Based Information Systems, February 2-4, 2006, Gulbarga University, Gulbarga

3. http://drupal.org
4. http://dspace.org
5. http://enterprise.linux.com
6. http://obiblio.sourceforge.net/
7. http://refbase.sourceforge.net/
8. http://savannah.nongnu.org/users/gimpy/
9. http://wordpress.org/
10. http: //www. ala.org/ala/pla/plapubs/ tech notes/ opensource.doc
11. http://www.brickscommunity.org/
12. http://www.eprints.org/
13. http://www.fedora.info/
14. http://www.indexdata.dk/keystone/
15. http://www.infotoday.com/it/oct01/poynder.htm
16. http://www. istl.org/05-spring/article2.html
17. http://www.opensource.org/
18. http://www.postnuke.com/
19. www.avantilibrarysystems.com
20. www.emilda.org
21. www.greenstone.org
22. www.koha.org
23. www.learningaccess.org
24. www.oss4lib.org

9

Digital and Virtual Library Resources for Veterinary Science Education: An Overview

K. Veeranjaneyulu
University Librarian & Professor
Prof. Jayashankar Telangana State Agricultural University
Hyderabad – 500 030, Telangana State

G. Rathinasababapathy
University Librarian
Tamil Nadu Veterinary and Animal Sciences University
Chennai – 600 051

INTRODUCTION

The history revealed that veterinary cult existed in Indian subcontinent as far back as 3000 to 4000 years ago. In the post-vedic period, the teaching of veterinary medicine was included in the curricula of medical schools. Evidences are available to prove the existence of veterinary hospitals during the rule of Chandra Gupta Maurya (300-298 BC) and King Ashoka (237-232 BC) and it is believed that King Ashoka erected the first veterinary hospital in India. However, there are evidences that Veterinary Hospitals were erected by Pandiya Kings of Tamil Nadu before 232 BC. Chanakya has also written a lot about veterinary medicine and formulated various rules and regulations in respect of veterinary practice.

However, the modern veterinary education in India began in 1862 with the establishment of an army veterinary school in Pune. The first civil veterinary school was started in Babugargh (Hapur) in Uttar Pradesh in 1877. Subsequently, the first veterinary college was started in 1882 at Lahore (now in Pakistan). To meet the requirements, veterinary colleges were established in various parts of the country and the Madras Veterinary College which was established in 1903 took the lead to offer a graduate degree programme in veterinary medicine with its affiliation to University of Madras in 1936. As on date there are about 55 veterinary colleges in India (including private veterinary colleges).

Considering the need for a full-fledged university to impart quality veterinary education and ensure cutting edge research in this area, the ever first veterinary university was established in Tamil Nadu in 1989, probably the first of its kind in the entire South East Asia.

The Tamil Nadu Veterinary and Animal Sciences University (TANUVAS) paved the way for establishment of more universities for veterinary science and as on date there are about 12 veterinary universities in India and it is hoped that in the future, there would be at least one such university in each state. The Veterinary Council of India (VCI) is the apex body at national level which takes care of the quality of veterinary education in India.

ROLE OF LIBRARY IN EDUCATION

"Library is considered as the Heart of University system' as it plays a vital role in education and research and extension activities of the university. Especially, the veterinary medicine is a life saving science and the updates taking place around the globe need to be imparted to the veterinary students and teachers for which an effective and efficient library system should be established. Realising the importance of libraries, almost all veterinary universities and veterinary colleges in the country have established its own library and information system to cater to the increasing information requirements of its stakeholders viz., students, research scholars, faculty and scientists.

The Indian Council of Agricultural Research (ICAR) is also helping the veterinary college libraries by sanctioning Development Grant exclusively for Library Strengthening to ensure seamless access to knowledge resources to the stakeholders of the university. Apart from development grants, the ICAR also gives priority for strengthening and modernisation of the veterinary libraries through various projects viz., AHRDP, NATP, NAIP, etc.

DIGITAL LIBRARY

The advent of the Internet has changed a lot in the information storage, processing and retrieval methods of the libraries and libraries started using the latest technologies such as networking, digitization, etc. to meet the ever increasing information requirements of the stakeholders in the networked digital environment.

As rightly pointed out by Dr. APJ Adbul Kalam, our Former President of India "Digital library is the place where the past meets the present to create the future". Digital Library is accessible from anywhere by anybody, if it is available online. This is not only useful for the students and research scholars undergoing full-time programmes in colleges and universities but for the field veterinarians who are working in remote area, the digital and virtual libraries are really boon to update their professional skills and knowledge. The virtual library and digital library play a vital role in continuing professional education of the field Vets.

Since the younger generation is IT savvy and using various IT tools such as Desktop PC, Laptop, Tablet PC, Android Mobiles, etc. to access information in the networked digital environment, the librarians should concentrate more to provide the information through these channels so as to reach the stakeholders.

THE INTERNET – A VAST DIGITAL LIBRARY

The Internet may also be considered as a vast digital library as it has built in a very rich collection of various types of information resources useful for veterinary education. But, using Google type general purpose search engines will not be much helpful to the students, research scholars and practicing veterinarians to get the appropriate, authenticate and reliable web resources to support their academic and research related information requirements as reliable and malicious contents coexist on the Internet. So, it is always better to use effective and efficient search tool such as *http://scholar.google.co.in/* to mine authenticated and reliable information from the Internet for education and research purposes. A test search performed for a keyword using Google and Scholar Google will clearly indicate the vast difference between the two search engines. Scholar Google is definitely one of the best search engine available for academicians and researchers.

MAJOR OPEN ACCESS ONLINE RESOURCES FOR VETERINARIANS

Open Access Online Databases

PubMed

Though many veterinary colleges and universities have access to CABDIRECT Online database through CeRA, still some important databases which are useful for veterinary education are available online in open access. PubMed is not only useful for the medical students but also for the veterinary students and research scholars. Produced by the U.S. National Library of Medicine in Bethesda, Maryland, this extensive database includes over 22 million citations to journal article citations back to the 1940s. The citations have been indexed from over 4,900 human medical, nursing, dentistry, **veterinary,** and related biomedical journals. It is a major resource that may be helpful to you now or in the future.

AGRIS

AGRIS is a global public domain Database with 4337000+ structured bibliographical records on agricultural science and technology. 77.29% of records are citations from scientific journals. The bibliographic references contain either links to the full text of the publication or additional information retrieved from related Internet resources. It can be accessed at *http://agris.fao.org*

WAHID (World Animal Health Information Database)

The WAHID Interface provides access to all data held within OIE's new World Animal Health Information System (WAHIS). A comprehensive range of information is available on this database which are highly useful for the veterinary fraternity. It is available at *http://www.oie.int/wahis_2/public/wahid.php/Wahidhome/Home*

ADW (Animal Diversity Web)

Animal Diversity Web (ADW) is an online database that collects the natural history, classification, species characteristics, conservation biology, and distribution information of thousands of species of animals. It includes thousands of photographs, hundreds of sound clips, and a virtual museum. It is available at *http://animaldiversity.ummz.umich.edu*

AVIBASE

Avibase is an extensive database information system about all birds of the world, containing over 9 million records about 10,000 species and 22,000 subspecies of birds, including distribution information, taxonomy, synonyms in several languages and more. This site is managed by Denis Lepage and hosted by Bird Studies Canada, the Canadian co-partner of Birdlife International. Avibase has been a work in progress since 1992. It is available at *http://avibase.bsc-eoc.org*

ONLINE DIAGNOSTIC SUPPORT SYSTEM

CONSULTANT (from Cornell Veterinary College)

Consultant is a database designed to link over 500 clinical signs and symptoms to nearly 7,000 possible diagnoses or disease conditions. Thus, it can help you find summary information about animal diseases. In addition, it can assist in compiling lists of diseases with certain clinical signs, such as all of the dog diseases that have "diarrhea" as one of the clinical signs. *Consultant* also contains a selected list of up-to-date journal articles on each diagnosis.

Hints for using Consultant : For a known disease or condition, click "Search by Diagnosis". Then choose the "Species" from the pull-down menu, and enter one or more disease terms. From there, click on your choice of diagnosis to see a brief description of the disease, its clinical signs, species affected, and some recent journal article citations and/or web page links of potential interest. For identifying possible diseases with one or more clinical signs, click "Search by Signs". Then, choose the "Species" from the pull-down menu, and enter the first clinical sign, such as "vomiting". Additional clinical signs can be added before searching the database to obtain a list of diagnoses exhibiting those particular signs. It is available at *http://www.vet.cornell.edu/consultant/consult.asp*

CaDDiS (Cattle Disease Diagnostic System)

CaDDiS is designed to serve as a component of a larger decision support system which will provide information to decision makers on the relative likelihood of a cow having different diseases given that you have observed that it exhibits particular clinical signs. The objective of this decision support module is to facilitate better differential diagnosis of tropical diseases which is available to use at *http://external.cis.strath.ac.uk/caddis/*

ELECTRONIC JOURNALS

Electronic journal is a boon for the educators and researchers in the field of veterinary science. Gone are the days where one has to go to the library to refer to a print journal. Nowadays, almost all journals are available online. Among the e-journals, there are two types i.e. subscription based e-journals (for which we have to pay subscription) and open access e-journals (e-journals available online free). Nowadays, good number of open access e-journals are available online. The following are the major directories from where we can identify the open access e-journals.

DOAJ

The Directory of Open Access Journals (DOAJ) service covers free, full text, quality controlled scientific and scholarly journals. There are now 10,000+ journals in the directory. Currently 2467 journals are searchable at article level. About 120+ journals are related to veterinary and animal Science, really a great resource for veterinary education and research. Even the resource poor veterinary libraries may make use of this resources besides veterinarians who are working in remote areas who don't have access to the veterinary library. It is available at *www.doaj.org.* Some other directories which provides collection of full-text free e-journals are:

- http://highwire.stanford.edu
- http://www.freemedicaljournals.com
- http://www.biomedcentral.com/browse/journals
- http://www.bioline.org.br
- https://www.plos.org
- http://scielo.org/php/index.php

ELECTRONIC BOOKS

Veterinary students and teachers can make use of the vast amount of e-books available online. The following are some of the important directory sites from where we can download full-text e-books.

Gutenberg

Project Gutenberg offers over 42,000 free ebooks: choose among free epub books, free kindle books, download them or read them online. Over 100,000 free ebooks are available through our Partners, Affiliates and Resources. It is available at *http://www.gutenberg.org*

ELECTRONIC THESES AND DISSERTATIONS (ETDS)

Electronic Theses and Dissertations (ETDs) are important source of information for veterinary students and research scholars. One can download full-text theses from the Internet using a number of directory sites. Networked Digital Library of Theses and Dissertations (NDLTD), an international organization dedicated to promoting the adoption, creation, use, dissemination, and preservation of electronic theses and dissertations (ETDs). It is available at *http://www.ndltd.org*

E-LEARNING AND DIGITAL LIBRARIES: ICAR's INITIATIVES

Realising the importance of e-learning and digitization of libraries in India to ensure effective and efficient access to library resources to the agriculture and veterinary science students, research scholars and faculty, the Indian Council of Agricultural Research (ICAR) has taken a lot of initiatives during the past few years. The following are the major online products available for the students and teachers which were possible by the efforts of ICAR under NAIP project.

E-Courses in Veterinary Science

The project on 'Development of e-courses for B.V.Sc. & A.H. degree programme was sanctioned by NAIP of ICAR to the TANUVAS, Chennai to create e-learning modules to enable students to acquire a more effective learning system. The project envisaged to create e-learning modules for 79 courses offered under Veterinary Council of India pattern of education. The well developed e-courses in veterinary and animal sciences are available at *http://www.elearnvet.net/*

Consortium for e-Resources in Agriculture (CeRA)

Consortium for e-Resources in Agriculture (CeRA) is an e-Consortium of Agricultural Libraries under the Indian Council of Agricultural Research for National Agricultural Research System (NARS) libraries to share the e-resources among Indian Agricultural and Veterinary Science Universities. CeRA, the Consortium for e-Resources in Agriculture, has been established for facilitating accessibility of select scientific journals related to agriculture and allied fields, to all researchers in the National Agricultural Research System (NARS). The foundation for this initiative was made by providing internet connectivity to most of the Indian Council of Agricultural Research (ICAR) institutes under the National Agricultural Technology Programme (NATP) over a decade ago. This was done with the ultimate objective of providing access to information, specially access to on-line journals, which is crucial for excellence in research. CeRA is available through institutional access to all SAUs /SVUs at *http://jgateplus.com/search/login/*

Online Union Catalogue (AGRICAT)

"AgriCat" brought to you by ICAR under NAIP Project on e-Granth is a Union Catalogue of the holdings of 12 major libraries (IARI, IVRI, UAS, GBPUAT, CCSHAU, ANGRAU, NDRI, CIFE, CSKHPKV, MPKV, TANUVAS, DIPA) of the ICAR Institutes and SAUs combined together. AgriCat lets you to : Search many libraries at once for an item and then locate it in a library nearby ; Find books, thesis and dissertations, journals, back volumes of journals and non-book materials to check out; Contact the Librarian of a particular university for further help. It is available at *http://egranth.ac.in/AgriCat.htm*

Online Electronic Theses Database (KRISHIPRABHA)

KrishiPrabha is a full-text electronic database of Indian Agricultural Doctoral Dissertations submitted by research scholars to the 45 State/Deemed Agricultural Universities during the period 2000 to 2014. This database, listing about 7900 Doctoral Dissertations with a full text of about 6250 Dissertations has been created by Nehru Library, Ch. Charan Singh Haryana Agricultural University, Hisar with financial support from Indian Council of Agricultural Research, New Delhi under its National Agricultural Innovation Project. It is available at *http://14.139.232.167:8080/equestthesis*

Online Institutional Repository (KRISHIKOSH)

KrishiKosh, is an Institutional Repository under NARS funded under NAIP of ICAR. The repository of knowledge in agriculture and allied sciences is having a rich collection of old and valuable books, records and various documents spread all over the country in different libraries of Research Institutions and State Agricultural Universities (SAUs). It is available at *http://krishikosh.egranth.ac.in*

CONCLUSION

There are enormous amount of digital information are available for veterinary science students and teachers across the information superhighway. Starting from useful web sites to huge databases and big data, they are very much useful for them to update their knowledge and professional skills. Though the ICAR has taken the initiative to digitize institutional repositories under e-granth project, the Krishikosh veterinary universities and colleges should ensure sustainable development of Krishikosh by contributing regular uploading of new digital resources. Further, the ICAR should also fund for creation of more digital resources in the field of veterinary medicine to ensure seamless access to the stakeholders across the country. The Librarians should conduct regular information literacy programmes to sensitize the veterinary fraternity about the latest digital resources available to enrich their knowledge and skills.

REFERENCES

- Jehn CT, Perzak DE, Cook JL, et al. Usefulness, completeness, and accuracy of Web sites providing information on osteoarthritis in dogs. J Am Vet Med Assoc 2003;223:1272-1275.
- Kogan, L., R. Schosnfeld-Tacher, A. Simon and A. Viera. (2010). The Internet and Pet Health Information: Perceptions and Behaviours of Pet Owners and Veterinarians. The Internet Journal of Veterinary Medicine, Vol. 8: (1). Available at *http:// http://ispub.com/IJVM/8/1/12921. Accessed on 10.11.2015.*
- Rathinasabapathy, G and L.Rajendran (2009). Web-based Digital Resources for Small Animal Medicine Professionals. Asian Journal of Library and Information Science, Available at http://hdl.handle.net/10150/299578. Accessed on 30.10.2015
- Sethuram R, Weerakkody AN. Health information on the internet. J Obstet Gynaecol 2010;30:119-121
- Short, N (2002). The Use of information and communication

technology in veterinary education. Research in Veterinary Science, 72; (1): pp.1-6

- Taggart R, Wardlaw J, Horstman CL, et al. An Analysis of the Quality of Canine Cranial Cruciate Ligament Disease Information Available on the Internet. Veterinary Surgery 2010;39:278-283.

10

Open Access and Digital Repositories in Scholarly Communication : An Institutional Experience

Y M Patil
Girija Srinivasa
Raman Research Institute
Banglore — 80

INTRODUCTION

Since last three centuries, the basic model for scholarly communication in science and technology has remained unchanged with the journal playing a pivotal role. The publication of the first journal was in French - Le Journal des Savants started in 1665, followed by the Philosophical Transactions of the, Royal Society, London. The journal number reached to 750 by the turn of the 18th century and at present the figure has reached to a staggering number of 2,80,000 by the end of 2006. (Lawal, I., 2002 and Ratnakar, A., 2006)

There have been tremendous changes in printing from Gutenberg to Internet era in publication, which has directly affected the trinity of publishers, researchers and the end users. The impact of ICT has completely changed the publishing landscape. There emerged the desktop publishing during 1980s as a viable alternate to traditional printing. By 1990s, we could see that any one could share his ideas with rest of the world through Internet, and this opportunity could give countless writers-in-search-of-publishers a platform in which one could share his thoughts with others. (Misek, ML, 2004).

The literature is growing astronomically. With the advent of ICT, the journals are being printed in both print and electronic forms. This has added fuel to existing costs and increasing more than the inflation rates. There cannot be any librarian who is not affected by the so called "serials crisis". Rising journals costs and falling library budgets are order of the day. (Gedye, R., 2004). This has directly affected library subscriptions with dwindling library budget resulting in drastic cuts in subscription. Several studies carried out during 1990s indicated that the subscription rates have increased over 80%.

As a result of proliferation of electronic resources and cuts in library budgets, the library professionals have started looking into other means so as to share precious information resources with others. There emerged consortium concept, where like-minded professionals came together and negotiated with publishers for access to more information with optimum payment. The consortium approach was one of the modes as far as access to all available information is concerned. Added to this, there have been demands for open access to literature published by authors in different journals, as authors are the sole originators of the piece of information generated, for which libraries have to pay and subscribe and access to information. (Patil,Y.M.,2006). Due to barriers of access and copyright, there emerged Open Access Movement, with three distinct parameters attached, viz. Open Access Journals, Open Archives and

Institutional Repositories to facilitate scholarly communication.

WHAT IS OPEN ACCESS?

Traditionally, scholars carry out research and report their findings in the form of articles, which appear in peer-reviewed journals published by academic societies or commercial publishers. These journals are sold to libraries at regularly hiked prices. The usage is restricted and only those who afford the subscription can have access to information and it does not reach to all end users. In addition, authors have to sign away copyrights and publishers have complete control over such writings. This holds good for restricted access publishing. On the other hand, in an OA, articles published are available on the Internet free of cost to all users. In such situations, authors are holding partially or fully copyright. Thus scholarly works are no longer restricted to any user either at institutional or individual level. Full access to generated fund of knowledge is a vital aspect for any effective research. As a matter of fact, not only free access, but dire need to further distribution, dissemination, use in course materials, data mining, and re-examination is required for crystallization of knowledge. (Waller, A. and Morrison, H.; Velterop, J., 2004).).

OPEN ACCESS: WHY?

The scientists conduct research and put across their results in the form of papers. The experience shows that the results of research normally do not reach to end-users due to various reasons like cost factor or access problems. Keeping this in view, the concept of Open Access (OA) has emerged as a major development in the world of scholarly communication. The very basic concept of OA is to facilitate free access to information without any barriers. The Open Access has become a buzzword amongst authors, publishers, and librarians, involving issues like copyright, funding mechanisms, business models, peer review, access to content and all issues are addressed to government agencies. The only solutions could be that every scientist and librarian's dream is to access perpetual, unfettered access to all scholarly content in the world without restrictions or any barrier. (Chesler, A., 2004).

Benefits of Open Access

The following could be the benefits one can derive from Open Access Movement.

- Libraries can cope with subscription costs and stable budgeting;
- Remove access barriers to research and use by all strata of the society;
- Researchers can have more control over their research work;
- To bridge the knowledge gap;
- To maximize impact of research by facilitating access to information;
- Greater support for the researchers having made their research out-put publicly accessible.

IMPACT OF OPEN ACCESS

Open access, now dominates discussion everywhere due to major shift in the landscape of publishing. We see major discussions bringing about new declarations by major societies, publishers, consortium, or governmental agencies supporting open access. As a matter of fact, several new open access journals are emerging in the horizon with new publishing models to test new ways to increase readership and access. Several studies have been made to establish a clear correlation between openly accessible materials and citation impact and it is established that the materials available in the open access or subject/institutional repositories is more often cited than that available as journal article. Therefore, self-archiving or posting in subject or institutional repository is no less as compared to non- OA sources. In order to establish impact factor of OA sources, further studies are to be undertaken. (Thompson ISI, 2004; Hamad, S. and Brody, T, 2004; Hajjem, C, et al., 2005; Brown, C, 2001; Eysenbach, G, 2006).

OPEN ACCESS INITIATIVES

Open Access became a movement after the Information Program of the Open Society Institute convened a meeting in Budapest in December 2001. Later several rounds of meetings were held in different places with elite groups of scholars in order to propose and implement Open Access Movement and declarations of policy statements at each meeting, which are briefed as below:

Budapest Open Access Initiative (BOAI) was released on **14 February 2002.**
(http://www.soros.org/openaccess/index.html)

There were over 100 institutions and 2000 individuals who have joined the original signatories to commit to promoting open access to peer-reviewed journal literature. Open access to peer-reviewed journal literature is the goal. Self-archiving and a new generation of open access journals are the ways to attain this goal. (ARL, 2002).

To achieve this, the following two complementary strategies were proposed:

Self-Archiving - to deposit referred articles in the archives conforming to standards mooted by OAI so that search engine and other tools can treat the separate archives as one when searches are made for content access;

Open Access Journals - Scholars need the means to launch a new generation journals committed to open access and to help existing journals that elect to make the transition to open access.

Glasgow Declaration on Libraries, Information Services and Intellectual Freedom, IFLA, Glasgow, 19th August 2002.

"At a meeting in Glasgow on 19th August 2002, IFLA proclaimed the fundamental right of human beings both to access and express information without restriction.... IFLA asserts that a commitment to intellectual freedom is a core responsibility of the library and information profession worldwide, expressed through code of ethics and demonstrated through practice ... IFLA therefore calls upon libraries and information services and other staff to uphold and promote the principles of intellectual freedom and to provide uninhibited access to information" (Glasgow Declaration.2002)

Bethesda Statement on Open Access Publishing (BSAOP), released on June 20, 2003.

The meeting was held on April 11, 2003 on Open Access Publishing. The purpose of the meeting was to stimulate discussion within the biomedical research community on how to proceed, as rapidly as possible, to the widely held goal of providing open access to the primary scientific literature. The document could bring aspects relating to: definition of Open Access Publication, statement of the Institutions and Funding Agencies Working Group, Statement of the libraries and Publishers working Group and Statement of Scientists and Scientific Societies working Group. (BSOAP, 2003).

Berlin Declaration on Open Access to Knowledge (BDOAK) in the Sciences and Humanities, October 22-23, 2003.

In continuation to BOAI and BSOAP declarations, the Berlin Declaration drafted document to promote the Internet as a functional instrument for global scientific knowledge base and human reflection and to specify measures which research policy makers, research institutions, funding agencies, libraries, archives and museums need to consider. The goal was to realize the vision of global and accessible representation of knowledge; the future web has to be sustainable, interactive and transparent. Content and software tools must be openly accessible and compatible. (BDOAK, 2003).

IFLA Statement on Open Access to Scholarly Literature and Research Documentation, 5th December 2003.

(http: //www. ifla. org/ V/cdoc/open-access04. html

The International Federation of Library Associations and Institutions (IFLA) is committed to the widest possible access to information for all peoples in accordance with the principles expressed in the Glasgow Declaration on Libraries, Information Services and Intellectual Freedom. This statement was adopted by the Governing Board of IFLA at its meeting in The Hague on 5th December 2003.

Washington D.C. Principles for Free Access to Science, March 16, 2004.

(http: //www. dcprinciples. org/statement. htm)

A group of not-for-profit publishers endorse the declaration during a meeting held on March 4, 2004 to continue to support broad access to the scientific and medical literature through the following publishing principles and practices:

- Mission is to maintain and enhance the independence, rigor, trust and visibility that have established scholarly journals as reliable filters of information emanating from clinical and laboratory research;
- That we reinvest all of the revenue from our journals in the direct support of science worldwide, including scholarships, scientific meetings ... and improvements in scientific publishing.

Through numerous organizations that serve the entire scholarly publishing community, not- for - profit publishers have freely shared their ideas and innovations, with the common goal of improving the dissemination of vital scientific and medical information throughout the world. (Washington D.C. 2004).

Salvador Declaration on Open Access: the developing Countries perspectives, Salvador, Brazil, **20-23 September 2005.** (Parallel meeting held with 9th World Congress on Health Information and Libraries).

The meeting emphasized the need for open access in the context of developing countries and urged governments to make open access a high priority in science policy including (SDOA, 2005):

- Requiring that publicly funded research is made available through open access;
- Considering the cost of publication as part of the cost of research;
- Strengthening the local OA journals, repositories and other relevant initiatives;
- Promoting integration of developing countries information in the worldwide body of knowledge.

Bangalore Declaration - Workshop on Electronic Publishing and Open Access: Developing Countries Perspectives, 2- 3 November 2006

Keeping in view all previous declarations, another meeting was held in Bangalore where more than 30 experts attended the workshop from developing countries like India, China, Brazil and South Africa and some from developed countries. Besides presentations of articles reflecting developing countries scenario, the workshop ended with discussion on a proposed national policy that should promote acceptance of the open access strategies as declared in the Budapest Open Access Initiatives and based on what was envisaged in Salvador Declaration for

Open Access for Developing Countries. The proposed National Open Access Policy for Developing Countries should provide a major fillip in adopting open access as the way to release all publicly funded research publications from financial and other barriers, thus facilitating wider access to scientific information worldwide. (Kirsop, (B., 2007). Many such meetings have declared unequivocal support for open access to literature.

STRATEGIES TO ACHIEVE OPEN ACCESS

The Budapest Open Access Initiative has recommended two complementary strategies to achieve open access to scholarly journal literature (BOAI, 2002). They are:

I. "Self-Archiving : First, scholars need the tools and assistance to deposit their referred journal articles in open electronic archives, a practice commonly called, self-archiving. When these archives conform to standards created by the Open Archives Initiative, then search engines and other tools can treat the separate archives as one. Users then need not know which archives exist or where they are located in order to find and make use of their contents. referred journals.

II. Open-access Journals : Second, scholars need the means to launch a new generation of journals committed to open access, and to help existing journals that elect to make the transition to open access. Because journal articles should be disseminated as widely as possible, these new journals will no longer invoke copyright to restrict access to and use of the material they publish. Instead they will use copyright and other tools to ensure permanent open access to all the articles they publish. Because price is a barrier to access, these new journals will not charge subscription or access fees, and will turn to other methods for covering their expenses. There is no need to favor one of these solutions over the others for all disciplines or nations, and no need to stop looking for other, creative alternatives".

OPEN ACCESS JOURNALS

Due to rapid growth in ICT, there has been tremendous scope to publish articles in a new breed of media, i.e. Open Access Journals (OAJ). The basic criteria of OAJ is to be available freely on the Web to any one to read, download, to save and down load either on Institutional Archives or Central Archives with no barriers of any kind. There are journals with online access but majority of them are accessible only on subscription. It has been estimated that there are about 5 % of scholarly publishing, which follow open access model. It is to be noted that OA journals also follow all rigorous treatment of peer review as of non-OA journals.

The *Directory of Open Access Journals* is hosted and maintained by Lund University Libraries. There are now 2588 journals in the Directory. Currently, 773 journals are searchable at article level. As of March 2007, there are 127571 articles included in the DOAJ service. (DOAJ, 2007). Informatics India's OpenJgate lists about 3750 open access journals of which 1750 are referred journals.

Characteristics of Open Access Journals

The characteristics of open access journals as identified by Suber, P (2005) are:

- OA journals conduct peer review;
- OA journals typically let authors retain copyright;
- OA journals levy fee from the authors or his employer;
- Some OA journal publishers are not-for-profit (e.g. PLoS) and some are for-profit (e.g. BioMed Central or BMC);
- OA journals are economically viable and disseminate information at a faster rate;

Some publishers of Open Access Journals

Cost wise, OA journals are not for free. The up - front subscription fee is avoided as in traditional journals. One model is to charge authors for a submission fee. There are a few publishers, who initiated publishing altogether new journals keeping in view Open Access Initiative, which grew out of a meeting convened by the Open Society Initiative in Budapest in December 2001. Some important publishers are given as below:

Public Library of Science (PLoS) (http://www.plos.org)

PLoS is a non-profit organization established in October 2000, engaged in publishing eight leading biological journals with high Impact Factors and citations and provides Open Access as per the mandate. The business model is - expenses are recovered in part by charging publication fee to authors or research sponsors for each article they publish. It also offers complete or partial waiver of fees to authors who do not have funds to cover publication fees. Also, it has institutional memberships that allow all scholars at the member institution to submit articles free of charge.

BioMed Central (BMC) (http://www.biomedcentral.com)

BMC is a publisher of more than 170 peer-reviewed open access journals in the field of medical and allied sciences. It is an independent publisher dedicated to making the results of scientific research freely accessible. Like, PLoS, some funding for the project is provided by page charges. Sales of supplemental products such as reprints and paper copies of journals to libraries and individuals generate additional funding. They are immediately and permanently available online without charge and are open access. A number of journals require an institutional or a personal subscription to view other content, such as reviews or paper reports. Free trial subscriptions to these journals are available.

BMJ Group of Journals (Selective titles)

http://journals.bmj.coin/nusc/aboutijs.shtinl

The journals.bmj.com website is owned by BMJ Publishing Group Limited, a private limited company. The low income and low-middle income countries are entitled to free access. They include 113 developing countries, areas and territories included in the HINARI Initiative. There is no need to subscribe to access the full-text, which automatically qualify for free access.

Indian Academy of Sciences, http://www.ias.ernet.in

The Academy, founded in 1934, aims at promoting the progress and upholding the cause of science in pure and applied branches. Major activities include publication of journals and special volumes, etc. The Academy's eleven journals are open access and full text is available as pdf files on each journal's website.

Indian National Science Academy, http://www. insa.ac. in/html/home.asp

The Indian National Science Academy was established in January 1935 with the object of promoting science in India and harnessing scientific knowledge for the cause of humanity and national welfare. Keeping this in view, the importance and impact of electronic publishing aids in Science and Academy's mandate of promoting and publishing scientific knowledge, the INSA being a premier scientific body took the initiative to propose a project on "Building Digital Resources: Creating facilities at INSA for hosting S & T Journals Online". The six journals published by them are available for open access.

The other known Indian Open Access Journal publishers are: MedKnow, Indian Medlars Centre (NIC), Kamala-Raj-Enterprises and IndianJournals.com which cover a few journals in the area of science and technology, medicine and humanities.

OPEN ACCESS INITIATIVES BY SOME OTHER WELL-KNOWN PUBLISHERS

Some leading societies and commercial publishers are supporting open access to articles published by authors in some of the journals based on payments either by sponsorship or by the authors/institutions and some representative examples are given below:

The American Physical Society has announced release of FREE TO READ (APS, 2006)

The APS has announced its Open Access (OA) Offering articles published in Physical Reviews (PR): A to E, Physical Review Letters (PRL), and Reviews of Modern Physics (RPM), It is in operation since September 2006, which can be applied to any article or group of articles published in the above said journals back to 1893. Any one may, by paying a one-time fee, make articles published in APS journals available to all readers at no cost and without subscription. Readers will have access to pdfs and postscript versions of the FREE to READ articles through APS online journals.

The FREE TO READ fees will initially be $975 for articles in PR; $1300 in PRL. Articles in RMP differs depending upon size of the paper and is considered on a case-by-case basis. This initiative represents a path by which APS would gradually move to full open access.

American Chemical Society offers ACS *AuthorChoice* Open Access Option (ACS, 2006)

ACS now offers an important publishing option in support of the Society's journal authors who wish or need to sponsor open access to their published research articles. The ACS *AuthorChoice* was launched in October 2006, provides a fee-based mechanisms for individual authors or their research funding agencies to sponsor the open availability of their articles on the Web at the time of online publication. Under this policy, the ACS as copyright holder enables unrestricted Web access to a contributing author's publication from the Society's Website, in exchange for payment from the sponsoring author. ACS *AuthorChoice* also enables such authors to post electronic copies of published articles on their own personal websites and institutional repositories for non-commercial scholarly purposes. The option is extended to authors only after peer-review and editorial acceptance of their articles for publication. The base fee set is at $3000 through 2007, with significant discounts applied for contributing authors who are members of ACS and/ or who are affiliated with an ACS subscribing institution.

As per latest news, there is a very interesting program for ACS authors, which can be used to make articles open access. They have what is called *Articles on Request* program (ACS, 2007).

As an extension to author's e-print service, ACS permits within the first 12 months of publication up to 50 complimentary article downloads to interested readers who are not already ACS subscribers; at 12 months and there after, reader access via author - directed links is unlimited. Under this scheme, the authors are at liberty to e-mail or post links to final published articles as published by the society. Articles access via the links is from the ACS web site only, and is provided without charge to the reader, with no access limitations after 12 months.

Springer Open Choice: Open Access Publishing: Springer, 2006

Springer operates a program called Springer Open Choice. It offers authors to have their journal articles made available with full open access in exchange for payment of a basic fee (article processing charge).

In this model, authors submit manuscripts for peer review as in the traditional system. When article is accepted for publication, the author does not transfer copyright, but, instead, arrange for payment of 'processing fee', which defrays the publisher's costs and as a result, the article will be published with immediate and permanent full open access online. The basic fee for Springer Open Choice is $3000.00. Springer Open Choice articles are freely available for any one to read, downloads, or print from SpringerLink. Here publisher is giving publishing service and the publisher is paid for, not content. In this model, the main customers are authors (and or sponsors). The aim is to make and keep the best option around for publishing with open access in established journals.

SELF-ARCHIVING

Self-archiving refers to the process wherein individual authors submit their articles to a server or any archive of their choice. The recent spurt in the growth of archives is due to common protocol for metadata retrieval defined by Open Archives Initiative (http://www.openarchives.org) enabling OAI- compliant archive to be searched seamlessly. (Chan, et al, 2005). The OAI which aims to develop and promote the use of a standard protocol, known as Open Archives Initiative Protocol for Metadata Harvesting (OAI - PMH), designed for better sharing and retrieval of eprints residing in distributed archives. With the OAI harvesting protocol, articles in OAI compliant servers will form a global library that facilitates searching, data retrieval, cross linking, as well as long term archiving.

The UK-JISC funded RoMEO Project (Rights Metadata for Open-Archiving) was carried out vis-a-vis IPR issues relating to academic author self-archiving of research papers. The study concluded that self-archiving is not best supported by copyright transfer to publishers and recommends that institutes must assert in copyright ownership in the long term, and that publisher consider new-ways of protecting the value they add through journal publishing. (Gadd, E. et al, 2003). The strong proponent of Open Access Movement, Stevan Harnad argues that research papers currently given away to "toll-gated" journals should instead be made openly available through free Web-based access.

There has been mixed reactions and apprehension about author's self-archiving, which may result in potential damage to journal subscriptions. There have been studies to show that there is little or no evidence to suggest that such posting is affecting journals as yet. In the realm of physics, where the arXiv preprint repository has been in operation since 1991, publishers of physics and related journals do not report any unusual drop either in submissions or in subscriptions. (Morris, S., 2004). As an example, for subject repository, arXiv is briefed below:

ArXiv for Literature in Physics (http://arXiv.org)

The e-print arXiv, which was implemented during August 1991, is the oldest archive, which facilitates free access to global resources of physics, mathematics, computer science and quantitative biology. Since inception, it has grown in size containing over 375,000 articles with more than 40,000,000 full text downloads per year. It is an international project, with dedicated mirror sites in 18 countries and has provided crucial lifeline for isolated researchers in developing countries.

This archive is entirely scientist driven and articles are deposited either before, simultaneous with or after peer review and articles are available immediately for access throughout the world. It has a heuristic steering mechanism, including a filter on institutional affiliation of submitter, or to ensure insofar as possible that submissions are at least "refereeable quality" (Ginsparg, P., 2006).

As per APS and IoP, it has been observed that in spite of the existence of arXiv for over 15 years, there has been no cut in subscription of journals they publish or they could not have any loss as a result of emergence of arXiv. (Swan A. and Brown, S., 2005).

INSTITUTIONAL REPOSITORY

With recent developments in scholarly communication, institutional repository concept is gaining momentum in making Open Access Movement a success. Raym Crow defines the institutional repository as a collection of digital material hosted, owned or controlled, or disseminated by a college or university, irrespective of purpose or provenance and the one capable of supporting two complementary purposes: as a component in a restructured scholarly publishing model, and as a tangible embodiment of institutional quality. Clifford Lynch (2003) defines IR as "a set of services that a university offers to the members of its community for the management and dissemination of digital materials created by the institution and its community members. It is most essentially an organizational commitment to the stewardship of these materials, including long-term preservation where appropriate, as well as organization and access to distribution".

With free access to some open source softwares for creating institutional repositories, several institutions around the world have developed institution-based repositories. Some of the open source softwares are: *Eprints* (http://www.eprints.org/), *FEDORA* (http://www.fedora.info/) and *DSpace*. The prominent software, which is used by many, is DSpace (http:// www.dspace.org/), developed by MIT, Cambridge in collaboration with Hewlett-Packard with a slogan of "durable digital documents", created to capture, distribute and preserve the intellectual output of MIT (Kwasik, Hand Fulda, P.O., 2005).

EVALUATION OF IRS

Institutional repositories are basically data providers and expected to provide full range of service to its potential user communities. As a service, IR needs to be subjected to periodic evaluation to ensure that it is fulfilling its basic institutional requirements and user needs for which it has been implemented in the organization. The basic aspects related to evaluation is: whether the IR is fulfilling needs defined; communities are well served; whether all communities represented in the IR are posted with articles by the faculty; if not what are the reasons; how best is the usage pattern; how concerned are the faculty for posting/ submission of their pre or post prints. (Davis, P.M. and Connolly, M.J.L., 2007).

INDIAN SCENARIO IN DEVELOPING INSTITUTIONAL REPOSITORIES

The Indian R & D organizations, which have the best facilities with all required infrastructure are developing institutional repositories as could be seen in the Directory of Open Access Repositories (open DOAR: http://www.opendoar.org/) where over a dozen prominent IRs have been listed. The Indian scenario is well documented in the paper by Ghosh and Das (2006). The important Indian Digital Repositories are given in Table: 1. Also there have been extensive discussion in the LIS forums and literature regarding open access and implementation of IRs and choice of hardware and software in the Indian libraries (Madalli, Devika P. and Seth,R.,2005; Krishnamurthy, M., 2005; Das R., et al, 2006; Rajashekar, T.B., 2006; Birdie, Christina and Vagiswari, A., 2006; Sukhdev Singh and Pandita Naina, 2006; and Girija Srinivasan, et al, 2007).

List of Indian Digital Repositories as given by the OpenDOAR:

http://www.opendoar.org/countrylist.php?c Continent= Asia

- *Indian Institute of Astrophysics* - http: //www. iiap. res. in/

  Indian Institute of Astrophysics Repository (DSpace@IIA) http: //prints. iiap. res. in/
- *Indian Institute of Management Kozhikode (IIMK)* - http://www.iimk.ac.in/
  1. *DSpace at Indian Institute of Management Kozhikode (DSpace@IIMK)* http://dspace.iimk. ac.in/
  2. *Indian Institute of Management Kozhikode Scholarship Repository (ePrints@IIMK)* http:// eprints.iimk.ac.in/
- *Indian Institute of Science, Bangalore (IISc)* - http:// www.iisc.ernet.in/
  1. *Electronic Theses and Dissertations at Indian Institute of Science (etd@IISc)* http://etd.ncsi. iisc.ernet.in/
  2. *Open Access Repository of IISc Research Publications (ePrints@iisc)* http://eprints.iisc. ernet.in/
- *Indian Statistical Institute, Bangalore Centre (ISI)* - http://www.isibang.ac.in/
  1. *Digital Library at Indian Statistical Institute, Bangalore (ISI Library)* http://library.isibang.ac. in: 8080/dspace/
  2. *Librarians' Digital Library (LDL)* https://drtc. isibang.ac.in/
- *Information and Library Network Center (INFLIBNET)* - http://www.inflibnet.ac.in/

  DSpace@INFLIBNET

http://dspace.inflibnet.ac.in/

- *Information Centre for Aerospace Science and Technology (ICAST)* - http://www.icast.org.in/

  National Aerospace Laboratories Institutional Repository (NAL Repository) http: //nal -ir. nal. res. in/

- *National Chemical Laboratory (NCL)* - http: //www. ncl-india.org/

  DSpace at National Chemical Laboratory

  (DSpace@NCL)

  http: //dspace. ncl. res. in/dspace/

- *National Informatics Centre (NIC)* - http: //home. nic. in/

  OpenMED@NIC http: //openmed.nic.in/

- *National Institute Of Oceanography (NIO)* - http:// www.nio.org/

  DRS at National Institute Of Oceanography (DRS@nio)

  http://drs.nio.org/

- *National Institute of Technology, Rourkela (NITR)* - http://www.nitrkl.ac.in/

  Dspace@NITR

  http: //dspace. nitrkl. ac. in/dspace/

- *OWSA (OneWorld South Asia)* - http://www. southasia.oneworld.net/

  OneWorld South Asia Open Archive Initiative

  http://open.ekduniya.net/

- *Raman Research Institute* - http://www.rri.res.in/

  RRI Digital Repository (Raman Research Institute Digital Repository)

  http //dspace. rri. res. in/dspace/

- *University of Delhi* - http://www.du.ac.in/

  DU Eprint Archive

  http://eprints.du.ac.in/

RRI DIGITAL REPOSITORY (E-SANGRAH)

http://dspace.rri.res.in

Keeping in view, the developments around the world, and to join the main stream for supporting Open Access Movement (OAM), we decided to develop institutional repository using the open source software, DSpace (http://www.dspace.org). It collects preserves and disseminates in digital format the research output of the RRI community. It facilitates RRI community to deposit their preprints, post prints and other publications using a web interface and organizes these digital products for easy access and retrieval. We are briefing in a nutshell about the RRI Digital repository.

Why need for the Repository

We had been thinking for a kind of system wherein we could accommodate the following materials, which could be archived for future use and for access and retrieval of required document with full text. The documents in question were :

- Newspaper clippings of C.V.Raman collected during 1930 - 1960s, which have become too fragile to handle;
- Collected pdfs of all RRI research papers from early 1990s since onset of online journals and also scanned articles from journals and conference proceedings dating back to early 1970s;
- To create an information centre for collected works of C.V.Raman and literature published on him by other scholars; and
- Institutional gray literature, including annual reports and other miscellaneous publications relating to RRI.

Software selection

In order to accomplish the above project, we were

looking for suitable hardware and software so that institute's research output is projected in a best possible manner. At the same time, few software, viz. GNU Eprints, Greenstone Digital Library Software (GSDL), FEDORA Digital Library and DSpace Digital Library were already in place and many libraries were using them across the world. Keeping in view our collection of varied nature, and exposure by way of training of library staff members, DSpace was selected for our library. The application of DSpace provides the ways for capturing, storing, indexing, preserving and disseminating digitally held objects. (Baudoin, P. and Margaret Branschofsky, 2003). It complies with the Open Archives Initiative (OAI) framework allowing publications to be easily indexed and searched by web search engines. The details of the Digital Repository hardware/software are as given below:

Configuration of RRI Digital Repository:

URL: http://dspace.rr.ires.in;

IR software: DSpace version 1.3.2;

Software: CentOS 4.0 Linux, Apache Tomcat 5.5.9, Apache Ant 1.6.5, PostgreSQL 8.0.0, Sun Java JDK 1.5.0_01;

Server: Intel 4, CPU 3 GHz, 1 GB RAM, 160 GB SATA Mirrored Hard Disks.

Contents of RRI Repository

The main scope of the IR is defined by Crow (2002) as "a digital archive of the intellectual product created by the faculty, research staff and students of an institution...". They may contain a wide range of digital materials that reflects the intellectual wealth of an institution - e.g. Preprints and working papers, published articles, enduring teaching materials, student theses, data sets, etc. Based on Institutional research output, the content essentially consists of the following digital products:

- Preprints/post prints;
- Published articles in journals, conference proceedings;
- Annual Reports;
- News Paper Clippings of C.V.Raman;
- Collected works of C. V. Raman;
- RRI - Masters/Doctoral dissertations/theses; and
- RRI Photo Gallery.

Benefits to the authors/institution and the society

There are many benefits, at many levels, to institutional repositories (Prosser.D.C), viz.

For the individual : Provide a central archive of their work; increase the dissemination and impact of their research; acts as a full CV; the papers could have higher citation than the traditionally published articles; can stamp priority of ideas;

For the institution : Increases visibility and prestige; acts as an advertisement to funding sources, potential new faculty and students, etc;

For Society : provide access to the world literature of research; ensure long-term preservation of institute's academic output; and they can accommodate increased volume of research output.

Content and Copyrights Issues

The major concern of DR is intellectual property rights. Normally, every publisher demands authors to sign copyright when paper is accepted for publication and this varies with publishers.

We have different categories of the documents posted in the repository and copyright for each has to be looked into differently. In case of News Paper Clippings and Raman's collected works, we had to seek copyright permission from each publisher. Wherever, we were trying to get copyright permission for such documents, publishers willingly permitted us for hosting the documents for the reason that the documents are of historical significance. In normal case of research articles, we have followed guidelines as given in each publisher's site and posted them accordingly without infringing copyright laws.

As a part of the survey process, the Project RoMEO compiled a list of journal publishers' copyright policies on "self archiving", a useful source that is currently maintained by the SHERPA Project, (http://www.sherpa.ac.uk/romeo.php). They have used a color code to classify the self-archiving policies of various publishers. *Green Publishers-allowing* archiving both pre-prints and post-prints; *Blue Publishers* - allowing archiving of post-prints but not pre-prints; *Yellow Publishers* - allowing archiving of pre-prints but not post-prints; *and White Publishers* - no archiving allowed. (Guedon, J-C, 2004 and SHERPA).

Policies and Guidelines for DR

We have identified different set of documents for our repository including not only research output of the institute but also the collected works of C.V.Raman, the founder of the RRI, and gray literature consisting of annual reports and theses. The following communities have been taken into our repository, which acts as Information Centre of RRI providing access to all scattered information at one place. There are over 2200 items held in the DR as of March 2007..

- Archives- consisting annual reports; Gandhi Memorial Lectures, News Paper Clippings (items available - 747);
- Astronomy and Astrophysics (382);
- Light and Matter Physics (44);
- Soft Condensed Matter (245);
- Theoretical Physics (148);

- C.V. Raman's Collected Work and articles on Raman (498)
- Theses and Dissertations (digitized 112 theses and expected to be posted soon);
- Photo gallery (this is being developed)
- Miscellaneous (63).

We have yet to formulate institutional mandate for the Digital Repository for posting of papers by researchers and the students. Our main contributors are the faculty members and the research students. To facilitate, online submission, we placed brief note on "Submission Guide" on our repository home page. To begin with, majority of the papers were posted by the project team of the library, where all submissions are checked including copyright clearance, correct format, edit of metadata, etc. In case, where copyright clearance is not there, we have posted articles for access with full bibliographic details indicating publisher site as an alternate location. We are trying to rope in all researchers/students to post their papers in the form of preprints/post prints or published and permitted papers from publishers in the repository. The growth of the DR is given in the following graph:

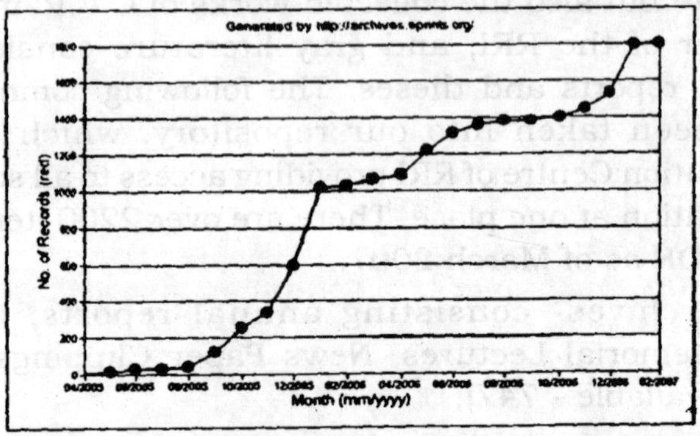

RRI Digital Repository records holding

Content Development

The success of the repository is largely defined by

quantity of content. The widespread feeling is that content development in an institutional repository is a painful exercise, as Gibbons (2004) puts it, "Recruitment of content, not technology, is the greatest barrier to success". The setting - up of institutional repository implies an institutional commitment to the ongoing management of information. Several studies have indicated that relying on self-submission from authors alone is not enough and the project staff have to have open mind to develop content in the repository. (Chan, 2005, Foster, 2005; Mackie, 2004; Hunter, P. and Day, M., 2005; and Gibbons, S., 2004). There are several reasons for authors' poor response for posting their papers, viz.

- Authors are not willing to take additional burden of posting work;
- They have apprehension of violating copyrights and are not well versed with different publishers' copyrights;
- Fear of plagiarism; and
- Benefits not immediately obvious with a reason as to why to deposit in an institutional repository when their papers are archived in a well-known subject repository like arXiv.

Mark and Shearer (2005) have strongly advocated a multi-pronged approach in order to promote submission to the repository. They have identified and classified these strategies into six categories, viz. general promotional activities, mediated depositing services, content harvesting, researcher bibliographies, usage information and self-archiving policies. These strategies will enhance submission to repository (Girija Srinivasan, et al, 2007).

CONCLUSIONS

The journals crisis has forced the stakeholders in scholarly communication, i.e. publishers, researchers, librarians and the users of information to look for ways and means for free and open access to literature published, as research is funded by the society and the society has right to free access to information generated. As a result, the Open Access movement has emerged. This has given the way for developments in self-archiving, publishing Open access journals and creating institutional repositories to achieve the set goals.

The Institutional Repository will better serve the authors and the users by way of wider dissemination and by removing access barriers to the information they seek. The purpose for which the repositories are created is to maximize the impact of research, visibility of authors and the institutions. This will enhance research and education worldwide and society is benefited for the investments made. RRI Digital Repository supports open access movement; collects, preserves all research output at a central place; showcases institutional gray literature and enhances visibility of authors and the institution.

11

A Catalogue of E-Resources in Social Sciences with a Special Reference to Sociology

Jivesh Bansal
Deputy Librarian, Panjab University Library, Chandigarh-160014
Vinod Kumar
Senior Library Information Assistant, Indian Institute of Technology Mandi, Mandi (H.P.)

ABSTRACT

The technological developments have led to the tremendous increase in the production of scholarly literature in the present era. But on the positive side, the new electronic information environment has also provided new options of freely publishing and disseminating the scholarly literature which is termed as Open Access (OA), free access, open domain, public domain, etc. A decade ago, this new invented phenomenon was strengthened by launching a worldwide campaign in Budapest known as Budapest Open Access Initiative. The aim behind open access is to bridge the gap between information rich and information poor nations emerging as 'Digital Divide'. 'Social Sciences' and especially 'Sociology' which is described as 'Queen of Social Sciences' has come up with many successful open access initiatives in recent past. The focus of this paper is to discuss various important open access information sources of social sciences in general and sociology in particular. The listed electronic information resources were accessed in January, 2016.

1. INTRODUCTION

The Internet as a publishing medium has opened new vistas of publishing the scholarly content freely and for wider accessibility among its users. The movement although started with the start of new publishing medium, it gained momentum with certain breakthrough initiatives such as Budapest Open Access Initiatives (2002) and Berlin Declaration on Open Access to Knowledge in the Sciences and Humanities (2003). The third world countries representing 80% of the world population cannot access the research findings from the developed nations as well as research conducted by them is largely invisible to the global research community due to financial and governmental constraints (National Knowledge Commission). The Open Access (OA) movement is aimed at bridging this gap, emerging as 'Digital Divide' among the information rich and information poor nations. Besides this, the creators of information are also benefited in term of more use and better citation impact for their works. There are two main ways of OA – 'Self Archiving' in which authors make their scholarly content freely available on the web or deposit it in institutional repositories termed as 'Green' road to OA; whereas 'Open Access Journals' involves publishing and making free availability to scholarly articles immediately after the publication known as 'Golden' road to OA. In the two, the green road is realized more viable and plausible route to OA (Perakakis et.al, 2010).

2. OPEN ACCESS IN SOCIAL SCIENCES

E.R.A. Seligman (1930) defined Social Sciences as, "those mental or cultural sciences which deal with human in their social relations". Social Sciences consist largely of economics, anthropology, psychology and sociology. The other disciplines which come under the domain of social sciences are criminology, communication, library science, education, geography, history, linguistics, laws, cultural studies, philosophy and social policy, etc. August Comte termed Sociology as 'Queen of the Social Sciences". Although, OA initiatives as seen in social sciences are less in number as compared to sciences even then OA literature in social sciences is available in many forms such as digital repositories, OA journals, information gateways, e-reference sources, etc. Haridasan and Khan (2009) reported awareness and effective use of the available e-resources by the social scientists in Indian environment.

2.1. Disciplinary Repositories

2.1.1. Social Science Research Network (SSRN) (http://www.ssrn.com/en/)

SSRN is network of social science research with an aim to disseminate the social science research at world level. It is composed of a number of specialized research networks in each of the social sciences. SSRN has rich response from journal publishers and social science institutions. SSRN e-library consists of two components; 'Abstract Database' containing 646200 records and an 'Electronic Paper Collection' having 540200 downloadable full text documents. SSRN provide detailed author contact information including e-mail address for personalization with the authors.

2.1.2. Social Science Open Access Repository (http://www.ssoar.info/en/home.html)

Social Science Open Access Repository (SSOAR) is an OA repository of electronic fulltext collection funded by German Research Foundation (DFG) in the field of social sciences. SSOAR stands for the archiving and dissemination of quality-checked texts. The repository has certification from DINI (German Initiative for Networked Information). It has 35361 fulltext documents in the various fields of social sciences.

2.1.3. Social Science Cyber Library (http://socsccybraryamu.ac.in/)

The Social Science Cyber Library is collection of e-books, e-journals, conference proceedings, in-house publications, video lectures, useful websites, subject gateways, databases, softwares, e-theses, etc. in the field of social sciences. The purpose of Social Science Cyber Library is to bring all open access resources in social sciences at one platform, so that the students, research scholars and faculty members belonging to various disciplines of social sciences may make optimum use of them. The Social Science Cyber Library hosted by Aligarh Muslim University is an important venture in the field of social sciences in India.

2.2. Online Journals

2.2.1. Scientific Research Publishing – Social Sciences and Humanities

Scientific Research Publishing is an academic publisher of open access journals. It also publishes academic books and conference proceedings. Under the section, Social Sciences and Humanities, 22 open access journals are being published. For example, Open Journal of Social Sciences (*http://www.scirp.org/journal/jss*), Advances in Applied Sociology (*http://www.scirp.org/journal/AASoci/*), Sociology Mind (*http://www.scirp.org/journal/sm*), etc.

2.2.2. Bentham Open (http://benthamopen.com/)

BENTHAM OPEN publishes over 50 plus peer-reviewed open access journals. These free-to-view online journals cover all major disciplines of science, technology, medicine and social sciences. In the subject of social Sciences, from this publisher. For example – The Open Psychology Journal, The Open Family Studies Journal, The Ergonomics Open Journal and many more are available.

2.2.3. Open Access Journals Search Engine (http://oajse.com/)

The Open Access Journals Search Engine (OAJSE) service covers free, full text, quality controlled journals. OAJSE covers journals in all subjects that are published in English language. There are now 4,775 journals in the directory. All are searchable at article level. The aim of this project is to increase the visibility and ease of use of OA journals thereby promoting their increased usage and impact. The 112 and 54 journals are available under the heading 'Social Sciences' and 'Sociology' respectively.

2.2.4. Socjournal (http://www.sociology.org/)

Socjournal is a new media journal offering to sociologists a window into the world of new media communications. The journal was founded by Lightning Path Press, Canada in 2010 recognizing that traditional scholarly publications is limited, slow, and isolated. Socjournal aims to bring sociology to the world by providing blog space, regular columns, and academic reports designed to popularize and disseminate the fascinating world of sociological research.

2.2.5. Postmodern Culture (PMC) (http://pmc.iath.virginia.edu/)

PMC is founded as an experiment in scholarly publishing on the Internet by Johns Hopkins University Press with support from the University of California, Irvine, and the University of Virginia in 1990. PMS is a leading electronic journal of interdisciplinary thought on contemporary cultures, publishing the works of noted authors like Kathy Acker, Charles Bernstein, Bruce Robbins, Bell Hooks, Susan Howe, etc. As an entirely web-based journal, PMC combines images, sound, animation, and full-motion video as an aid to the text.

2.3. Information Gateways

2.3.1. Understanding the World Today: A Website of 'The Global Social Change Research Project' (http://gsociology.icaap.org/)

The website is supported by The International Consortium for the Advancement of Academic Publication (ICAAP). ICAAP is supported by Athabasca University. The website organized information resources in two parts – Reports and Resources. In the Report section, the website provides *Reports, Basic Guides to the World, Data sets and Presentations.* Besides this, it also covers all about major global social, demographic, economic and political trends in the last several decades, about topics such as aging, poverty, globalization, democracy, terrorism, literacy, quality of life, etc. We also have a report about theory of change, how to understand all the changes that have been happening.

In Resources Section, the website links to other sites with *Theory, Research, Data, Basic Profiles & History, and Softwares* that can remain useful in studying social change. The website also provides links to organizations, journals, History Videos, educational classes pages, etc. The important critical topics such as such as global warming, terrorism, sustainable development, etc. are also covered.

2.3.2. SocioSite (http://www.sociosite.net/)

SocioSite (Social Science Information System – University of Amsterdam) is designed to provide a comprehensive listing of information resources which are relevant for sociologists and other social scientists. SocioSite is a project based at the Faculty of Social Sciences at the University of Amsterdam. It has become a very popular yellow guide for social scientists from all over the world because of its comprehensive, easy to use and regular updation features. The website presents the resources and information that are important for the international sociological scene. It contains high quality resources and texts that can be used as wheels for the sociological mind.

2.3.3. Digital Common Network (http://network.bepress.com/social-and-behavioral-sciences/)

The Digital Commons Network is a growing collection of free full-text articles from peer-reviewed journal, book chapters, dissertations, working papers, conference proceedings, and other original scholarly work. The collection is curated by university librarians and their supporting institutions from hundreds of universities and colleges worldwide. Under the general heading, 'Social and Behavioral Sciences' 384 institutions have contributed more than two lac fulltext articles in the Network.

2.3.4. Social Criticism Review (http://www.socialcritic.org)

Social Criticism Review (SCR) presents selected readings on modern society and its ills. The critical reviews on alienation between man, nature and a dysfunctional scientific-technical complex is the main focus of the website. In this way, SCR offers an outstanding selection of 1,000 online readings on the crisis of modernity: progress, science for sale, megatechnology, third world debt, counterproductive economy, globalization, corporate rule, anti-democratic media, advertising consumerism, environmental destruction, genetic manipulation, sustainable development, human rights, ethics, responsibility, citizenship, community building, arms race, war on terrorism, resurgent totalitarianism, and much more. The website constitutes a useful resource for a unified protest movement.

2.4. E-Reference Sources

2.4.1. Online Dictionary of the Social Sciences (http://bitbucket.icaap.org/)

The website is publication of Athabasca University

along with International Consortium for the Advancement of Academic Publication. This dictionary has 1000 entries covering the disciplines of sociology, criminology, political science and women's study. It is Canadian biased in citing examples, events and names.

CONCLUSION

Open access movement is gaining momentum in social sciences with the success of many initial initiatives in many sub-disciplines of the subject. Universities, societies, associations, libraries and government agencies should come forward to promote awareness about internet resources among social scientists. These organizations should provide funding and encourage for establishing subject repositories and open access journals in social sciences so that scholars in different fields could be benefited from new means of scholarly communication. The Internet has provided a viable solution to the research communities to expand the horizons of information through own scholarly ways.

REFERENCES

- Haridasan, S., & Khan, M. (2009). Impact and use of e-resources by social scientists in National Social Science Documentation Centre (NASSDOC), India. *The Electronic Library.* 27 (1), 117 -133.
- Perakakis, P., Taylor, M., and Trachana, V. (2010). The road to open access. In: *World Social Science Report 2010.* Paris: UNESCO Retrieved on January 2, 2016 from http://unesdoc.unesco.org/images/0018/001883/188333e.pdf
- Report of the Working Group on Open Access and Open Educational Resources. Retrieved on January 2, 2016 from http://www.knowledgecommission.gov.in/downloads/documents/wg_open_course.pdf.
- Seligman, E.R.A. (1930). What are the social sciences. Edwin R.A. Seligman (Ed.), *Encyclopedia of the social sciences.* New York: The Macmillan. p.3.

12

Excelling Communications Through E-Governance and E-Learning

Bibha Prasad Panda
Dilip K Swain
IBS, Bhubaneswar

INTRODUCTION

E-governance involves the use of information and communication technologies (ICTs) to transact the business of government. At the level of service, e-governance promises a full service available 24 hours a day and seven days a week. Greater accessibility, the capability to obtain government services without visiting government offices, and reduced service cost. At all level of basic factors (government accountability and general acceptance of state institutions, e- governance contributes to the functioning of democracy by online provision of government information which would otherwise be difficult to obtain or unavailable, and through online debates and plebiscites (Saxena. 2006; Teicher et al., 2002). At the same time, electronic learning (e- learning) seems to have taken the world by blizzard and is fast becoming a major form of learning. It is an approach to teaching and learning that is now used widely by schools, colleges, universities and distance learning cells, and academic institutions. In this regard, if e-learning is a process, e-governance is a means. However, all forms of e-learning do not come under the purview of e-governance. Though 'e-learning' and 'e- governance' are two different connotations, they are just two pictures on same paper. Nevertheless, successful implementation of e-learning and e- governance policy helps in bridging the digital divide through a wide-ranging approach to digital environment across the world. If implementation of e-learning addresses some of the fundamental issues, for instance, infrastructure, digitization, curriculum designs, content developments, evaluation of students' needs, etc, then e-governance possesses some other additional issues. This unfastens a stimulating research prospect. Therefore, it is vital to assess some of the assorted facets of web enabled digital environment before being endemic to the situation.

E-GOVERNANCE

Torres et al. (2005) define governance as the rules, processes and behaviors that affect the way public administration function, that is, the organization and culture of public administration. It is believed that governance itself is much more than the physical authoritative institutions, organizations and process within the public sector. The effectiveness of systems of governance he argues is particularly important because, if failure occurs, then government will ultimately be held accountable. Torres et al. believe that e- governance should now be at the heart of national ICT strategies to make the development of e-Government sustainable, encompassing the wide-ranging challenges to corporate management brought about by technological advancements (Wong et al., 2007).

E-government commonly refers to the processes and

structures pertinent to the electronic delivery of government services to the public (Saxena. 2006). As a concept, e-governance can be perceived to be contextually inclusive of "electronic democracy (Okot- Uma, 2001). In this context, e-democracy refers to the processes and structures that encompasses all forms of electronic communication between government and the citizen, such as information, voting, polling, or discussion, thereby enabling citizens to participate in the governments policy making (Gronlund, 2001)

E-governance goes beyond simple service provision to build external interactions (Heeks, 2001), enhance democracy by improving representative participation in political decision making (Lenihan, 2002), strengthen democratic institutions and processes, and involve the public in political choices so that their needs and priorities are respected (Kolsaker, 2008; Council of Europe, 2007). In addition, the growth of an online public sphere may require a reassessment of traditional conceptions of the role of the citizen and citizen and the nature of government-citizen relations (Kolsaker, 2008; Lips, 2006) that makes the concept of e-governance pervasive.

FEATURES OF E-GOVERNANCE

E-governance provides the following three major functions:

E-Administration : improving government processes by cutting costs, by managing performance, by making strategic connections within government, and by creating empowerment

E-Citizens and e-Services : connecting citizens to government by talking to citizens and supporting accountability, by listening to citizens and supporting democracy, and by improving public services

E-Society : building interactions beyond the boundaries of government by working better with business, by developing communities, by building government partnerships, and by building civil society

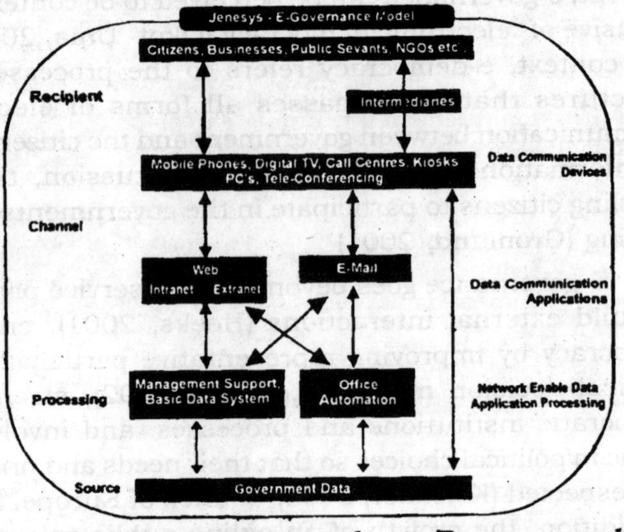

Source : *http://www.jeltesystech.com/E-governance.html*

IMPACT OF E-GOVERNMENT

Some developing country governments have been eager to utilize these new technologies to enable efficiency gains, cost savings, and improvement of service delivery. Schware and Deahe (2008) have expressed in brief the impact of e-government on society as presented in Table No. 1.

Table 1. E-government impact

Impact	*Definition*	*Project Example*
Direct citizen Value	Government functional value Citizens gain value from increased access and reduced delays, improved service delivery, and less interaction with intermediaries	Government functional value India: Andhra Pradesh: Land registration: Payment of property taxes and issue of land titles at 230 locations. Process takes five minutes instead of 15 days
Social	Improved trust in	Estonia: TOM Portal:

value	government. Increased sharing of information. Monitoring of regulatory compliance, greater visibility	Citizens participate in government decision making; citizens review and comment on draft legislation online and send proposals online to the government
Govt. operational value	Improvement in current performance and in participation for future requirements: on- time, completion rate, redundancy, network congestion flexibility	Philippines e-customs: Quick clearance of major transactions has brought down the cost of trade significantly. Cargo is released in four hours to two days as opposed to eight days in the previous system
Strategic/ political value	Organization perceived as moving toward fulfilling its mission: improved public image, legislative guidelines met	Mexico: Declarant: requires civil servants to declare their patrimonial assets online
Govt. functional value	Benefits that impact organizational and other federal government budgets: reduced cost and steps per transaction, decreased cost of materials, reduced cost of correction	Chile: e-procurement system estimated to provide government with efficient gains of $ 200 million per year, a total of 1.38 percent of government expenditure.

Source: *Schware and Deane (2008)*

E-LEARNING: THE CONCEPT

Different terminologies have been used for e-learning, a fact that makes it difficult to develop a generic definition. E-learning, defined as instructional content or learning experiences delivered or enabled by electronic technology (Aydin and Tasci, 2005), Terms that are commonly used include "online learning", "internet learning", "distributed learning", "networked learning", "tele-learning", "virtual learning", "computer-assisted learning", "web-based-learning" and "distance learning". All of these terms imply that the learner is at a distance from the tutor or instructor and other learners, and that some form of support is provided to learners (Sharifabadi, 2006). Therefore, in brief e-leaming can be redefined as an electronic technology with wide acceptability and can reach the learners with a telephone line, a modem, internet connectivity at least to a desktop.

MERITS OF E-LEARNING

Educational institutions are moving towards the use of the Internet for delivery, both on campus and at a distance. However, for institutions to make this often expensive move, there must be a perception that e-governance provides major benefits. Some of the benefits pointed out by Sharifabadi (2006) are given as under:

- For learners, e-leaming knows no time zones, and location and distance are not an issue,
- In asynchronous e-learning, students can access the online materials at any time,
- Synchronous e-learning allows for real time interaction between students and the instructors,
- E-leamers can use the internet to access up-to-date and relevant learning materials, and can communicate with experts in the field in which they are studying,
- Situated learning is facilitated, since leamers can complete online courses while working on the job of in their own space, and can contextualize the learning,
- Online materials can be updated as per the needs of the learners, and learners are able to see the changes at once, and
- When learners are able to access materials on the

Internet, it is easier for instructors to direct them to appropriate information based on their needs.

The advantages of e-learning must outweigh its disadvantages for its implementation to be worthwhile. Amongst the many advantages of e-learning are that it is less expensive to deliver. E-leaming is self-paced, provides consistent content, faster and works anywhere at anytime for learners. The instructional materials are easily updated and permit the use of multimedia which leads to reinforced learning through the use of video, audio, quizzes and other forms of interaction. E- learning can improve retention, provide immediate feedback and allows learners to customize learning materials to meet their individual needs (Uhomoibhi, 2006; Kirsh, 2002, Turk and Robertson, 2000).

DIGITAL LIBRARIES AND E-LEARNING

One of the natural responses to the challenges of e-learning environment consists of introducing the digital library to support e-learning as a learning environment and resources network, designed to meet the needs of the learners, in both individual and collaborative settings, constructed to enable the dynamic use of a broad array of materials for learning primarily in digital format, managed actively to promote reliable anytime, anywhere access to quality collections and services, available both within and outside the network (Lippincot,2002).

The introduction of digital libraries into the education process was made easier by distance education, which has developed over the years. With the Internet and the World Wide Web, distance education programs can mount sets of materials on web servers to support online courses. One of the basic ideas is to join learning materials on various topics, written by many educators, in a digital library of courseware. Digital libraries have the potential to significantly change fundamental aspects of the classroom in ways that could have an enormous impact on teaching and learning. New pedagogical methods should accompany digital libraries as an emerging technology for education to reach the compelling vision of education (Sharifabadi, 2006). Therefore, for an ideal e-learning situation digital libraries are regarded as the hub of the library collections and services that function together in the real e-learning environment.

E-LEARNERS' EXPECTATIONS FROM LIBRARIANS

Communication is not just important to break the isolation of students in an e-learning environment but also for a much more basic reason: whatever one person says or writes, the receiver of the information will always interpret the information in the receiver's personal context, created through upbringing, culture, language, etc. This does often lead to deep misunderstandings. The only way to make sure that information is properly understood is not by reading, hearing, seeing, but by being able to check if things have been understood and asking questions: this is why an e-learning system that ignores the importance of communication will not work.

What do e-learners need from librarians? Suggestions advocating change in librarians' role in support of e-learning in information age appear throughout the literature: librarians must assert themselves as key players in the learning process thereby changing their roles from information providers to educators (Cooper and Dempsey, 1998), and they have been transferred from "information gatekeepers" to information gateways (Sharifabadi, 2006; Haricombe, 1998). Lippincot (2002) advocates librarian involvement in teaching communities that the librarian can shift the focus from explaining library resources to meeting the ongoing information needs of the students in the broad information environment.

In responding to the need to provide ongoing digital library support, librarians have worked at translating what they do in a traditional library into virtual or digital environments, while customizing their services and resources for e-learners. The traditional role of academic library services has always been to provide information resources for the teaching and learning activities within the academic sphere. Its role in supporting the virtual learning environment is no different. The linking of digital libraries and virtual library environments is required to provide a meaningful connection between learning activities and learning resources. The digital libraries can help provide information content to teaching staff who are engaged in e-learning. Traditionally, libraries offer circulation services, interlibrary loans, course reserves, an information desk, a reference desk, and library instruction. To serve learners connected to their institutional libraries primarily through a computer network, librarians are providing remote access to, and delivery of, library resources and are using communication technologies to deliver electronic reference services and instructional support.

As the literature suggests, e-learners are a wider community of learners than "students". An academic library's learners may include students, faculty, staff, teachers, and so on. The library is scen as a source of training and guidance to a community of learners who are concerned with navigating the complexities of locating and using digital resources and services. Moreover, the move towards a digital environment has resulted in a shift from the systematic one-to-one information flow of the past to a new model in which the users and the providers of information are able to relate in a many-to-many, dynamic relationship. For example, in the traditional model, a librarian provides a bridge between learners and information providers by selecting and cataloguing resources and by providing assistance with these resources. In the new model, the library serves as a facilitator by offering ongoing support enabling learners to interact and exchange knowledge with others, to communicate directly with the publishers and vendors of information resources, and to participate in a collaborative endeavor to make available rich collections of online scholarly information resources (Sharifabadi, 2006).

PARAMETERS OF SUCCESS IN E-LEARNING

The success of e-learning depends on how learning takes place online, that is the underlying pedagogy and the real value of e-learning lies in our ability to deploy its attributes to train the right people to gain the right knowledge and skills at the right time. The successful implementation of e-learning depends on the adherence to underlying principles that are embedded in the e-learning experiences. Though these principles apply to both the e-learning and the traditional classroom delivery method, they are yet to be included in the former. These pedagogical principles should form the basis for inclusion of features in e-learning management systems. Bixler and Sports (2000) have identified seven parameters affecting the successful implementation of e-learning. They are: institutional support; course development; teaching and learning; course structure; student support; faculty support; and evaluation and assessment

The availability of strong institutional support is crucial for e-learning deployment and success. The changing roles of staff must be recognized and acknowledged. Support Strategies must be developed for management of the transformation processes. Standards must be set and applied consistently. Although the teaching and learning process encourages a flexible and independent approach to knowledge acquisition, the notion of student support is markedly different from the traditional method.

Assessment reinforces the learning approach a student adopts and is an indispensable part of teaching and learning. Evaluation and assessment of learning should be based on higher order thinking skills, so that students may adopt a deep holistic approach to e-learning (Uhomoibhi, 2006; Twomey, 1996). Basing upon the underlying parameters, the authors have devised a conceptual e-model, which is depicted in Figure No. 2.

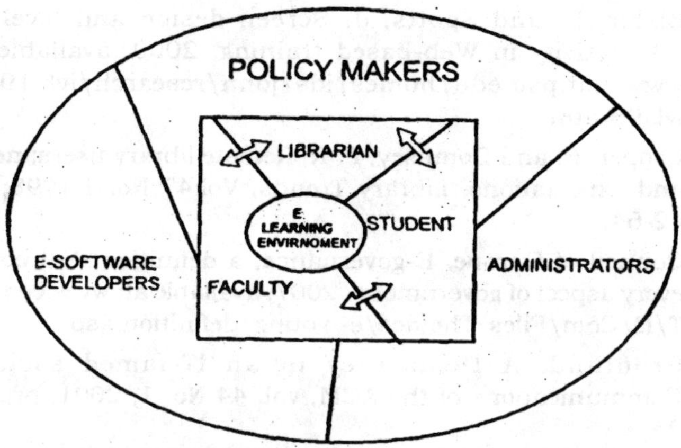

Fig. 2. A conceptual e-learning model

CONCLUSIONS

Governments' initiatives for e-governance and academic implementation of e-learning are two hot issues which have been prioritized these days for the welfare of the general public and students respectively. In this regard, Government of India has taken right e-government initiatives for making different systems and procedures transparent by setting Up different information Kiosks at block levels so that rural people can get information online and put their subsequent feedbacks on different issues. At the same time, institutions are gradually building up their e-resources, digitizing their contents, subscribing online databases for providing truly qualitative and cost effective online services to the students. Therefore, it is deduced that e-government initiatives for general public and implementation of e-learning in academic sphere will shortly bring an absolutely saturated global electronic world to bridge the gap of digital divide.

REFERENCES

1. Aydin, C. H. and Tasci, D. Measuring readiness for e-learning: reflections from an emerging country, Educational Technology & Society, Vol.8, No.4, 2005, pp. 97-101.
2. Bixler, B. and Spotts, J. Screen design and levels of interactivity in Web-based training, 2000, available at: www.clat.psu.edu/homes/jds/john/research/ivla1998/ivla98.htm
3. Cooper, R. and Dompsey, P. R. Remote library users; needs and expectations, Library Trends, Vol.47 No. 1,1998, pp. 42-64.
4. Council of Europe. E-governance, a definition that covers every aspect of government', 2007, available at: www.coe.int/T/E/Com/Files?Themes/e- voting/definition.asp
5. Gronlund. A Democracy in an lT-famed society', Communications of the ACM, vol. 44 No. 1, 2001, pp. 23-26.
6. Haricombe, I. J. Analytical Review of the library of the future, Council on library resources, Washington, DC. 1998.
7. Heeks, R. Understanding eGovernance for Development Institute for Development Policy and Management, Manchester. 2001.
8. Kirsh, D E-learning, metacognition and visual design, paper presented at the International Conference on Advances in Infrastructure for e-Business, e-Education, e-Science, and e-Medicine on the Internet L'Aquila, Italy, 29 July-4 August. 2002.
9. Kolsaker, A. and Lee-Kelly, L. Citizens attitudes towards e-government and e- governance: a UK study, *International Journal of Public Sector Management,* Vol.21 No 7, 2008, pp.723-738, available at www.emeraldinsight.com
10. Leninhan, D. Realigning governance: from e-governmen! to e-democracy, OECO Center for Collaborative Government, 2002, available at: www.collaborativegovernment.com
11. Lippincot, J. K. Developing collaborative relationship: librarians, students and faculty creating learning communities, College and Research Libraries News, Vol.63

No.3, 2002, pp. 190-192.

12. Lips, A.M.B. eGovernment under construction: challenging traditional conceptions of citizenship, in Koutrakou, V. and Nixon, P. (Eds), Re-booting the State via e-Government, Routledge, London, 2006, pp.33-37.
13. Okot-Uma, R. W. Electronic governance: (leading to good government), Electronic Governance and Electronic Democracy: Living and Working in the Connected Work), The Common Wealth Center for Electronic Governance, Ottawa, 2001, available at www. Electronegov.net
14. Saxena, K.B.C. Towards excellence in e-governance', International Journal of Public Sector Management Vol. 18 No.6,2006, pp. 498-513, available at www.emeraldinsight.com
15. Schware, R and Deane, A. Deploying e-government programs: the strategic importance of "I" before "E" Info, Vol.5, No 4, 2008, pp. 10-19.
16. Sharifabadi, S. R. How digital libraries can support e-learning, The Electronic Library, Vol.24 No.3, 2006, pp.389-401, available at www.emeraldinsight.com.
17. Teicher, J., Hughes, O. and Dow, N. E-government: a new route to public sector quality, Managing Service Quality, Vol. 12 No. 6, 2002, pp. 384-93.
18. Toress, L, Pina, V. and Acerete, B. eGovernance developments in EU cities: reshaping government relationship with citizens, 2005, available at: www.unpan.org/government.asp
19. Turk, M and Robertson, G. Perpetual user interfaces', Communications of the ACM, Vol.43 No.2, 2000, pp.33-40.
20. Twomey, E. Is there a role for computer-based assessment?, 1996, available at: http://sdence.universe.edu.au/mirror/CUBE96/twomey.html.
21. Uhomoibhi, J. O. Implementing e-learning in Northern Ireland: prospects and challenges, Campus Wide Information Systems, Vol. 23 No. 1, 2006, pp. 4-14, available at: www.emeraldinsight.com
22. Wong, K Fearon, C. and Philip, G. Understanding eGovernment and eGovernance: stakeholders, partnerships and CSR, *International Journal of Quality & Reliability Management.* Vol.24 No.9,2007, pp. 927-943, available at www.emeraldinsight.com

Websites

1. http://science.univerthe.edu.au/mirror/CUBE96/twomey.html.
2. http://www.jenesysle4n.com/E-governance.html

13

Information, Knowledge, Wisdom : A Value Added Pyramid

M P Satija
Ex-UGC Emeritus fellow
Guru Nanak Dev University, Amritsar

ABSTRACT

The paper lists problems in defining information and knowledge and also in differentiating between the two. It separately describes physical, economic and cognitive properties of information and knowledge. A long drawn comparative chart of the nature, characteristics and properties of knowledge and information is given. In addition it explains their relation with wisdom. Paper emphasis that knowledge is only a human preserve. Also it finds common grounds and mutual dependence between information, knowledge and wisdom. Purpose is to clear confusion between knowledge and information, and find their relation with wisdom and tradition by placing these in value added evolutionary pyramid: Signals—data—Information—Knowledge— Wisdom— Tradition.

Keywords : Cognition, Data, Information, Knowledge, Memory, Tradition, Wisdom.

INTRODUCTION

Data, facts, information, intelligence, knowledge and wisdom being airy intangibles are elusive entities to define. Comparison is like entering a blind alley. All these consist of the same cerebral stuff that is ideas. Even though the terms are used interchangeably by many (Ranganthan, 1967, Sec.CR21), the entities are different indeed in structure, properties and functions.

INFORMATION: DEFINITION

Matter and energy are all-pervasive and constitute the only two elemental components of this universe (Satija,2013). This is what Chapter 13, Verse 26 of the Bhagavadgita means. Lord Krishna says: Arjuna, whatsoever being, the moving or unmoving, is born, know it as emanated through the union of Matter and the Spirit. Next to these two all-pervading entities is the information which is composed of these two. Information is considered as next stage of transmutation of energy (Curras,2014,p.94). Information is a pattern of matter and energy (Singhal and Roger, 1989) which acts on the mind. It is the live wire of any system be it mechanical, biological, celestial or social. Without a constant feed of information any system will die. Despite being all pervasive it is not easy to define information. When used loosely it means everything and nothing. Consensual definition of information is a problematic area of philosophy and science. Its definitional essence is elusive due to its all pervasiveness, broadness and vagueness (Weller, 2008, p.14). It is the much overused but least understood term of our times (Bawden, 2001).

INFORMATION: PROPERTIES

Information and communication are almost synonymous in action. What is communicated is information; information when not communicated is not information *per se*. Information needs a physical medium for its communication and storage. It can be communicated at the speed of light. Its storage density varies with media and increases tremendously with technology (Liu, 2004). In the electronic form it has acquired a few more wonderful properties. Information is a resource as well as a commodity in the information society. It is a resource of all resources and is the ultimate substitute. It is the ultimate input in decision making in every organisation from government to business, and from family affairs to research (Al-Hawamedeh, Suliman, 2003). Above all it is an essential input for policy making, for governance, and gaining and maintaining power. It is the most superior source of power – other being violence and money (Toffler, 1990). No surprise then that a government in any country is the single largest collector, producer, disseminator and controller of information.

KNOWLEDGE DEFINITION AND PROPERTIES

"Knowledge is ambiguous, unspecific and dynamic phenomena intrinsically related to meaning, understanding....."(Alvesson and Karreman, 2001). It is a fluid mix of information, experience, skills to provide context or to interpret the new experience and information (Davenport and Prusak, 1998). As to its properties, Ranganthan (1967,Sec.PM7) writes, it is always fragmentary and remains ever in a dynamic continuum. That is a clue to its limitless growth. Broadly speaking knowledge is of two kinds: Tacit and expressed

TACIT KNOWLEDGE IS KNOWLEDGE PER SE

Peter Drucker, as quoted by T. Kontzer (2001), aptly says that "Knowledge is between two ears, and *only between two ears*"(Emphasis mine). Tacit knowledge is mostly formed with public knowledge by a ruminating mind. In fact knowledge by definition is implicit or latent. Explicit knowledge is simply information. Knowledge when externalised becomes information—like ice becomes water when taken out of refrigeration machine. T. D. Wilson (2002) asserts that M. Polanyi who coined the term tacit knowledge had a misunderstanding that tacit knowledge can be managed. All knowledge is rooted in acts of comprehension, which is a sort of inside neuro-physiological process, and is still subject to much speculation in bio and medical sciences. Mental processes of knowledge formation and memorising are not yet fully understood by any one. Being intangible it can only be demonstrated through our acts, both physical and mental. In facts all acts are initiated and controlled by our mental models created by knowledge. Knowledge shapes the views, values and further thinking of any person. Knowledge though personal is not private. Private knowledge is not knowledge *per se.* It could be something spurious claimed by quacks or claimants of esotericism or *tantric* powers. Intuition and mysticism are two dubious sources of private knowledge in fact these two concepts cannot be objectively defined .

KNOWLEDGE IS HUMAN DEPENDENT

There cannot be any knowledge without a knower. The knowledge is knower dependent. Man is the creator and consumer of information and knowledge. Knowledge is created to solve problems facing mankind. Its creation and use leads to new systems, products, action, services, values, and ultimately the outlook to life and living. Every byte of new knowledge is an addition to human power. The society which is the conservator of knowledge has devised contraptions like books and established libraries, archives and other memory institutions to conserve and preserve it. Education and socialisation perpetuate information and knowledge, and the society consequently.

KNOWLEDGE IS OUR WORLD

It has aptly been said that the distinction between knowledge and action is flimsy and slippery. "Action is knowledge and knowledge is action" (Baumard, 2010, p.3189). There is nothing so practical as a good theory, paradoxically but aptly said Kurt Lewin (1890-1947). Knowledge leads to form our viewpoints, beliefs and values which ultimately define our worldview. Knowledge in the sense of justified belief guides our behaviour in totality. Jesse Shera (1970,p.93) quotes Kenneth Boulding to say "Knowledge is the individual's or society's image of the world". This knowledge is indeed individual, so is the world that it is perceived with it. Even when transferred from one individual to another, as in the Knowledge Management process, the transferred knowledge is not the same. It is not the mirror image of the source. That is why every human being is somewhat unique in totality of his/her worldview. It is automatically edited and coloured by the beliefs and values of the receiving individual. In non-literate cultures the knowledge is transmitted orally from generation to generation which is a very slow process and is mostly done in the form of imitating others (following their footsteps), and giving precepts by elders to the chosen ones over a period of time. Orally transmitted knowledge inevitably gets transmuted to some degree, if not corrupted. But ultimately it takes the form of proverbs and folklore for living by norms in a society. It metamorphoses into tradition – a force which helps a society into continuity.

Characteristics of Knowledge : There is a unity in entire knowledge, says Jesse. H. Shera (1903-1981). All assorted chunks of knowledge can be unified into a single big whole—like pieces into a big jigsaw. There is a continuity in the evolution of knowledge without any hiatus. In other words, the entire body of knowledge is a dynamic system having its definite characteristics:

- Knowledge is not independent; it is dependent upon the knower, the human being for its creation and use. It resides in the mind and is thus subjective; though personal it cannot be private.
- It is created from information by the treasured experiences of an individual person.
- Knowledge is the rock bed of innovations and

research. Thus is an intellectual property which empowers the holder.

- It is conserved by human society. Thus it is social in character. It is not natural; even the knowledge of the natural world is not natural. Knowledge of Natural sciences is not natural—it is social and human creation
- Technology, social advancements and knowledge creation are mutually dependent.
- Society is the ultimate adjudicator inheritor and proprietor of knowledge.
- Knowledge is never complete. It is eternally fragmentary. It is dynamic, multidimensional and evolving. It grows and changes with time and society. Growth is both quantitative and qualitative (Satija, Madalli and Dutta, 2014). If a teacher is teaching the same thing for a long time then either the teacher is not updated or the subject is dead and irrelevant.
- Though its quality improves constantly, quantity of knowledge cannot be measured by any true means. In the present days its growth is in geometric progression.
- It tends to be infinite. Only constraints are the limited span of individual's life, and the unknown but certainly limited capacity of the human brain. Thus it is inexhaustible, i.e. never ending.
- Knowledge growth is pyramidal in structure, especially in so called natural science where knowledge is cumulative. In such areas growth is both qualitative and quantitative. Qualitative growth implies constant obsolescence of some knowledge. Rate of obsolesce depends on the speed of research. More the speed of research ,more the obsolescence of knowledge
- Knowledge is a catalyst and enzyme for future

knowledge—knowledge does not grow in vacuum, intuition notwithstanding..

- It is non-exclusive. Magically, you can give it to someone and you still retain it. More it is used , communicated or distributed more it grows.
- It is never decimated, though some of it may become obsolete with discovery of new facts.
- Though knower dependent, it finds its own discoverer sooner or later. It is absurd to say that there would have been no knowledge of gravity if Newton were not born, or not sitting under the (apocryphal?) apple tree on that particular day and time. It is not to say knowledge discovery follows fatalism theory. It only means natural phenomena exists though may not be known at a given time. Nature is incremental in revealing its secrets! There seem secrets within secrets like layers of an onion. Earth did orbit the sun before Galileo discovered and told us so.

KNOWLEDGE FORMATION

Knowledge originates from the environment, both physical and social. Human being is the knower and knowledge creator. The Nature, including society, is the ultimate source of knowledge. Our sense organs are window to perceive raw knowledge in the form of data and signals, and work as tools to transmit signals as neuro-electrical pulses to our brain. (Satija, 2004)

Information is generated when the knower interacts consciously or unconsciously, voluntarily or involuntarily with the environment through the sense organs. Information thus received, gained or intercepted is first given a context by in brain by the previously conserved knowledge for its use and validation. Thus information is a construct which does not pre-exist.(Curras,2014)Thus knowledge is socio-psycho-biological in nature. Society is the producer and consumer of knowledge, while knowledge is the prime mover of society. Thus society and knowledge are locked in mutual influence on one another. Technology, social advancements and knowledge discovery are mutually dependent. It is not possible to isolate the one way influence. Knowledge grows as society grows; whereas society changes, develops and progresses in multidimensional ways as new knowledge is generated. It is the society which decides which kind of knowledge it is going to have, in which direction and with what speed, and in how much quantity of particular knowledge we need, and also determines the value scales for the different disciplines of knowledge. Particular lines of knowledge are encouraged or impeded by the political, economic and social interests in particular times and places (Daniels, 1966, p.40). Therefore thrust areas in research to develop new knowledge will depend on the values and priorities of society —which change from time to time. During the world wars whole of the western industry was intensively engaged in manufacturing defense material. After the war that very industry turned its machines to produce consumer goods and household amenities. That in turn produced a consumer and affluent society. Need for new knowledge is unending for a civilised and progressive society. Conservative and orthodox societies and persons do not live to their full potential.

KNOWLEDGE IS CAPRICIOUS: WE DO NOT KNOW WHAT WE KNOW

Knowledge resides in the human memory—animals, even primates have no knowledge though they have memory. Animals lack the power to synthesise. They lack creative powers. Humans and animals have inborn genetic information in the form of DNA molecules which guides internal (bio) actions while external (daily living) actions are guided by externally acquired information (Satija, 2004). Though every bit of knowledge is memory, but every act of memorising does not create knowledge.

Latter requires understanding first and then retention. Knowledge on the other hand is difficult to manage except by the individual knower, that too somewhat imperfectly. How our brain organises and retrieves knowledge is not fully known. This process is ambiguous and amorphous. Paradoxically, it is a common saying that we do not know what we know. Memory mechanism is another hazy area of psycho-biology research. But for certain, there can be no education, no progress of thought and no knowledge without memory. Memory being elusive, capricious and undependable may not recall what may be required at a time. Yet "something may only emerge when we need to employ knowledge to accomplish something" asserts Wilson (2002). On the other hand it is a common experience that we are not able to express exactly what we feel and want to convey. It is mostly due to the fact that knowledge in the form of feelings, emotions and experiences is tacit and very personal while the tool to convey it, which is our language, is common, public and socially shared. Growth of language is slow but that of knowledge is very fast. Thus there is always a gap between thought and its expression.

Between the idea
And the reality
Between the motion

And the act
Falls the Shadow

wrote T S Eliot (1888-1965) in his Hollow Men (1925). All these make creativity a least understood process.

THE CHAOS AND CONFUSION

In the literature of business management studies, or as used by laypersons, the terms knowledge and information are freely used interchangeably. This makes the term knowledge management somewhat fuzzy, broad and vague. Authors have used it over a wide and diverse range of topics from knowledge engineering, artificial intelligence, networked information, knowledge portals, data mining, tapping indigenous knowledge, knowledge sharing to team learning, and acquiring knowledge for decision support systems. But for a researcher it is imperative to define their usage so that the field of philosophy of information science has a clear and unambiguous vocabulary. This intentional confusion leads to selling ducks for swans and information management easily passes as Knowledge Management. Business and Industry always use high sounding terms as public relations strategy or to aggrandize their products, services and brand name. Professor T D Wilson (2002) castigates that it is knowingly never distinguished between the two by the knowledge management consultancies. No wonder that some library science schools prefer to designate themselves as Schools for KM.

CLEARING THE CONFUSION

It is ironical to do knowledge management without knowing the nature of knowledge unambiguously or defining it formally. Being a theoretician and LIS professional it quite clear to T D Wilson when he writes "Knowledge is what we know: knowledge involves the mental processes of comprehension, understanding and learning that go on in the mind and only in the mind, however much they involve interaction with the world outside the mind, and interaction with others." The consequence of this analysis is that everything outside the mind that can be manipulated in any way can be defined as 'data', if it consists of simple facts, or as 'information', if the data are embedded in a context of relevance to the recipient. Data and information can be easily managed as we do in databases, libraries, archives or information centres or even at a personal level. But knowledge management is an uncertain process.

COMMON GROUNDS

Data, information and knowledge all comprise of ideas and cannot be neatly separated, as said earlier. However, the following evolutionary chain depicts the increasing maturity, enhanced organisational value and more enduring life span of each link. Though hierarchical in evolution the chain is circular in nature and steps are reversible. They are mutually dependent and are derivable from one another:

Signals → Data → Information → Knowledge → Wisdom → Tradition → Social norms → Laws

Knowledge : Information : A Broad Comparison

Knowledge	*Information*
• What I know	• What I am able to convey
• Historical and Durable. Sum total of ideas conserved after filtering through value system	• Current and Transient Message
• Information + Knowledge + Experience	• Data and or Facts
• General and personal	• Specific but common
• Theoretical	• Practical
• Cultural	• Applied/Business like
• Power	• May be Instant power, Subversive
• Descriptive	• Instructive
• Context free, or provides the context	• Context dependent
• Vertical/Hierarchical/ cumulative/Pyramidal	• Horizontal/Additive
• Rule like	• Case like
• Prescriptive	• Diagnostic
• Expresses relations between variables	• Expresses values
• People oriented	• Document oriented
• One could keep it oneself, and ceases with the death of its holder.	• Leaks and ultimately howsoever sealed and secretively it may be kept.
• Resides in the mind	• Resides externally in documents and needs physical media for storage

• Accretes in the mind with experience over time	• Cultivated with R & D
• Ii is expertise	• It is a commodity
• Cannot be replicated absolutely, replication is hyper slow.	• Can be easily, instantly, and perfectly replicated
• When communicated becomes information	• Is the essence of communication and can lead to knowledge formation
• Is harvested through knowledge management (KM)	• Communicated through numerous media and channels.
• Our knowledge makes what we are	• Information is the product of our consciousness
• Is central to mind, thought and feelings	• Communication is vital to life socially and biologically.

COMPREHENSION AND UNDERSTANDING

It is clear that information answers questions of what, which, who, how and many other types. Knowledge answers why and how-to questions. Use of information presupposes a perspective and purpose of the enquirer. In medical parlance, diagnosis is information while prescription is knowledge. Understanding is the completion of data processing by the mind. Understanding is comprehension and results in learning. It is explanatory; it answers all questions. Understanding presupposes prior knowledge of the field of input information, and its current relevance. Intelligence is the capacity and efficiency of the brain to apply knowledge and information quickly. It is also defined as capacity to make sense of things and situations and to learn (Baumard, 2010, p.3185).

MUTUAL DEPENDENCE

Proper use of Information needs knowledge and experience, in other words, familiarity with the idiom of the field, to give it a context for its effective use. Without knowledge information cannot be used to make decisions or solve problems. Man's judgment, which essentially applies knowledge, cannot be better than the information on which it is based. Knowledge in itself is not only comparatively perennial and of universal value, but also helps to evaluate and enjoy other human values such as goodness and beauty (Radovan, 2013). It increases operative power of the mind. It needs an astronomer to fully appreciate the grandeur and beauty of a starry night. To a botanist a flower looks more a thing of beauty and a peace of wonder than to a layperson. Data tables require background knowledge to be interpreted meaningfully. Information is current, but knowledge is historical. To quote Daniels (1966, p.39) "Since everything that exists in the past is history and since everything we know is already in the past, all knowledge in a way is historical." Without current and authentic input of information mere knowledge may lead to disastrous decisions. To use knowledge without current information is autocratic. That is why it is said history teaches no lesson. Using information without knowledge makes a decision maker priggish. Old generation has knowledge but may lack in current information. It invariably leads to clash of opinions between the old generation and the new one – latter has lot of information but less knowledge.

KNOWLEDGE AND WISDOM ARE EXCLUSIVELY HUMAN PRESERVES

A computer can store tremendous amount of data and information, but is not knowledgeable. Not even the entire knowledge in the world can help us to discern the difference and discriminate between the good and the evil. Here only wisdom can help which is the socially correct application of knowledge. Wisdom, being social and cultural, is the preserve of human beings only — animals and computers have no knowledge and wisdom. What is technically possible with information and knowledge may not be socially correct and morally acceptable — human cloning is still banned. Information is received and or transmitted by every system while knowledge is applied only by human beings. Wisdom is mostly advisory and guides in making ethical and socially acceptable judgments by the experienced few.

WISDOM

Wisdom is the socially correct application of knowledge. Spiritualist and moralist (very wise people) advise the scientists (knowledgeable people) not to play God. Nobody has made a better distinction in the Info-Knowledge-Wisdom trio than the Nobel laureate poet T S Eliot:

- Where is the wisdom we have lost in knowledge?
- Where is the knowledge we have lost in information?
- Knowledge is proud that it knows all, but it is wisdom that makes us bit humble by informing us of our infinite ignorance.

REFERENCES

- Al-Hawamedeh, Suliman (2003). *Knowledge management: cultivating knowledge professionals.* Oxford, U K : Chandos,222p.
- Alvesson, M. and Karreman, D.(2001) Odd couple: Making sense of curious concept of knowledge management. *Jl. of management studies* 38(7) : 995-1018
- Baumard, P. (2010). Knowledge: Tacit and explicit In: *Encyclopedia of Library & Information Science,* 3rd ed./ ed. by Marcia Bates and Mary N. Maack. New York: Taylor & Francis, pp. 3184-3194.
- Bawden, D. (2001). The shifting terminologies of information. *Aslib proceedings* 53(3) : 93-98.
- Davenport, T.H. and Prusak, Lawrence (1998). *Working knowledge: How organisations manage what they know.* Cambridge, MA: Harvard Business School, p.5.
- Curras, Emilia(2014) The nature of information and its influence in human cultures. *Knowledge organisation* 41(1): 92-96
- Daniels, R.V. (1966) *Studying history: how and why,* 2nd ed.

Englewood Cliffs, N.J.: Prentice-Hall.

- Kontzer, T. (2001) Management legend: trust never goes out of style. *Call Center Magazine*. available at <http://callcentermagazine.com/article/IWK20010604S0011> [Site visited December, 2014]
- Liu, Ziming (2004) The evolution of documents and its impacts. *Journal of Documentation*. 60(3): 279-288.
- Radovan, Mario (2013) ICT and Human Progress. *The Information Society*. 29: 297-306.
- Ranganathan, S.R. (1967). *Prolegomena to library classifcation*,3rd ed. Bombay: Asia.
- Satija, M.P. (2004): Man as an Information Processor. *SRELS Jl. of Info. Mgmt.* 18(3) July: 9-18.
- Satija, M P (2013) Information: Nature, importance and functions. *Annals of lib.sc inf. studies* 60(2): 128-133
- Satija, M P, Madalli, D and Dutta, B (2014) Modes of growth of subjects. *Knowledge Organisation*, 41(3): 195-204.
- Shera, J.H. (1962) *Sociological foundations of librarianship*. Bombay: Asia.
- Singhal, Arvind and Rogers, E.M (1989). *India's information revolution*. New Delhi: Sage, p.244
- Toffler, Alvin (1990) *Power shift: Knowledge, Wealth, and Power at the Edge of the 21st century*. New York: Bantam Books, 585 p.
- Weller, Toni (2008). *Information history: an introduction*. Oxford, U K : Chandos
- Wilson, T.D. (2002, Oct.) "The nonsense of 'knowledge management'" *Information research* 8(1) Available at <http://informationr.net/ir/8-1/paper144.html> (Accessed Dec 2014)

Further Readings

- Barber, Bernard and Hirsch Walter, (1962) *Sociology of Science* Illinois; the Free Press.
- Bhattacharyya, G. (1997). Information: Its definition for its service professionals. *Lib. sc. with a slant to documentations*. 34 (2): 69-83.
- Boulding, Kenneth (1956). *Image*. Ann Arbor: University of Michigan Press.

- Cassier, Ernest (1950). *Problems of Knowledge.* New Haven: Yale University Press.
- Chide, V.G. (1956). *Society and Knowledge.* New York: Harper.
- Curras, Emalia (2014) The nature of information and its influence in human cultures. *Knowledge Organisation* 41(1):92-96.
- Godert, Winfried (1996) Information as a cognitive construction: A communication theoretic model..... *Knowledge org.23(4): 206-212.*
- Grene, Marjori (1956) *Knower and the Known.* London: Faber.
- Kent, A (1979) Information as power. *Aslib Proceedings* 31(1): 16-21.
- Kochen, Manfred, Ed. (1967) *Growth of Knowledge.* New York: Wiley.
- Koestler, Arthur (1966) *Act of Creation.* New York: MacMillan.
- Liebenau, Jonathan and Backhouse, James (1990). *Understanding information: An introduction.* London: MacMillian, ix, 125p.
- Lovejoy, Arthur O (1956) *Great Chain of Being.*
- Machlup, Fritz (1962) *Production and Distribution of Knowledge in the United States.* Princeton, N.J.: Princeton University Press.
- Maritain, Jacques (1959) *Degrees of Knowledge.* Chicago: Scribner.
- McGarry Kevin (1993). The *changing context of* information: *an introductory analysis*, 2nd ed. London: LA Publishing, p.11-16
- Meadows, Jack (2001). *Understanding information.* Munchen: KG Saur, p.112.
- Nitecki, Andre (1995). Information: its sources and role in nation building. *Int. Inf. Commu. and Edu.* 14(2):160-172.
- Nonaka, I and Takeuchi, H. (1995). *The knowledge creating company.* Oxford: OUP, p.60.
- Polanyi, M (1958) *Personal Knowledge.* Chicago: University of Chicago Press.
- Polanyi, M (1966) The logic of tacit inference. *Philosophy: The Jl. of Royal Institute of Philosophy* 41(155):1-18

- Popper, Karl R. (1963) *Conjectures and Refutations: The growth of scientific knowledge.* London: Routledge and Kegan Paul.
- Scarrott, Gordon G.(1994) Some functions and properties of information. *Jl of Info. Sc.*20(2):88-98
- Wood Ledger (1940) *Analysis of Knowledge:* London Allen and Unwin.

14

Contributors, Users and Benefits of Institutional Repositories of Delhi and NCR : A Case Study

Nazrul Islam Azmi

College Librarian, Ramanujan College,

(Delhi University) Kalkaji, New Delhi -110019

ABSTRACT

Institutional repositories are online databases of scholarly materials such as articles, reports, datasets to enable and foster sharing, discovery, and archiving of scholarly resources produced at a given institution. IRs provides immense benefits to their parent institutions. In the present study, it is found that IRs of Delhi and National Capitol Region of India are benefiting their institutions, increases the prestige of their institutions, provides opportunity for better service and helps in preserving intellectual output of their institutions.

INTRODUCTION

Institutional Repositories (IRs) play a fundamental role in centralizing, preserving, and making accessible institution's intellectual capital and, at the same time, they form part of a global system of distributed and interoperable repositories that provide the foundation for a new disaggregated model of scholarly publishing ((Johnson, 2002). Institutional repositories (IRs) are digital collections that capture and preserve the intellectual output of a single or multi-university community. Their aim is to provide access to scholarly material without the economic barriers that currently exist in scholarly publishing. If successful, IRs hold the promise of being very advantageous to researchers everywhere, especially those in the developing world (Shearer, Kathleen, 2003).

LITERATURE REVIEW

The emergence of IRs provided the way for hassle less access to research output throughout the world. Institutional repositories are online databases of scholarly materials such as articles, reports, datasets to enable and foster sharing, discovery, and archiving of scholarly resources produced at a given institution. As a scholarly communication mode, institutional repositories represent a particularly interesting case to examine as they incorporate both normative and ideological agendas and illustrate how technical products embody social goals and power relationships. Although the analysis is based on institutional repositories, the theoretical approach is relevant to various information and communication technology development efforts aiming to introduce new tools in support of scholarly communication (Rieger, Oya Y, 2008). Repositories are services that can help an institution manage content and preserve the intellectual work of the campus. Repositories are the means by which an institution can distribute information in an open access mode that makes that research accessible throughout the world. The repository then is a tool to manage the image of the university by showcasing the research work of the faculty and students. For libraries, repositories were seen as a way to combat increasing serial prices and collect and manage the work of their own constituencies (Furlough, 2009). In spite of all the obstacles to successful implementation, including associated negative perceptions, IRs have been increasingly recognised as a vital tool for scholarly communication and an important source of institutional visibility and a viable source of institutional knowledge management (Jain, Priti , 2011). IRs at small institutions exist in significant numbers, and they exhibit some unique patterns, particularly in the benefits (Nykanen, Melissa , 2011). Open accesses IR are the most viable means of ensuring the global visibility and impact of Nigerian scholarship (Ezema, Ifeanyi J. , 2011). IRs are defined most often as a set of services that are offered by an institution for the management and dissemination of digital materials created by the members of the institution or scholarly community (Giesecke, Joan , 2011). Institutions need to give due attention to policies related to two aspects of publication, especially those related to quality and copyright issues and to the academic value of research output. Other policy-related topics include citation in other publication with due acknowledgement, inclusion in indexing systems for retrieval, interoperability with other IRs, and Permanent storage (Paul, Shampa, 2012). Little is known about the costs academic libraries incur to implement and manage institutional repositories and the value these institutional repositories offer to their communities (Burns, C. Sean, Amy Lana, and John Budd, 2013). Institutional repositories represent extremely innovative technology, but repository managers still struggle to bring together a critical mass of content and to demonstrate their overall impact on research (Cassella, Maria , 2013).

OBJECTIVES

A study of seventeen IRs in Delhi & the National Capital Region of India was conducted to: identify benefits of IRs. The IR mangers of the selected following seventeen institutions are the population of the study.

1. Indian Agricultural Research Institute (IARI), New Delhi

2. National Physical Laboratory (NPL), New Delhi
3. National Informatics Centre (NIC), New Delhi
4. National Institute of Immunology (NII), New Delhi
5. Management Development Institute (MDI), Gurgaon (NCR)
6. Indian National Science Academy (INSA), New Delhi
7. VV Giri National Labour Institute, Noida (NCR)
8. NIPFP (National Institute of Public Finance And Policy), New Delhi
9. Delhi Technological University (DTU)
10. Delhi University (DU)
11. J.P. Institute of Information Technology (JIIT), NOIDA (NCR)
12. Indira Gandhi National Centre For Arts (IGNCA), New Delhi
13. Jawaharlal Nehru University (JNU), New Delhi
14. Guru Gobind Singh Indraprastha University (GGSIPU)
15. NOPR, NISCAIR
16. NSDL, NISCAIR
17. Indian Institute Of Technology, New Delhi

Various questions were identified on the basis of knowledge gained through reading of available literature as well as various studies conducted in the area of benefits of institutional repositories. The IR managers were asked about the wide range of questions related to benefits of institutional repository.

DATA ANALYSIS & FINDINGS

The survey data was grouped according to different questions representing the various benefits of the institutional repository. The data collected in the survey was analyzed using frequency distribution that included mainly percentages which were reported in form of tables and graphical charts.The collected data has been tabulated and analyzed with findings that are shown in

Table. Institutional Repositories have immense benefit to the institutions in which they are created. IR Benefits of IRs of Delhi and NCR in the opinion of IR managers are grouped as for data collection.

- Enhances your institution's prestige / visibility
- Better service to contributors and institution's learning community
- New Services to learning communities beyond your institution
- Maintaining control over your institution's intellectual property.
- Capturing and maintaining the intellectual assets of your institution.
- To encourage Open Access.
- Contributing to reform of entire enterprise of scholarly communication and publishing.
- A reduction in amount of time between discovery and dissemination of research findings to scholarly communities.
- An increase in citation counts to your institution's intellectual output.
- Exposing your institution's intellectual output to researchers around the world who would not otherwise have access to it through traditional channels.
- An increase in the accessibility to knowledge assets such as numeric, video, audio and multimedia datasets.
- Providing maximum access to the results of publicly funded research
- A solution to the problem of preserving your institution's intellectual output.
- An increase in library's role as a viable partner in the research enterprise
- Reducing user's dependence on your library's print collection.
- Others

Table : Benefits of IRS of Delhi and NCR (Y= Available)

DTU	*DU*	*GGSIPU*	*IARI*	*IGNCA*	*IITD*	*INSA*	*JIIT*	*JNU*	*MDI*	*NIC*	*NII*	*NIPFP*	*NOPR*	*NPL*	*NSDL*	*VVILI*	*TOTAL IR (%)*
BENIFITS																	
Control over intellectual property.	Y					Y	Y						Y				4 (27%)
Reducing dependence on print collection.			Y		Y		Y						Y				4 (27%)
Accessibility to knowledge assets	Y				Y	Y					Y						1 (7%)
Discovery and dissemination of research	Y			Y	Y			Y					Y				5 (33%)
Maximum access to research.		Y															1 (7%)
Scholarly communication and publishing	Y		Y	Y	Y			Y					Y				6 (40%)
New Services to learning		Y	Y	Y	Y	Y		Y							Y	Y	8 (53%)
Increase in your citation counts			Y		Y		Y	Y		Y	Y		Y			Y	8 (53%)
Maintaining the intellectual assets	Y		Y		Y	Y	Y	Y			Y		Y			Y	9 (60%)

Encourage Open Access	Y	Y		Y	Y	Y	Y	Y				Y		Y	Y	10 (67%)
Exposing intellectual output	Y	Y	Y	Y	Y		Y			Y	Y		Y		Y	10 (67%)
Increase in library's role			Y	Y	Y	Y	Y	Y		Y	Y		Y		Y	10 (67%)
Preserving intellectual output	Y	Y		Y	Y		Y	Y		Y	Y	Y	Y			10 (67%)
Institution's prestige	Y	Y	Y	Y	Y	Y	Y	Y	Y		Y	Y	Y	Y	Y	14 (93%)
Better service	Y	Y	Y	Y	Y	Y	Y	Y	Y		Y	Y	Y		Y	13 (87%)

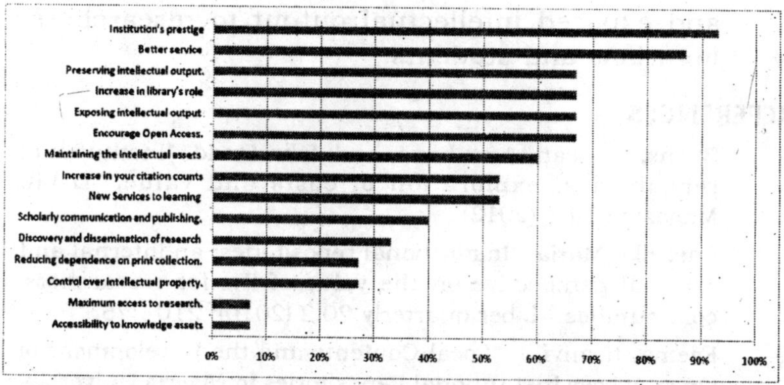

Fig. IR Benifits – Opinion of IR Managers of Delhi and NCR

The Benefits study of IR by the managers of IRs of Delhi and NCR are tabulated in Table and shown in Figure.

The benefit study of IRs of Delhi and NCR finds that more than 75% IR managers of the opinion that institution's prestige and better services are prime benefits that IR provides. More than 50% managers think that IR provides opportunity to preserve the contents and increases the library's role as information disseminator.

More than 30% managers are of the opinion that IR is helpful in exposing the intellectual ouput of the institution and encourages the open access, maintains intellectual assets as well as increases citation counts of the authors.

CONCLUSION

It is found that IRs in Delhi and NCR;

- Benefited their parent institutions.
- Increases the prestige of institution.
- Provides opportunity for better service.
- Helps in preserving intellectual output of the institution.
- Increases library's role; encourages Open Access,

and exposed intellectual output to researchers, librarians and students.

REFERENCES

- Burns, C. Sean, Amy Lana, and John Budd. "Institutional repositories: exploration of costs and value." D-Lib Magazine 19.1 (2013):
- Cassella, Maria. "Institutional repositories: an internal and external perspective on the value of IRs for researchers' communities." Liber quarterly 20.2 (2010): 210-225.
- Ezema, Ifeanyi J. "Local Contents and the Development of Open Access Institutional Repositories in Nigeria University Libraries." Library Hi Tech 31.2 (2013): 323-40.
- Furlough, M. 2009. What we talk about when we talk about repositories. Reference and User Services Quarterly, 49(1): 18–23.
- Giesecke, Joan. "Institutional repositories: Keys to success." Journal of Library Administration 51.5-6 (2011): 529-542
- Jain, Priti. "New trends and future applications/directions of institutional repositories in academic institutions." Library Review 60.2 (2011): 125-141
- Nykanen, Melissa. "Institutional repositories at small institutions in America: Some current trends." Journal of Electronic Resources Librarianship 23.1 (2011): 1-19.
- Paul, Shampa. "Institutional Repositories: Benefits and Incentives." The International Information & Library Review 44.4 (2012): 194-201.
- Rieger, Oya Y. "Opening Up Institutional Repositories: Social Construction of Innovation in Scholarly Communication." JEP: The Journal of Electronic Publishing 11.3 (2008).
- Shearer, Kathleen. "Institutional repositories: towards the identification of critical success factors." Canadian journal of information and library science 27.3 (2003): 89-108.
- Westell, Mary. "Institutional repositories: proposed indicators of success."Library hi tech 24.2 (2006): 211-226.

15

Knowledge Audit of Social Mobile Applications

P.B.Jain
Ex. Librarian, VMV Commerce,
JMT Arts & JJP Science College, Nagpur

ABSTRACT

This Paper outline the integration of social web applications and mobiles technologies in sharing. The inherent characteristics of mobile technology sharing in organizations with ease. Mobile Phones become the new hub of social computing. The World is also witness the huge increase in the use of social web technology. Many innovative startups have pioneered mobiles social networking in the last few years. This paper is an attempt to explore the possibility of knowledge sharing through social web and mobile technology.

INTRODUCTION

Cell phone is the constant companion for today's world. New generation is not ready to fritter away time to log onto the pc to communicate with the world. The network friendly phone is the gadget they rely upon to share knowledge instantaneously. Handset manufacturers are trying to integrate online Social experiences in their devices. With the current software that is available interactions within mobile social networks are not limited interactions within mobile social networks are not limited to exchanging simple text messages bur are constantly evolving towards the sophisticated interactions. Of social web. The convergence between mobiles and social computing is gaining attraction of large stakeholders.

ROLE OF MOBILES COMPUTING IN KNOWLEDGE SHARING

Knowledge sharing culture is the attitude to work together more effectively, to collaborated and to share-ultimately to make knowledge more productive. One of the serious problems in knowledge sharing is unwillingness of to give away their hard knowledge because knowledge is perceived as power. One of the challenges of Knowledge sharing is the attitude of people that, why should they give up their hard-won knowledge, when it is one of their key sources of personal advantage.

The emergence of social web technologies restructured the old paradigm "Knowledge is power" in to sharing knowledge is power" sharing tacit knowledge in an interactive sea of knowledge helps to find solution, which is people's wisdom. In the age of social web and mobiles technology, there are no boundaries for knowledge. The competencies of social web provide collaboration opportunities of relationships. In the co context of social web the avenue to share information is tremendous. The New generation of smart phones add fuel to the sharing culture by providing ambiance to share reflection of thoughts that promises quickly connecting with problems and solutions.

PERSONAL COMPUTER TO MOBILE TECHNOLOGY

Most of the digital revolution has taken place on the Pc. So far, with the emergence of email, instant messaging, wikis, blogs, photo and video-sharing sites, and social

Networks : Now the ubiquitous nature of mobiles phones has changed the away we live and communicate.

Letters, diaries, address books, and memories have gone digital, while communication with friends, relatives, and colleagues never involved such a mix of technology. However, now mobile phones are not only communication tools. Mobile phones have unique characteristics that will enhance and modify existing PC based Social experiences. Mobile devices are the preferred tools by social network site(SNS) users over PCs now. The next big trend for social networking is the rise of the Mobiles social network. The Young generation's cell phone addiction has gives way too proliferation of these mobiles networks. The number of users on these services is growing fast. The information sharing potential of social mobiles web applications. Somehow simplifies knowledge building and there by liberates the knowledge seekers. The interactive and collaborative nature of social web helps to create new knowledge, the people's wisdom.

SOCIAL WEB AND MOBILE TECHNOLOGY AS A FACILITATOR FOR KNOWLEDGE SHARING

The social web or web 2.0 the, user-centered web based tool revolutionized the way the interned was tool revolutionized the way the internet was conceptualized and used. These tools include: blogs, wikis, Image-sharing, video-sharing, etc.

Social web is the need of the hour for universal sharing of Knowledge. The main difference from the earlier context of internet is its multidimensional platform where the users meet new social content and quality. The mobile friendly social web tools, to create this environment include blogs, image and video sharing, social network instant messaging micro blogging etc. The combination of two exciting technologies the social web and the mobiles technology build a novel social interaction among stakeholders. The social mobile content sharing and distribution is familiar Phenomenon now because more than a billion and a half people around the world are now consumers of mobile phone services. This gives the opportunity to explore the possibility of making the mobiles phone an important tool in information sharing. Mobiles social web technologies offer exciting new opportunities for information exchange by making their own contributions, sharing ideas, exploring, investigating, experimenting and discussing.

SOCIAL MOBILE TECHNOLOGY IN LEARNING

The rapid global diffusion of social mobile technology creates exciting new avenues for academic environment. Over the past two decades there appear to be a paradigmatic shift from teacher- centered learning to student centered learning. Combined with social web technologies, mobile devices are today seen as offering new learning potential. There is considerable interest from educators and technical developers in exploiting the matchless capabilities and characteristics of mobiles technologies to enable new and appealing forms of learning.

The recent trends in education shows that mobile social web technology devise have been accepted as a promising learning tool due to the portability and connectivity. Mobiles learning implies several possibilities for learning. Instead of sitting in front of a computer screen, learners can move around and feel the physical environment for gaining tangible knowledge. Mobile social web technology is bridging the gap between formal and informal and informal learning.

WIKIS AND BLOGS AS KNOWLEDGE SHARING TOOLS

Wiki is a website where any user has the right to crate, edit and delete content. System abuses are avoided by a revision control system that tracks changes, enabling reverting to previous versions. The potential of wikis as open knowledge exchange systems is illustrated by the rise of Wikipedia which started in January 2001 as a multilingual project to create a complete and accurate open content encyclopedia. Wiki allows the creation and linking of multiple web pages. It is often used for collaborative projects and in knowledge management systems.

The usefulness of the wiki relies on its ability to aggregate knowledge from the users themselves. Wikis can be used to develop and update information that is useful for many users who, individually, only hold parts of it. Wikis are often used to create collaborative websites and to power community websites. Generally speaking, wikis can be divided into three basic categories: public, protected, and private. Wiki is a system that allows once or more people to build up a corpus of knowledge in a set of interlinked web pages, using a process of creating and editing pages.

Wikis provide a dashboard of relevant content with the user able to search for specific information relevant to the project they are working on. The wiki approach enables to mange remote tears globally and improve the efficiency of information management by centralizing content.

Wikis are ideal for organizations with remote tears operating globally where information regency is essential and decisions need to be made quickly, leveraging the existing knowledge base. They also help reduce duplication of effort where one team may not be aware of available knowledge from another terms

A blog is a website, usually maintained by an individual, with regular entries of commentary. It consist primarily of periodic articles, usually in reverse chronological order. Early blogs were simply manually updated components of common websites. However, the evolution of tools to facilitate the production and maintenance of web articles posted in a chronological dashion made the publishing process accessible to a much large, less technical population. Ultimately, this resulted in the distinct class of online publishing. Millions of blogs around the world share information about diverse subjects. Blog can be powerful communications vehicle which can keep followers informed whit organization's latest news. If an organization has a limited budget this can be a great promotional tool ? A group of bloggers using their individual blogs can build up a corpus of interrelated knowledge via posts and comments.

Blogging is a great way for senior management and departments to share latest news and developments with other teams. During the heat of battle, organizations often lose touch of internal communication and feeling isolated from the business is a key driver in demotivation , By providing regular blog, information can quickly be disseminated; keeping people in touch with the business and sharing good news to maintain moral. Blogging can go beyond core knowledge management and help drive change.

MOBILE SOCIAL NETWORKING

A current trend for internet social networking websites such as is to turn mobile. Mobiles phones is increasingly becoming the glue that holds the social graph together, offering creative tools and immediacy, presence, location and context when interacting with the real world. The Social networking tools enable sharing ideas across geographical boundaries. There are an ever increasing number of tools that are described by the term social web tools. Digital workspaces use the advantages of social networks in order to create a virtual common area to work together. All of these have one thing in common the use of technology to try and build group effort and share tacit knowledge.

CONCLUSION

Application of Social web technologies through

mobiles gadgets have profound implications in the corporate world in formal, informal, work based knowledge gathering and sharing. The positive aspect to be noted over in this juncture is the attitude to share and exchange the hard earned knowledge. Mobile technologies has emerged as a viable information sharing environment, particularly with the advent of the iphone and other sophisticated devices with the ability to collaborate easy to use social web tools for creating and sharing collaborative content. The interactive web added fuel to the sharing culture and enriched the collaborative knowledge building process. Social web technology through mobile is driving the re-engineering of information exchange in a fast pace.

REFERENCES

- Alavi. M. & Leidner D.E. "Review: knowledge management and knowledge management systems: conceptual foundation and research issues" MIS Quarterly 2001. Vol, 25, No 1 PP 107-136
- C. O' Dell and C. Jackson Grayson, "If only we knew what we know: identification and transfer of internal best practice" California management Review, Vol. 40 No. 3., PP.154-174, 1998.
- Hansen, M. T., and Tierney. T., " What's Your Strategy for Managing Knowledge?" Harvard Business Review, (77.2) 1999 PP. 106-116
- Nonaka, I. "A Dynamic Theory of Organizational knowledge Creation," Organization Science 5:1 1994 14-37
- R.M Gran, " Toward a knowledge-based theory of the fire' Strategic Management Journal, Vol. 17, pp. 109-122, 1996
- V.P. Ardichvilli and T. Wentling, "Motivation and barriers to participation in virtual knowledge sharing teams" journal of knowledge management, 2003 vol 7 no 1 pp. 64-7-
- W.R.King, P.V. Marks, and S. McCoy, "The most important issues in knowledge management" communications of the ACM vol. 45, No. 9, PP.93-97 2002.

16

Online Reference Management Software : An Overview

Shalini Lihitkar

Sr. Asst. Professor, Department of Library and Information Science Rashtrasant Tukadoji Maharaj Nagpur University, Nagpur.

Archana More

Research Scholar, Department of Library and Information Science, Rashtrasant Tukadoji Maharaj NagpurUniversity, Nagpur.

ABSTRACT

This article derives from an overview of online reference management software's that are most useful for researchers to manage their bibliographic citations. There are a number of different types of software packages that you can use to manage the bibliographic details of information and the documents you find during your degree or research. This article gives twenty nine number of reference management software's, name of software developer and latest version of software. When we begin our research for any piece of work, it is important that we record the details of the entire information that find by us, Reference Management Software's helps us to manage the bibliographic citations and also fulfills 4th law of S.R.Rangnathan "Save time of users" but everyone are not aware about the Reference Management Software's.

Keywords : References, Reference management, Reference Management Tools.

1. INTRODUCTION

Today references also called citations are not just books and journal articles. They can include websites, e-publications, videos and more. Using a reference management tool we will make it a lot easier for us to not only collect and store our items, but also to organize and tag them (add Meta data). A good tool will also provide us with the correct format for citing references in our papers. It's important to remember that we don't have to wed yourself to any one tool. They each have pros and cons, and we can use different ones for different things. We can sometimes also exchange references between tools pretty easily.

Reference management software, citation management software or personal bibliographic management software is software for scholars and authors to use for recording and utilizing bibliographic citations (references). Once a citation has been recorded, it can be used time and again in generating bibliographies, such as lists of references in scholarly books, articles and essays. The development of reference management packages has been driven by the rapid expansion of scientific literature. Reference Management Software's are used by researchers in academics to manage the bibliographic citations they encounter in their research. With these tools, scholars keep track of the scientific literature they read, and to facilitate the editing of the scientific papers they write. Several different software packages exist, with sometimes different features and purposes. Most of this process can be automated by using a reference management tool. It can help us keep track of our citations and it makes sure that all our citations are put in us bibliography as well. All this according to the standard we choose. A reference management tool will saves our time, since we do not have to spend time on manually typing all the references for our bibliography and we do not have to struggle with commas, parentheses etc.[2]

2. DEFINITIONS

2.1. References

"Reference is a relation between objects in which one object designates, or acts as a means by which to connect to or link to, another object. The first object in this relation is said to refer to the second object. The second object – the one to which the first object refers – is called the referent of the first object".[3]

The term reference is used in many spheres of human knowledge, adopting shades of meaning particular to the contexts in which it is used.

2.2. Reference Management

Reference management is how you organize the references you use in your written papers e.g. It is to cite correctly in your papers, assignments etc. You can do all this manually or by using a reference management tool, For example it is a good idea to create your bibliography and to cite your references according to a specific method/ standard. Your bibliography and your citations will look the same and it will make it easier for anyone to find the references, the literature you cite in your paper, assignment etc.[4]

2.3. Reference Management Software

According to Telstar's definition, a Reference Management Software "enables an author to build a library of references by entering the details of each reference in a structured format." They usually support mechanisms for organizing sets of references by tagging or use of 'folders', and will generate references, citations or bibliographies in a range of referencing styles. Most packages support ways of importing records.[3]

"From library catalogues and other bibliographic data sources in order to facilitate the generation of references. In addition, many packages offer plug-ins or add-ons for Word processing software which enable authors to insert references from their 'library' directly into a document as they are writing" (JISC & Open University, 2010).

3. NEED OF THE STUDY

When we begin our research for any piece of work, it is important that we record the details of the entire information that find by us, Reference Management Software's helps us to manage the bibliographic citations and also fulfills 4th law of S.R.Rangnathan "Save time of users" but everyone are not aware about the Reference Management Software's. Less Awareness about Reference Management Software's by the research scholars

4. Objectives

- To explore and identify of the Reference Management Software's tools for the researchers to utilize and manage bibliographic citations/ references.
- To find out evaluation criteria of Reference Management Software's for search out which Reference Management Software's are user friendly so that many research students may rely on that software's.

5. DEVELOPMENTS IN RMS

Reference Management is perceived to be tedious and time consuming by many researchers, especially when it is done manually. In the past, references used to be written on index cards and stored in boxes. Reference management software allows for the digitization of a personal collection of relevant scholarly publications. The earliest programs to manage the basic task of storing references and adding them to manuscripts have been around for over 25 years (including Endnote and BibTeX/ LaTeX-based programs still popular today), but each individual entry had to be typed in by hand. In the last 15 years we have seen a number of significant developments that have made reference management much easier for the researcher:

- Retrieval of reference information from online bibliographic databases
- DOIs and other persistent identifiers for bibliographic information
- Automated management of PDF files
- Open Access for easier access to full-text content
- Web-based reference management easier for collaboration and use across multiple devices.

We will need these details to provide accurate references, and to enable to locate the information again at a later date, should it be necessary to do so. Reference management (or bibliographic) software allows to manage all the references we need for papers, reports, essays or thesis by enabling to keep them in our own personal database or library. It allows us to:

- Search easily for a particular reference to which need to refer back
- Print or save a list of references
- Insert citations into our document and automatically produce a bibliography in whatever style we require.

These software packages normally consist of a database in which full bibliographic references can be entered, plus a system for generating selective lists of articles in the different formats required by publishers and scholarly journals. Modern reference management packages can usually be integrated with word processors so that a reference list in the appropriate format is produced automatically as an article is written, reducing the risk that a cited source is not included in the reference list. They will also have a facility for importing the details of publications from bibliographic databases.

6. DEFERENCE BETWEEN REFERENCE MANAGEMENT SOFTWARE'S AND BIBLIOGRAPHIC DATABASE

Reference management software does not do the same job as a bibliographic database, which tries to list all articles published in a particular discipline or group of disciplines; examples are those provided by Ovid Technologies (e.g. Medline), the Institute for Scientific Information (e.g. Web of Knowledge) or mono disciplinary learned societies e.g. the American Psychological Association (PsycINFO). These databases are large and have to be housed on major server installations. Reference management software collects a much smaller database, of the publications that have been used or are likely to be used by a particular author or group, and such a database can easily be housed on an individual's personal computers. Reference Management allows us to:

- Create, store and organize a personalized database of our references
- Enter references manually or import from library catalogues or databases
- Generate bibliographies/reference lists, choosing from 100s of bibliographic styles.

Although we may or may not consider them 'social media', reference management tools are one of the single most useful digital tools for a researcher today. Gone are the days of painstakingly changing each of our in text citations to a footnote or changing each full stop in a reference to a comma because a journal required it. Online reference management tools allow us to:

- Import references from different sources (e.g. websites, library catalogues, bibliographic databases)
- Manage and/or edit the references once they're in the system, and add manually any references that we cannot find online

- Export references into a document, either as a single bibliography, or individually (often called 'cite while we write') which generates a list of references.
- Format the bibliography according the referencing style of our choice, and re-format if/when necessary.[20]

7. TWO MAIN FUNCTIONS OF REFERENCE MANAGEMENT SOFTWARE'S

a. Building a database of citations, useful for keeping track of and organize the documents useful for one's research

b. Formatting bibliographies and citations when writing paper.

7.1. Other functions of Reference Management Software's:

- Import citations from bibliographic databases and websites
- Gather metadata from PDF files
- Allow organization of citations within the RM database
- Allow annotation of citations
- Allow sharing of the RM database or portions thereof with colleagues
- Allow data interchange with other RM products through standard metadata formats (e.g., RIS, BibTeX)
- Produce formatted citations in a variety of styles
- Work with word processing software to facilitate in-text citation.[7]

Table 1. Reference Management Software's

Sr. No	Name of Software	Name of Software Developer	Latest Version of Software
1	Aigaion	Aigaion developers	2012-01-18 (2.2)
2	Bebop	ALaRI Institute	2009-11-10 (1.1)
3	BibBase	Christian Fritz	2013-07 (v3)
4	BibDesk	BibDesk developers	2013-05-04 (1.6.1)
5	Biblioscape	CG Information	2012-04 01 (9.0.8.8)
6	Bibsonomy	University of Kassel	2013-11-18 (2.0.37)
7	Bibus	Bibus developers	2009–10 (1.5.0)
8	Bookends	Sonny Software	2012-1-14 (11.2.4)
9	Citavi	Swiss Academic Software	2014-02-17 (4.3)
10	CiteULke	Oversity Limited	
11	Colwiz	colwiz Ltd	2013
12	Decear	Otto-von-Guericke University Magdeburg and University Cali	2013-10-17 (1.0)
13	EndNote	Thomson Reuters	2013 (X7)
14	JabRef	JabRef developers	2013-01-12 (2.9.2)
15	KBibTeX	KBibTeX developers	2013-12-29 (0.5)
16	Mendeley	Elsevier	2012-11-15 (1.5.2)
17	Papers	Springer	2012-11-22 (2.4.0)
18	Pybliographer	pybliographer developers	2010-10-14 (1.2.14)
19	Qiqqa	Qiqqa	2012-07 (v44)
20	refbase	refbase developers	2014-02-28 (0.9.6)
21	RefDB	refdb developers	2007-11-05 (0.9.9)
22	Reference Manager	Thomson Reuters	2010 (12.0.3)
23	Referencer	Referencer developers	2013-05-07 (1.2.0)
24	RefWork	RefWorks / ProQuest	2013
25	SciRef	Scientific Programs	2012-11-20 (1.0)
26	Sente	Third Street Software, Inc.	2013 (6.6)
27	Wikindx	Mark Grimshaw	2013-05-13 (4.2.1)
28	WizFolio	WizPatent	2011-01 (Avatara)
29	Zotero	Roy Rosenzweig Center for History and New Media at GMU	2013.12.18 (4.0.17.1)

8. EVALUATION CRITERIA'S OF REFERENCE MANAGEMENT SOFTWARE'S ARE

1. Operating system support
2. Export file formats
3. Citation styles
4. Reference list file formats
5. Word processor integration
6. Database connectivity
7. Password "protection" and network versions
8. Ease of Use / Usability
9. Help
10. Compatibility
11. Costs
12. What features should my reference management software offer?
13. Where do I usually work?
14. Mobile Access
15. Personal Storage Space
16. Syncing Documents
17. Syncing Citations
18. Import file formats
    - Primary Importing Process ,
    - Secondary Importing Processes,
    - Importing from catalogues and discovery layers
19. Access and Subscriptions
20. Platform

9. SOME VERY USEFUL REFERENCE MANAGEMENT SOFTWARE'S

9.1. Zotero

Zotero is the free open source reference management software to manage citations such as PDF files. The website for free download zotero sofeware *https://www.zotero.org/* Zotero 4.0, released in April 2013, includes new features such as automatic journal abbreviations, colored tags, on-demand file syncing.

Fig.1. Home page of zotero

9.2. Endnote

Endnote is the commercial reference management software produced by Thomson Reuters. They give 30 days' free trial for the users. The official website of endnote is *http://myendnoteweb.com.* In the Endnote software having several ways to add a reference to a library: manually, exporting, importing, copying from another EndNote library, connecting from EndNote.

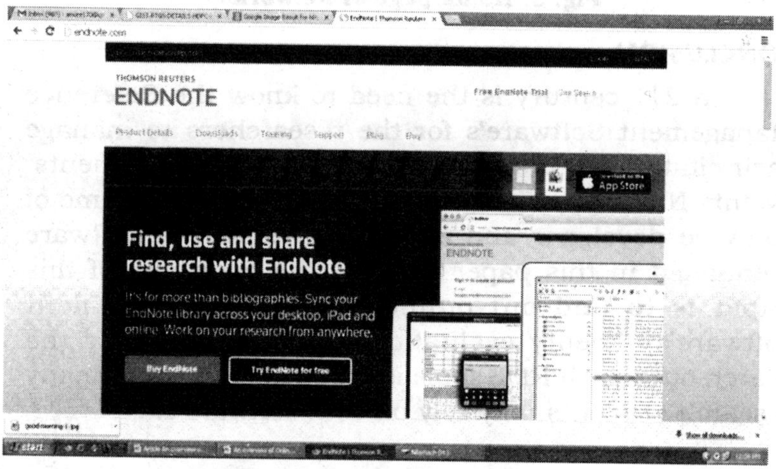

Fig. 2. Endnote homepage

9.3. Refworks

RefWorks is an online research management, writing and collaboration tool is designed to help researchers easily gather, manage, store and share all types of information, as well as generate citations and bibliographies. The official website is *https://www.refworks.com/*.

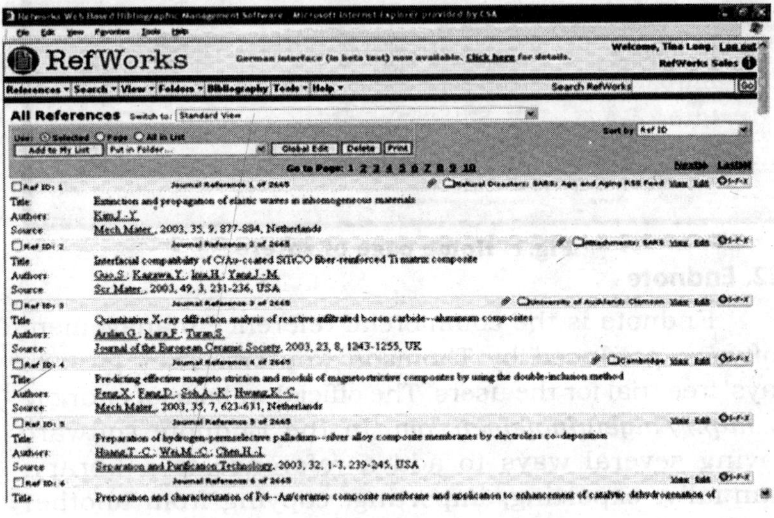

Fig. 3. Home page of Refworks

CONCLUSION

In 21st century is the need to know the Reference Management Software's for the researchers to manage their citations or bibliographic details of the documents. Twenty Nine reference management software's, Name of software developer and also latest version of software mentioned in this paper because the main aim of this paper is to find out online reference management software's. Twenty evaluation criteria's found for the search out which RMS tools is most useful so that many research students may rely on that software's.

REFERENCES

- Francese, E., "Mendeley, dal social bookmarking al reference management: unostrumentoinnovativo per la gestioned ellecitazionibibliografiche", *BibliotecheOggi*,
- http://en.wikipedia.org/wiki/Reference_management_software(23/04/2014)
- wikipedia.org/wiki/Reference(26/6/2014)
- http://www.jisc.ac.uk/whatwedo/programmes/institutional innovation/telstar.aspx)(25/4/2014).
- http://www.open.ac.uk/library/training-and-events/introduction-to-reference-management-tools(05/05/2014)
- http://guides.library.harvard.edu/reftools(14/05/2014)
- http://blogs.bodleian.ox.ac.uk/23things/thing-(19/04/2014)

17

Emerging Open Access Environment Vis-à-vis Copyright

Amitabha Chatterjee
Retired Professor & Head
Department of Library & Information Science
Jadavpur University, Kolkata 700032

INTRODUCTION

Scientific and technical journals play a vital role in scholarly communication. Scholars need these journals for acquiring new knowledge and information and applying those in their work. They also need these journals for publishing the results of their own research work. Scholarly communication has been facing some sort of a crisis in the recent decades as the scholars faced problems in accessing required resources. The problems that are responsible for creation of such a situation are:

- Continued increase in world production of published materials;
- Rise in costs of research publications at unprecedented rate;
- Non-rise in the acquisition budget of libraries commensurate with rate of inflation, particularly

for journals;

- Acquisition of academic/society publications by more expensive commercial publishers; and
- Bundling of scholarly journals by aggregators.

The idea of Open Access (OA) was mooted as a mechanism to overcome this crisis. Gradually the concept has become very popular and has taken the shape of a movement.

1. OPEN ACCESS (OA)

It is gathered that one of Mahatma Gandhi's earliest publications, *Hind Swaraj,* which was published in Gujarati in 1909 and is recognized as the intellectual blueprint of India's freedom movement, was translated into English the next year, with a copyright legend that read "No Rights Reserved", indicating that no copyright was claimed for this work and hence could be used by anybody freely. However, the modern Open Access movement (as a social movement) emerged in 1960s, but became much more prominent in 1990s with the advent of the digital age. With the spread of the Internet and the ability to copy and distribute electronic data at no cost, the arguments for open access gained new importance. Today a huge quantity of peer reviewed scientific periodical literature is published on open access platform.

1.1. Benefits of OA

Placing research results on open access has three main benefits [4]:

Accelerated discovery : With open access, researchers can read and build on the findings of others without restriction.

Public enrichment : Much scientific and medical research is paid for with public funds. Open Access allows taxpayers to see the results of their investment.

Improved education : Open Access means that

teachers and their students have access to the latest research findings throughout the world.

2. COPYRIGHT

Copyright is the exclusive right of the author to derive economic benefits from his own writing or artistic performance or creative work. Copyright regulation basically protects the interest of creator from commercial exploitation by others. As nobody can own or perpetuate vested interest in knowledge, even the copyright regime throws every creative writing open after certain prescribed period [13]. Besides, copyright law in almost every country has a 'fair use' provision to allow use of limited portion of the copyrighted work for the purpose of education and research free of cost. But often none of these provisions is sufficient for the aforesaid purpose. For use of any work beyond the limit and before the expiry of copyright period, one has to pay required fee, which is collected by the copyright holder or a copyright clearance organization created for the purpose.

3. OA VIS-À-VIS COPYRIGHT

"The Open Access (OA) movement has greatly stimulated the debate on copyright in the scholarly communication system. Stakeholders in the system – publishers, on the one hand, and academic institutes and libraries, on the other – participate in this debate, often taking up diametrically opposing positions. However, the voice of probably the most important stakeholders – the academic authors themselves – is relatively little heard in the debate" [9]. Nevertheless, a survey of such authors has shown that 71 per cent of them prefer to keep the copyright with themselves and thus are not in favour of providing open access to their works [9]. But does it really make any difference if an article is made available to all and should we be concerned? The answer is both yes and no. "To all intents and purposes, the fact that journal articles are being made available to all through open access, or to subscribers under the subscription model, should not really affect things. Issues can arise, however, as there is a common misperception that open access means anyone can do anything with an article – in fact, the rights in the content must still be understood and upheld" [16]. There is no doubt that copyright helps to prevent plagiarism, multiple submission and fraud in journal articles. Copyright does not actually detect these ills; it acts as a protective measure to uphold the quality of journals. Some believe that in an open access world these factors become blurred and journal articles are easier to copy and incorporate into other works. For example, open access journals offer additional usage rights which may introduce some confusion in relation to copyright. These factors may threaten the rights of the author and make it difficult for publishers to enforce copyright policy [16].

4. RIGHTS AT STAKE

In fact, copyright is a bundle of rights, automatically assigned to the author(s) by legislation in most countries. It is a combination of moral rights (most important of which is the right as an author to be properly and fully acknowledged) and exploitation rights. Moral rights are well acknowledged in the scholarly communication system and are upheld even when the copyright is transferred from an author to a publisher. Therefore, moral rights are not at stake in the copyright debate; rather, the debate centres on exploitation rights. Exploitation rights raise potential issues of ownership in the use and reuse of scholarly material. In the traditional publishing model of scientific periodicals, exploitation rights are generally transferred in full to the publisher. This means that reuse of the original article, fully or partly, in any form, by someone other than the publisher, is limited or dependent on the publisher's permission. This limits access to the material for author and reader alike.

Exploitation rights are in themselves a bundle of rights, and they reflect the needs and requirements of the parties involved, as well as the mode of exploitation. In scholarly communication the exploitation options for research articles are in fact rather limited: the two main options are reuse for educational purposes and for commercial purposes. The right to reuse is the key to the definition of Open Access: effectively, Open Access means free online access and permission to use the information for any responsible purpose [9].

5. COPYRIGHT MODELS

The Open Access environment has created a number of entirely new copyright models, which stand in contrast to the traditional academic journals in which the copyright has to be transferred from the author(s) to the journal publisher. The following emerging copyright models in OA journals have been identified [9]:

- A model in which the author keeps the copyright;
- Two models in which the author shares the copyright (with Creative Commons licences);
- A model in which the author transfers only the exploitation rights to the journal publisher.

Thus there are three choices with regard to copyright: retain it, share it or transfer it.

5.1. Retention of Copyright

Many scientific periodicals, such as *Electronic Journal of Comparative Law* (*EJCL*), allow the authors to keep copyrights of their research papers. Thus even if a paper is in open access, the copyright remains with the author, subject to fair use provision available in the copyright law of the land. Thus reuse of the paper requires written permission of the author concerned. But the author often has to give undertaking to the publisher of the paper that he will mention the name of the journal where it was first published whenever he republishes it on any other platform.

5.2. Licensed Sharing of Copyright

When any author wants to give people right to share his or her work, the author does so under a public copyright licence which enables free distribution of his copyrighted work. The licence gives the user right to share, use and build upon the author's work. The most used such licences are Creative Commons (CC) licences. These licenses were first introduced by Creative Commons, a US based non-profit organization [9]. The main features of CC licences are [10]:

- They provide flexible range of protections and freedoms for authors, artists, educators;
- They provide free easy-to-use legal tools;
- Tools give everyone from individual creator to large companies and institutions a simple standardized way to grant copyright permissions to his/ her/ their creative work;
- They enable people to easily change their copyright terms from "all rights reserved" to "some rights reserved".

Thus through CC licences creators can protect their works while still encouraging certain defined uses [9]. Many Open Access publishers now use Creative Commons licences "to ensure that the contents of the articles published in their journals are reusable in the widest sense: that is, they can be reproduced, abstracted, 'mashed up' with other material to produce new information, mined by text-mining and data-mining tools and so on" [11]. According to State of the Commons report, as of 2014 the number of CC licensed works is 882 million and in 2015, CC licensed works were viewed online 136 billion times [14]. A large number of UNESCO resources are now CC licensed.

5.2.1. Conditions of Licences

The CC licenses grant the "baseline rights", such as the right to distribute the copyrighted work worldwide for non-commercial purposes, and without modification [2]. The details of each of these licenses depend on the version, and comprise a selection out of four conditions [6]:

Attribution (BY) : Licencees may copy, distribute, display and perform the work and make derivative works based on it only if they give the author or licensor the credits in the manner specified by these.

Share-alike (SA) : Licencees may distribute derivative works only under a licence identical to the licence that governs the original work.

Non-commercial (NC) : Licencees may copy, distribute, display, and perform the work and make derivative works based on it only for *non-commercial* purposes.

No Derivative Works (ND) : Licencees may copy, distribute, display and perform only verbatim copies of the work, not *derivative works* based on it.

Six types of licences, with one or more of the above conditions, are issued by Creative Commons. It may be pointed out that Creative Commons licences are not alternatives to copyright. They work alongside copyright and enable one to modify one's copyright terms to best suit one's needs. The activities of CC are carried out by volunteers in different parts of the world through more than 100 affiliates working in over 70 jurisdictions [12].

5.3. Exploitation Rights

In this model, an author retains copyright of his or her work, but transfers all commercial exploitation rights to the publisher. *British Medical Journal* and *Nucleic Acid Review*, which are now available on open access platform, have adopted this model, in which the author is at liberty to use his work in any manner he or she likes without seeking permission from the publisher, as long as that does not affect commercial rights. The model provides for potential revenue for the authors as he or she becomes entitled for royalties if the publisher enters into a commercial republishing or redistribution deal on the basis of the author's paper [9].

6. INDIAN SCENARIO

Open access movement has spread in India too. The position of India in the list of open access journals is fifth, well ahead of the countries like Netherlands, China, Germany and Australia; while the position of the country with regard to open access institutional repositories is eighth as per registry of such repositories (ROAR) [3]. Many scientists are now also taking part in open access movement by publishing in open access journals and depositing their intellectual output in such repositories.

6.1. CC India

The India Chapter of CC was first launched in 2007 by IIT Bombay as a part of its technology fest, but it could not function effectively possibly because not enough groups were involved in promoting it as also because the CC movement, which had started to gain momentum in many parts of the world, did not have much effect in this country for some reason. Around six years later there was a lot more discussions and debate around the copyright regime as well as its implications, following which Creative Commons India was re-launched in New Delhi on November 12, 2013. Three organizations are mainly involved in this chapter, viz., Wikimedia India (with focus on outreach), Centre for Internet Society (with legal focus) and Acharya Narendra Dev College (with focus on open education resource). Creative Commons India aims at raising awareness and getting people to use CC licences and build a community of CC licence users in the country through its website, local activities and a mailing list. It also aims at developing a relationship with government and private sector that can benefit open access movement [7]. One of the most prominent CC licence holder in India is Pratham Books, a non-profit children's publishing house, which aims at achieving twin objectives of creating more reading content for children and at the same time ensuring maximum penetration [1, 12].

6.2. Legal Provisions

Another encouraging development is that the Copyright (Amendment) Act 2012 has incorporated some changes which have put Creative Commons and other open licensing models in a better footing in the country. While earlier one could only relinquish parts of one's copyright by submitting a form to the Registrar of Copyrights, now a simple public notice will be sufficient for doing so. Additionally, Section-30 of the Act, which earlier required licences to be in writing and signed, now only requires it to be in writing [5].

6. CONCLUSION

Today, Open Access is being increasingly recognized as a right rather than an abstract ideal. The case for rapid implementation of Open Access continues to grow. Open Access benefits research and researchers; increases the return to taxpayers on their investment in research; and amplifies the social value of research, funding agencies, and research institutions [17]. In this situation copyright should not serve as a barrier and at the same time the authors should not be robbed of their legitimate rights. Contrary to common misconception, there is no conflict between open access and copyright. The legal basis of open access is consent of the copyright holder (for newer literature) or the expiration of copyright (for older literature) [15]. Nevertheless, in view of the advantages of open access, the current copyright laws may be suitably amended, wherever necessary, to provide impetus to open access movement, without of course much affecting the rights of the authors. Meanwhile, libraries and academic institutes can stimulate the use of Creative Commons licences or similar licences that allow sharing of copyright, thus enabling the reuse of scholarly information for educational and scholarly purposes. Libraries and academic institutions can also influence publishers to adjust their present copyright policies with regard to the reuse of published articles [9].

REFERENCES

1. BAROOAH (Swaraj Paul). Creative Commons India relaunched. *http://spicyip.com/2013/11/creative-commons-india-relaunched.html*
2. Baseline Rights. *https://wiki.creativecommons.org/wiki/Baseline_Rights*
3. BIST (Rajendra Singh) and others. Indian open access: setting OA models for Asia. Open source movement – Asian perspective: Papers presented at the National Seminar of IASLIC, 22nd, Roorkee, 2016. p. 173-180.
4. The case for open access. *https://www.plos.org/open-access/*
5. CENTRE FOR INTERNET SOCIETY (India). Analysis of the Copyright (Amendment) Bill. 2012. *http://cis-india.org/a2k/blogs/analysis-copyright-amendment-bill-2012*
6. Creative Commons - Frequently asked questions: What are Creative Commons licences? *https://creativecommons.org/faq/#What_are_Creative_Commons_licenses.3F*
7. Creative Commons India. *https://wiki.creativecommons.org/wiki/India*
8. Creative Commons (CC) licence. *https://en.wikipedia.org/wiki/Creative_Commons_ license*
9. HOORN (Easther) and VAN DER GRAAF (Mautits). Copyright issues in open access research journals. *D-Lib Magazine.* 12, 2; 2006. (Available at *http://www.dlib.org/dlib/february06/vandergraaf/02vandergraaf.html*)
10. MUNSHI (Usha Mujoo). From All Right Reserved to Some Rights Reserved. A discourse on reprographic rights and copyrights: contemporary facets: Papers presented at the National Conference on Reprographic Rights and Copyright

Act – challenges and management, Kolkata, March 2013. p. 46-50.

11. OASIS Open Access Scholarly Information Sourcebook. Practical steps for implementing open access. *http://www.openoasis.org/index.php%3Foption%3Dcom_content%26view%3Darticle %26id%3D550%26Itemid%3D372*

12. RAMACHANDRAN (T). Creative Commons: thinking beyond copyright. *http://www.thehindu.com/opinion/blogs/blog-datadelve/article5380106.ece*

13. SRIDHAR (Madabhushi). The right to know and the copyright. *DESIDOC Bulletin of Information Technology*. 27, 4; 2007; 15-27.

14. State of the Commons. *https://stateof.creativecommons.org/report/*

15. SUBER (Peter). Open access overview. *http://legacy.earlham.edu/~peters/fos/overview. htm*

16. TEMPEST (David). Copyright in an open access world. *http://editorsupdate.elsevier.com/ issue-35-march-2012/copyright-in-an-open-access-world/*

17. We are open. *http://www.openoasis.org/*

18

Publishing anOpen Access Journal : An Introduction

M.R.Murali Prasad
Librarian, Centre for Economic and Social Studies,
Begumpet, Hyderabad – 500016

ABSTRACT

This paper describes the benefits and methods to host an electronic journal, which is suitable area in this electronic publication era. The author also discussed about some Publishing Management Software and required Software and Hardware to initiate an open access journal.

Keywords : open access, open access journal, online journals, electronic publishing, open journal system

OPEN ACCESS JOURNAL

An open access journal is a publication of content of a full text journal through online and making it free to the world to read. It should give access to their entire content, both archives and in the future, including present. Open access publishing is growing in the past five years very speedy, due to the hiking prices of print journal subscriptions in the world scenario.

ADVANTAGES OF OPEN ACCESS JOURNAL

The following are the some of the advantages with

open access journal:

1. Instant publication of the journal content
2. Reducing the time consumption and cost in publication and communication
3. Increase the visibility of the journal content and also authors and their affiliated institutions
4. Lot of scope to read, use and cite the journal content
5. Overall, the open access journal make significant contribution to the research

Some Challenges

There are some challenges (I do not want to say disadvantages) to bring out an open access journal, like:

1. Funding is a major problem in the absence of subscription prices
2. Resistance from the some Scholar communities
3. Content review problems with peer group
4. Abstracting and indexing problem with major influential publishing groups

HOW TO PUBLISH AN OPEN ACCESS JOURNAL

The following are the major and important requirements to publish an online journal:

1. Hardware
2. Software
3. ISSN
4. DOI

Hardware

1. A computer with good configuration
2. High quality, secure and reliable web server (either own or commercial)
3. Internet connection with high band width because net speed is an important issue.

Software

1. Publishing Management Software
2. PHP 4.2.x or later (including PHP 5.x) with MySQL or PostgreSQL support
3. A database server: MySQL 3.23 or later OR PostgreSQL 7.1 or later
4. A UNIX-like OS recommended (such as Linux, FreeBSD,Solaris, Mac OS X, etc
5. Desktop publishing software like office, pdf, etc.

After getting the above mentioned hardware and software, the journal authorities should know the procedure of installation of software and Publishing Managing Software. Also, they have to set the different configuration parameters on Publishing Management Software according to their procedures.The reference manuals and documentation are available to configure the open Journal system with the respective software websites.

ISSN (International Standard Serial Number)

An ISSN is an eight digit, standardized international code for any serial publication including electronic format. Every publication has its own unique ISSN, and it can be obtained it from local ISSN Centre with free of cost. ISSN International Centre is a network with its Headquarters at Paris. National Science Library (NSL) of NISCAIR is the national centre in India of ISSN international centre for assigning ISSN to serials published in India. (*http://nsl.niscair.res.in/issn.jsp*). For example, ISSN for an online journal called "International Journal of Library and Information Studies" is 2231-4911.

DIGITAL OBJECT IDENTIFIER (DOI)

In addition to an ISSN, the journal authority has to consider obtaining a Digital Object Identifier for online journal. It is different from ISSN, which gives unique identity to each of journal article as well as journal. It is also important to note that it will not change and it's a persistent URL to the journal content, if the server has changed, renamed journal, or even moved from one Publishing Management Software to another. But, it requires payment of an annual basis.

Publishing Management Software

There is lots of Publishing Management Software available online. The few are here:

1. Ambra (*www.ambraproject.org*) : Ambra is an Open Source Publishing system. It is developed by the Public Library of Science (PLOS) and is licensed under the Apace License, ver 2.0. This publishing platform is using by PLOS journals and Elementa journal.

2. Annotum (*www.annotum.org*) : Annotum, is an open-source, open-process, open-access platform for online publications based on WordPress. This is product of Solvitor LLC and supported by Crowd Favorite. This platform is using by National Library of Medicine/PubMed Journal Articles.

3. E-Journal (*www.drupal.org/project/ejournal*): E-journal is a powerful publishing system module of Drupal, which is content management software. It's distributed under the terms of GNU General Public License. This module prepared on the basis of Open Journal System.

4. Open Journal System (*https://pk.sfu.ca/ojs*) : This Open Journal System is a Journal management and publishing system of Public Knowledge Project (PKP), which is multi-university initiative open source software for scholarly publishing. It has lot of features like OJS is installed locally and locally controlled; Editors configure requirements, sections, review process, etc.; Online submission and management of all content; Subscription module with delayed open access options; Comprehensive indexing of content part of global system; Reading Tools for content, based on field and editors' choice; Email notification and commenting ability for readers; Complete context-sensitive online Help support. The majority of online journals are using OJS system in the world at present.

PROMOTING AND SUSTAIN A JOURNAL

It is very easy to start a new journal, but it is very difficulty gets wide readers and sustainability of the journal. To sustain a journal, it requires regular contributors, reviewers, readers, and more people discover the journal. The below strategies may helpful to sustain a new journal.

1. Marketing : Marketing is first and traditional method to get readers. For this, the journal authorities has to use social networking sites, professional networks, blogs, discussion lists, other forums to announce/call for papers for new issue/publication, using e-mail signature of editors, reviewers, etc; publicize in local libraries, contact libraries, etc. Another place to promote online journal on scholarly search engines like Google Scholar, Scirus, etc.

2. Indexing : The journal will reach more researchers by participating in an indexing service, such as Directory of Open Access Journals (DOAJ), AGRIS, PubMed, Scopus, Web of Science, etc.

3. Creating impact on journal : There are multiple ways to create impact of an online journal when compared to print journal. The following are few ways:

a. Requesting the users to registers with journal site.

b. Analysis of weblogs like visitors, geographical details, downloads, etc.

c. Increase the citation through promoting with librarians, authors, editors, etc.

4. Storing, technical support and security : The journal authorities ensure that they should host their journal on a secure and reliable web server to provide content to the readers 24x7x365. It may be their own server or third party or may free hosting providers who supporting Open Access movement. (For e.g. African Journals Online, *www.ajol.info* is providing free hosting to over 320 peer reviewed journal).

Other major issues toconcentrate while hosting an online journal are the continuous technical support, server speed, storage space and importantly backup of the journal content.

SCREEN SHOTS OF FEW OPEN JOURNAL SYSTEMS

1. Annals of Library and Information Studies

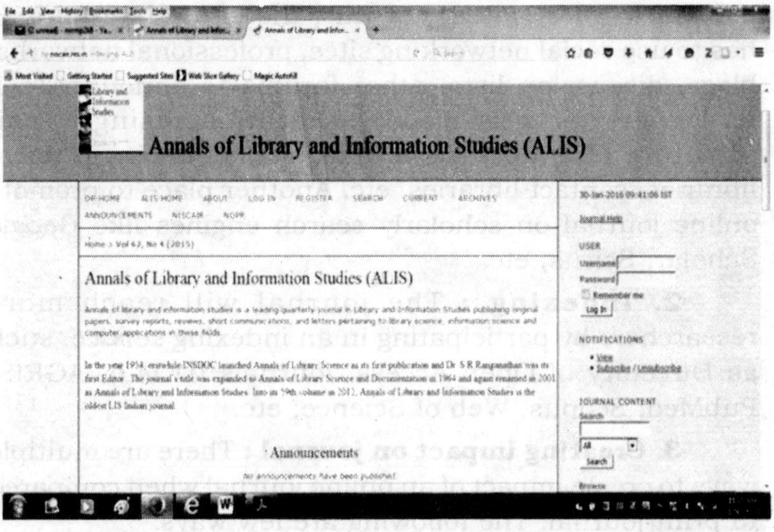

2. Asia Pacific journal of Library and Information Science

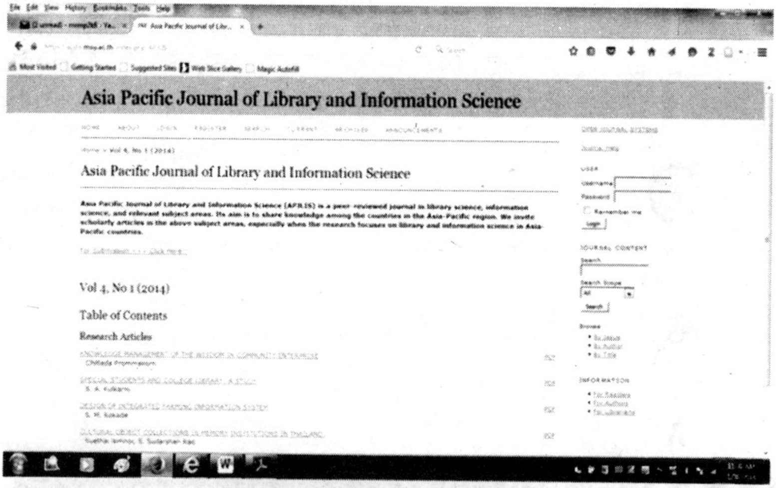

3. African Journals online

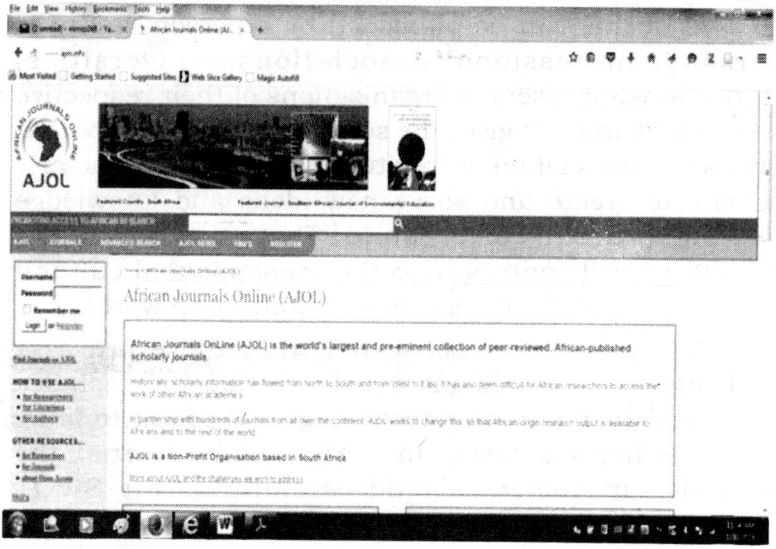

4. List of some journals hosted through OJS (website by INFLIBNET : *www.inflibnet.ac.in/ojs/*)

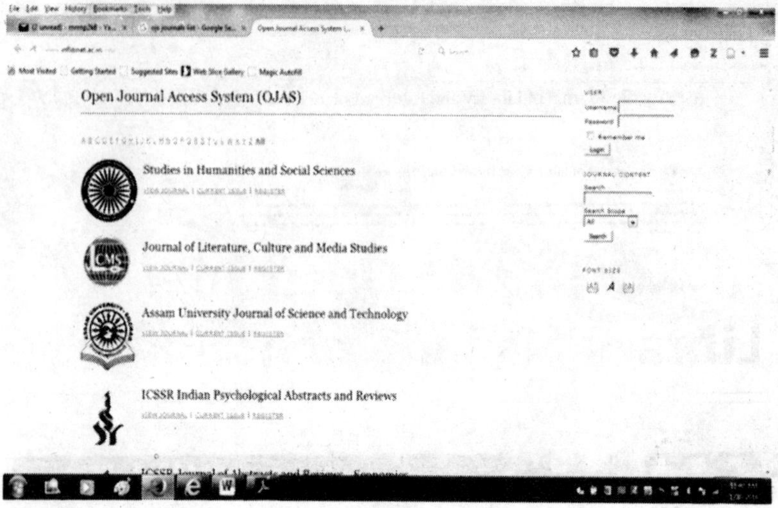

CONCLUSION

A journal can be published by a person, group of persons, professional associations, universities, institutions, or research organizations of their respective specialized areas. It gives the scholarly recognition to that person or association or institution. It also is a scholarly activity to create and share new ideas and knowledge (research output) to the world. These new ideas and knowledge will contribute to the economic and cultural development of the community, country and world.

Along with the above benefits, there are also challenges to maintain and sustain the journal, includes time, finance, manpower, technology and people to bring it all together successful. In starting a new journal, the journal management should carefully do the SWOT analysis of online publication and their models.

REFERENCES

1. *www.doaj.org*
2. *https://pkp.sfu.ca/files/AfricaNewJournal.pdf*

19

KOHA : An Open Source Library Management Software

Khaiser Nikam
Professor in Library and Information Science
University of Mysore
M Nandish Kumar
Librarian, Sadvidya PU College, Mysore

INTRODUCTION

Library Automation generally refers to the use and deployment of computers for house keeping activities such as circulation, serials control, cataloguing etc. Software for library automation have also moved from in house or home grown ones to off the shelf national or global software. There is a fair number of Library Automation Software to choose from in the Indian market too. Some examples include LibSys, SOUL, SLIM, Easylib, Alice, LibSoft. There have been some efforts to develop open source library automation software as well. The best available choice for the librarian now is to turn to Open Source software (OSS). OSS has grown tremendously in scope and popularity over the last several years, and is now in widespread use. One that has received good amount of attention is the Koha open source library system. It is essential to give emphasis to this aspect, as the library automation is yet to take off in majority of the Indian libraries(1). While justifying need for library automation more than cost effectiveness the benefits derived by the library users become the major consideration. To appreciate the advantages it becomes necessary to highlight the different levels of library automation. Automation provides many advantages over traditional library methods, in nearly all libraries, espcecially college libraries. Automation provides better services that are cumbersome to offer by means of traditional methods.

OPEN SOURCE SOFTWARE

Some of the well known and widely used open source library Software are

- Athenaeum Light
- Avanti Micro LCS
- Emilda
- Koha
- Learning Access ILS
- Library Manager
- OpenBiblio
- Openbook
- PhpMyBibli
- PhpMyLibrary

Advantages of Open Source Software

i. The availability of the source code and the right to modify it

ii. The right to redistribute modifications and improvements to the code

iii. The right to use the software in any way

iv. There is no one with the power to restrict in a unilateral way how the software is used

v. There is no single entity on which the future of the

software depends

vi. No per-copy fees can be asked for modified versions, and anyone can use the current code base to start new projects

vii. There are fewer conflicting priorities due to marketing pressures

viii. It provides a new forum for democratic action

KOHA

Koha is an integrated library system written in PERL and using MYSQL as the underlying database. KOHA makes it simple to create and manage a small integrated library system, equipped with acquisition, cataloguing, circulation and searching modules it provides much of the functionality of traditional catalogs. With the recent implementation of its Z39.50 interface, it is easy to enter ISBN numbers in to the system, and locate the MARC records. KOHA represents a major step in providing a catalog that is functional and usable for small libraries(l).

Key Features of Koha

Koha has all expected features of Integrated library System (ILS) software, including:

- Linux, UNIX, Windows and MacOS platform.
- Simple, Clear interface for librarians and members (patrons)
- Customizable search
- Reading lists for members
- Full acquisitions system including budgets and pricing information (including supplier and currency conversion)
- Simple acquisitions system for the smaller library
- Ability to copy with any number of branches, patrons, user categories, item categories, items, currencies and other data

- Serials system for magazines or newspapers
- Full-text electronic journal support
- Copy cataloguing and Z39.50.
- MARC21 and UNIMARC for professional cataloguers.
- Koha is multi-tasking and enables updates of circulation, cataloguing and issues to occur simultaneously.
- Web based OPAC system (allows the public to search the catalogue in the library and a home).
- Full catalogue, circulation and acquisitions system for library stock management
- Import/Export facility
- Printing barcodes

To successfully use Koha one need have some additional software

i. A webserver (It was built to work with Apache, but there is no reason it should not work with any other webserver).

ii. Perl

iii. MySQL (You could instead use postgres, or another SQL - Structured Query Language based database)

iv. DBI

v. DBD: Mysql (or Whatever database system you use)

vi. AuthenDBI (if you want to use Database based authentication)

vii. CDK (for the telnet interface)

INSTALLATION OF KOHA

The software can be downloaded from the site— http://www.Koha.org/download/. It is basically designed to work on Linux operating system. But it is possible to install and run Koha on windows platform. Koha is written in perl, stores its data in MYSQL database, and is accessed via an apache web server. All three of these supporting programs have distributions for windows and are not hard to install. And they are all available free of cost. To be clear, it is not yet as simple as a single install. But it is no harder than installing on a Linux box.

The following are the steps to install the Koha software.

The steps include the installation of apache server, MYSQL database server and Perl language, in which all the modules of the Koha are written. Koha checks for all the needs before installing the software and then configures them according to the need.

Installation on Windows

1. Installation of apache server : As soon as the destination directory is selected, the Apache server gets installed.

2. Installation of MYSQL Server : This server comes in a zipped package. It is to be unzipped using Winzip and clicked on the setup.exe file for initiating the process.

3. Installation of Perl : Here we have to decide that what features of Perl should be installed; and where it should be installed.

4. Installation of Koha : This is the final step in the process.

i) The installation wizard checks for the dependencies before starting the process.

ii) After agreeing to the license, it allows us to select the type of installation that we want. If we select the full version then all the functionalities get installed. However we can go for the custom version if we want some functionality.

Modules Supported by Koha

Koha Open Source Library software has the

following modules

a. Acquisition
b. Cataloguing
c. Members ("patrons")
d. Circulation
e. Online Public Access Catalog (OPAC)

CONCLUSION

This paper has attempted to give a picturesque view of the installation, application and use of Koha, a well-known open source software. This software is one of the most sought after open source software by many librarians of the modern genre. The qualities of **the** software suit a in-house library very well. A novice librarian can easily learn to install the software and start using it for library administration. The interesting part is a beginner in managing library can take to koha just like how fish takes to water. Infact, with this fecility of the software the authors were able to institutionalize at Sadvidya Semi-Residential Pre-University College library. Infact, it was a pleasure experimenting this. The authors are very sure that this paper acts as a guide to those who want to try it out in the respective institution.

REFERENCES

http://www.koha.org

http://koha.liblime.com/

http://www.kohadocs.org/

http://en. wikipedia.org/wiki/open_source_ software

20

Post Independence Childrens and Other Public Libraries in Delhi

Prof C P Vashishth
President, Delhi Library Association,
Naraina Vihar, New Delhi-110028

INTRODUCTION

After 1947 many public library-cum-reading rooms have come up in the city of Delhi. Total number of such Library-cum-Reading rooms may be around 250 in the city of Delhi. Their book collection ranges from less than 1,000 to 15,00,000 volumes or more. It is noteworthy that some of these libraries are exclusively for children. Also the school going children have access to their school libraries. Though the condition of school libraries under the administrative control of government is not very encouraging as most of them are one man libraries. However the situation in public schools is far better in terms of number of staff, seating capacity, infrastructure, book resources, budget and ICT tools.

The libraries attached to foreign missions/ embassies called contact libraries such as American Library Resource Centre at 24 Kasturba Gandhi Marg,

British Council Library at 17 Kasturba Gandhi Marg, German Library at Max Mueller Bhawan, Russian Culture Centre Library at Ferozeshah Road, etc are active libraries and providing quality library service to Delhi's elite public. The three akademi libraries (namely Sahitya Akademi, Lalitkala Akademi, Sangeet-Natak Akademi) at Mandi House and India International Centre Library at Maxmuller Marg are also providing good library service to Delhi public.

Indian publications in English and other regional languages have registered a steep rise after independence. Books are no more a scarce commodity. They are available in abundance and on almost all subjects and in all languages. This has facilitated in opening of more and more libraries. World Book Fairs organized in Delhi are a feat to book lovers. Readers and libraries buy a lot of titles in these book fairs.

NATIONAL BAL BHAWAN LIBRARY

National Bal Bhawan Library at Kotla Road, New Delhi was established in 1956 at the initiative of Pandit Jawaharlal Nehru, first Prime Minister of India with the aim of educating children between the age group of 5 to 16 and fostering in them the habit of lifelong reading. It is open from 9am to 5.30pm. It follows open access and can seat 60 children at a time. It has children specific collection of 35,000+ volumes. Though the Library does not use any Library Management Software, it does have a computer with Internet facility. Data conversion and Barcoding of collection is under way. DDC scheme of classification is being used to classify and organize the book collection.

In 1992 the Library got a new home which is very spacious and enough room for organizing various activities. The Library is fully funded by the Government and is supervised by a technically qualified lady librarian. There is separate room for the kids between the age group of 5-9. it is very well organized, quite attractive and fully decorated to suit childrens' taste.

There are two sections in the library – the Children's section and the Reference section. Children have easy access to the books in the library as they are kept in open shelves. The Reference section has a good collection of reference books related to arts, science, culture and literature. New books are regularly added so that children can keep themselves abreast with the latest developments in these areas.

National Bal Bhawan's Library is not confined to normal print collection alone. Most of the literary activities have been clubbed with the library activities. This is done by organizing various innovative and lively programmes such as:

1. Creative writing
2. Story Telling sessions
3. Poem Recitation and Kavi Goshthi (Poets' Meet)
4. Interaction with writers
5. Theme based discussions
6. Quiz programmes
7. Book reviews
8. Debates

(*http://www.nationalbalbhavan.nic.in/index2.asp?slid=1093&sublinkid=79&langid=1* accessed on 3rd March 2013)

DR B.C ROY CHILDREN'S READING ROOM AND LIBRARY

Housed in Nehru House at 4 Bahadur Shah Zafar Marg, New Delhi-110002 Dr B.C Roy Children'S Reading Room and Library is yet another children specific library in the city. It was established in 1964 on the initiative of famous cartoonist Shankar Pillai. It is funded and managed by Childrens Book Trust.

Library Membership is open to any child between the age of 5 and 18 years. Two types of memberships are available. Children residing beyond 20 kilometers from the Library may avail of the special membership by paying '1250 of which '1000 is refundable security deposit. The ordinary membership charge is ' 650 of which ' 500 is refundable security deposit. The security deposit is refundable at the time of withdrawing of membership. Every member is issued Photo Identity Card. Parents/ guardians can accompany the child member and guide him/her in selecting the books of interest. However, parents/guardians are not allowed to borrow books on behalf of the child member in his/her absence.

The books have been arranged under three different groups for different age groups. Group A provides books for children in the age group of 5 to 8 years. Group B provides books for children in the age group of 9 to 12 years. Group C caters to children of the age group between 13 to 18.

Library follows open access to facilitate free movement and browsing within the library. (*http:// www.childrensbooktrust.com/ lib.htm* accessed on 3rd March 2013)

Besides these two renowned children specific libraries in the city of Delhi, Delhi Public Library too has a very well organized and maintained Children's Section in Sarojni Nagar zonal library, Patel Nagar Library and at Main Library at Dr Shyama Prasad Mukherjee Marg opposite Delhi Railway Station.

DELHI PUBLIC LIBRARY

The most important land-mark in the history of public libraries in the city of Delhi has been the creation of Delhi Public Library (DPL). It was established in 1951 as a Public Library Project by the Ministry of Education, Government of India with technical assistance from UNESCO. Currently Delhi Public Library is functioning under the administrative control of Ministry of Culture, Government of India through Delhi Library Board, an autonomous body established under a special resolution of the then Ministry of Education, Government of India. It is housed in Auchinleck building opposite old Delhi Railway station. Initially the building was to serve as a transit camp and canteen for defence personnel. The building was gifted by Seth Ramkrishna Dalmia.

DELHI LIBRARY BOARD

Delhi Library Board (DLB), the Governing Body of DPL consists of 15 members, including the Chairman and Vice-Chairman nominated by the Ministry of Culture, Government of India. Director General of DPL – a new post created in 2010 is the ex-officio Member Secretary of the DLB, representatives of the Union Ministry of Education, Delhi Administration, Municipal Corporation of Delhi, New Delhi Municipal Council, UNESCO, and four co-opted members. In addition there are various sub-committees constituted by DLB to organize different activities of DPL such as

(i) Finance and Establishment Committee,

(ii) Books Advisory Committee,

(iii) Departmental Promotion Committee,

(iv) Selection/Screening Committee, etc.

DELHI PUBLIC LIBRARY SYSTEM

Besides Main Library at Dr Shyama Prasad Mukherjee Marg, the Delhi Public Library system comprises , one Regional Library at Sarojini Nagar, 3 branches (Karol Bagh, Patel Nagar, Shahdara), 24 sub-braches, 3 community libraries, 12 resettlement colony libraries, 22 deposit stations, 70 Mobile Library points. In addition it has a Braille Library which caters to the requirements of over 505 visually impaired readers. In all it served 73,467 members during 2010-11 (Delhi Public Library Annual Report 2010-11 p.2-30).

STAFF STRENGTH

DPL has a sanctioned staff strength of 449 personnel comprising 329 professionally qualified library staff and remaining 120 non professionals. Many of these positions are lying vacant. Staff is an important component of the library system. Its impact is clearly reflected in the quality of library services. Efforts are being made to recruit the staff to fill these vacant posts.

As per Unit number 6.4.5.6 of Library Systems of Vardhman Mahaveer Open Universty Kota presents the following picture of DPL staff:

Year	*Staff strength*	*Year*	*Staff strength*
1963-64	176	1977-78	286
1964-65	206	1978-79	295
1965-66	219	1979-80	300
1966-67	226	1980-81	301
1967-78	228	1981-82	308
1968-69	236	1982-83	311
1969-70	237	1983-84	444
1970-71	245	1984-85	454
1971-72	264	1985-86	454
1972-73	280	1986-87	454
1973-74	280	1987-88	463
1974-75	280	1988-89	467
1975-76	280	1989-90	469
1976-77	280	1990-91	483

Finance

DPL is fully financed by the Government of India. During 2010-11 it received grant-in-aid amounting to Rs. 16,66,00,000 under Non-plan head (Rs.12,41,00,000) and Plan head (Rs.4,25,00,000). It was spent under the following heads:

Head of Account	*Amount Spent Non-Plan*	*Amount Spent Plan*	*Total*
Books & Reading Material	6,83,000.00	84,81,000.00	91,64,000.00
Establishment	11,01,25,000.00	—	11,01,25,000.00
Other Items	1,61,37,000.00	2,84,84,000.00	4,46,21,000.00
TOTAL	12,69,45,000.00	3,69,65,000.00	16,39,10,000.00

(***Source:*** Delhi Public Library Annual report 2010-2011 p.2)

Breakup of Expenditure on Books & Reading Material during the financial year 2010-11 is as follows:

Name of Head	*Non-Plan*	*Plan*	*Total*
Books	—	84,81,089.00	84,81,089.00
Periodicals & Newspapers with Unesco Coupons	6,83,270.00	—	6,83,270.00
Binding	—	57,399.00	57,399.00
Gramophone Records	—	—	—
TOTAL	6,83,270.00	85,38,488.00	92,21,758.00

(***Source:*** Delhi Public Library Annual report 2010-2011 p.2)

DVD Corners have been set up in 7 libraries of DPL System. These libraries are located at Central Library (Dr Shyama Prasad Mukherjee Marg), Sarojini Nagar Regional Library, Patel Nagar Branch Library, Vinobapuri Branch Library, Janakpuri Branch Library, Karol Bagh Branch Library, and R K Puram Library. Together these seven libraries issued 19,374 CD/DVDs for home viewing during 2010-2011.

EXPENDITURE ON BOOKS AND STAFF

During the initial years, the expenditure on books and staff salaries used to be almost equal. But as the staff component started growing, the expenditure on staff salaries started showing an upward trend. The following decennial figures of expenditure compiled from various annual reports of Delhi Public Library are a testimony to this:

Years	*Expenditure on books*	*Expenditure on staff salary*
1951-52	40,783	40,564
1961-62	1,13,529	1,96,584
1971-72	2,09,751	10,16,248
1981-82	3,88,203	32,41,751
1991-92	1,90,627	1,32,54,987
2001-2002	34,84,878	5,21,89,878
2011-2012	N.A.	N.A.

TECHNICAL SERVICES

On the basis of selection done by Book Advisory Committees for English, Hindi, Urdu and Panjabi, the books are purchased, technically processed and transferred to respective service units. During the year 2010-11 as many as 33,868 books were procured, out of which 33,647 were purchased and rest 221 were received as gratis from various sources. Under Delivery of Book Act 10,711 titles were received.

READERS SERVICES

Any resident of NCT Delhi can avail free membership of DPL system without any annual subscription by filling a Membership Form obtainable from reception at a price of Rs. 2. The applicant has to make refundable security deposit of Rs.50 in case he/she is unable to secure the recommendation of a suitable guarantor such as a gazetted officer, elected public representative, MBBS doctor, lawyer, bank manager, chartered accountant, etc. Members are given 1 to 3 borrowers tickets depending upon the size of the library service unit against which books are issued for 14 days.

Total membership (Adults 56,544 & Children 16,923)	73,467
Number of books issued	11,69,734
Average number of books issued per day	3,378
Number of books consulted in reference section	20,659
Attendance of readers in Reading Rooms	2,44,499

(***Source:*** Delhi Public Library Annual report 2010-2011 p3)

CHILDRENS SECTIONS

Childrens Sections have been set up in Central Library at Dr Shyama Prasad Mukherjee Marg, Sarojini Nagar Regional Library, and Patel Nagar Branch Library. All these three Childrens sections have been revamped with new books, DVDs, toys, games and suitable furniture. These Childrens' sections are very well decorated and furnished with colourful chairs and tables.

EXTENSION SERVICES

DPL system is running two types of extension services i.e. (i) Deposit Stations, and (ii) Mobile Libraries.

Deposit Stations : This innovative scheme is being run by DPL in collaboration with housing societies/ resident welfare associations. Under this scheme books are lent to societies/associations and training imparted to their volunteers for keeping the issue and return record. At the end of March 2011 there were 22 such deposit stations in NCT of Delhi. The scheme served 2,451 members and issued 28,002 books.

Mobile Libraries : Since beginning of DPL, this scheme has been a very popular library service in colonies of Delhi and around. The Mobile Library Service was suspended for some years because of non availability of CNG mobile vans. This service has again been reintroduced since 2005. During 2010-11 it served 4,275 members in 70 colonies and issued 71,156 books. During the years 1964 to 1998 it served the following service points on 5 identified routes:

Years	*Routes*	*Service points*
1964-65	5	54
1981-82	5	65
1987-88	5	78
1988-89	5	81
1991-92	5	82
1992-93	5	86
1997-98	5	102

(***Source :*** MPLS-02 Library Systems, Vardhman Mahaveer Open University, Kota. 2009 p. 77)

BAJA GHAR

Delhi Public Library runs a gramophone records and music cassettes library where these are lent to registered borrowers of the Library. These music records/ cassettes comprise classical, instrumental, light music, bhajans, ghazals, filmy songs etc. The total stock of these music materials number 9,431.

BRAILLE LIBRARY

The Braille is the specialized service of DPL which caters to the reading requirements of visually impaired members of the library. It has a total collection of 15,699 books in English and Hindi. During 2010-11 the library issued 16,421 books to 505 blind members.

SERVICE TO PRISONERS

DPL provides library service to the prisoners of Central Tihar Jail of NCT Delhi. It served 570 registered prisoner members and issued them 15,839 books during 2010-11.

Practical Training in Library science : Under this service, technical advice and practical training is imparted to library & information science students and institutions to give them hands-on-experience in handling/performing different activities/jobs in libraries.

INTERNET Service

Internet service is being provided from three units of DPL. The following diagram shows the interest of users community in books and Internet among readers. It is found that on one side the interest of members is increasing in Internet, the record of issue of printed books is also increasing in three different libraries. This fact is to be considered carefully while bringing any change in purchase policy of electronic resources :

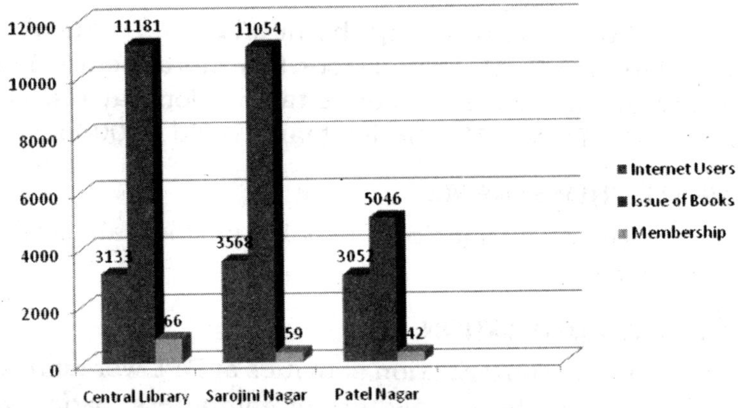

(*Source* : Library Systems. Vardhman Mahaveer Open University,Kota. 2009. P. 82)

BOOK RESOURCES

As on 31st March 2011 the collection of the DPL System stood at 16,08,813. Language wise breakup of books received under the provisions of Delivery of Book Act can be seen from the table given below:

S. No.	*Language*	*Stock as on 31-3-2010*	*Receipt during 2010-2011*	*Stock as on 31-3-2011*
1	Assamese	399	0	399
2	Bengali	8167	245	8412
3	English	96042	6193	102235
4	Gujarati	708	0	708
5	Hindi	89229	2970	92199
6	Kannada	7585	0	7585
7	Kashmiri	12	0	12
8	Malayalam	7448	0	7448
9	Marathi	20152	595	20747
10	Oriya	3058	0	3058
11	Punjabi	6469	400	6869
12	Sanskrit	1784	0	1784
13	Sindhi	562	0	562
14	Tamil	30978	0	30978
15	Telugu	5140	0	5140
16	Urdu	7564	308	7872
	TOTAL	285297	10711	296008

(*Source:* Delhi Public Library Annual report 2010-2011 p.5)

DPL is also receiving the publications of the Asian Development Bank as its Depository Library since 1994. These are available for consultation alone at the Main Library at Dr S P Mukherjee Marg, Delhi 110006.

SERIALS/NEWSPAPERS

Library subscribes to 110 periodicals and 29 newspapers.

LIBRARY AUTOMATION

The computerization activities at DPL were initiated in 1995 with the installation of computers loaded with UNESCO's CDS/ISIS software package which enabled the library to create bibliographic databases. From 1997 onwards books received under DBA provision are being inputted in computer database. By end of March 2011 bibliographic records of 52,681 books in English and 38,180 books in Hindi had been created using CDS/ISIS. DPL is now using KOHA open software for books received under DBA provisions.

PANJABI ACADEMY LIBRARY

Housed in DDA Community Centre, Sadar Thana Road, Motia Khan, Paharganj, the Panjabi Academy Library was established in 1983. It remains open from 9.30am to 6pm on all working days. It has 44 branches designated as Composite Libraries. It is fully funded by the Government of NCT Delhi. Its book budget is '6 lakhs per Annam spread in five districts of Delhi (8 Composite libraries are located in North District; 10 Composite libraries are located in South District). It has a staff strength of 40 professional librarians, 40 semi professional assistants and 38 other support staff.

The book collection comprising Panjabi language and literature of the main library consists of over 22,000 volumes. It subscribes/receives 10 periodicals and 18 newspapers. The collection is organized according to 20th

edition of *Dewey Decimal Classification.* Library is not yet automated. Catalogue cards are prepared manually using *AACR2*. Books are issued to members in a register. There are 2 sets of computer systems in the library with equal number of printers and one scanner.

Panjabi Academy helps in opening new libraries by providing free books, periodicals and furniture. It also provides free Punjabi books and periodicals to schools and colleges.

NEW DELHI MUNICIPAL COUNCIL (NDMC) CENTRAL LIBRARY

Founded in 1984, Central Library of New Delhi Municipal Council is housed in Palika Kendra, NDCC Phase II New Delhi-110001. It remains open between 10.30am to 7pm on all working days of the week. The Book collection consists of over 13,000 volumes. It subscribes to around 40 periodicals and 18 newspapers. Library is automated and has OPAC and Internet facility. Its reading room can accommodate 45 to 50 readers at a time. Photocopying, consultation, referral and reference services are provided by the library. Library has a budget of '7,00,000 ('3,00,000 for books, '2,50,000 for periodicals and '1,50,000 miscellaneous). The staff strength of library system consists of 13 professionals, 10 semi-professionals and 2 others. Beside Central Library it has 8 branch libraries. Six of these branch libraries are known as Palika Pustakalaya located in Aliganj Barat Ghar, Babar Road, Mandir Marg, North West Moti Bagh, Rohini and Laxmi Bai Nagar respectively.

Its Children Library is located in Kidwai Nagar and the Sports Library is located in Kaka Nagar.

RAMAKRISHNA MISSION LIBRARY AND READING ROOM

Ramakrishna Mission Library and Reading Room, New Delhi is housed in the campus of Rama Krishna Mission Ashram located at Pachkuiah Road, New Delhi.

It was established in 1956. It is open from 8am to 8pm. Its collection comprises 50,000+ volumes. Library subscribes/receives 150 periodicals besides 10 newspapers. It has a book budget of over '100,000 per annum. Its staff strength comprise three male professionals and 5 other male support staff who work under the supervision of an engineer monk. Beside there are quite a few other volunteer library workers too.

Library is fully automated and uses VLIS (Vivekananda Library and Information Software) for organising its various housekeeping operations. It has 15 computers, 2 printers, 1 scanner and 3 bar code readers. It is a member of library consortium. Its services comprise consultation, book loan, referral, photocopy, internet browsing and OPAC. There is separate seating arrangement for males and females.

PURUSHOTTAMDAS TANDON LIBRARY

Established in 1960 with a small collection of 3,360 books, it has grown into a fully developed library of over 70,000 books. It is an integral part of Servants of India Society, Delhi branch popularly known as Lok Sevak, Lajpat Bhawan Library. Library is located in Lajpat Nagar-IV, New Delhi. It is named after *Bharat Ratna awardee* Purushottamdas Tandon. The Collection of Library comprises ethics, philosophy, religion, social sciences, humanities, science, nature cure, arts, technology, history, biographies, etc. Library has about 7000 books for 1863 children members. Library has a special collection on Gandhian Literature. Library subscribes to 35 periodicals and 13 newspapers in English, Hindi and Urdu. Over 10,000 members utilize its services. Library has 260 Life members.

"The income of the library comprises of small annual grant from governmental agencies and for the rest it depends on donations received from friends and well wishers of the Servants of People Society, Library lovers and philanthropic individuals and institutions."

—*Purushottamdas Tandon Library Brochure. p 3*

For various housekeeping operations Library is using LibGuru Library Management Siftware. Staff strength of the Library is only three

DYAL SINGH PUBLIC LIBRARY

Dyal Singh Public Library is named after the name of Sardar Dyal Singh Majithia, son of Sardar Lehna Singh, a General in the army of Maharaja Ranjit Singh. Dyal Singh Public Library was originally established in 1928 at Lahore in Punjab in pursuance of the WILL of Dyal Singh Majithia (1848-1898) - a philanthropist and social reformer of the 19th century Punjab. After partition of India, with the efforts of Late Dewan Anand Kumar, the first Vice Chancellor of Panjab University, the Dyal Singh Public Library was established once again in free India in 1950. The Library was re-established in its new building at 1 Deen Dayal Upadhyay Marg, New Delhi in 1957.

B K Nehru had once said that Dyal Singh Majithia was "undoubtedly one of the most remarkable pioneers who led India out of the darkness of ignorance to the enlightenment of modernity through liberal education". India celebrated the 150th Birth Anniversary of Dyal Singh Majithia in 1998 as well as his 100th Death Anniversary as Majithia died on September 9, 1898. Dyal Singh Majithia established the *Tribune* newspaper and a Public Library well endowed with books, which were made available to general public free of cost.

Dyal Singh Public Library was registered under the Societies Registration Act, 1860 on 2.8.1948 at Kalka (then in east Punjab) in accordance with the 'WILL' of the donor of the Trust Late Sardar Dyal Singh Majithia. Justice R.S. Sarkaria says that "Dyal Singh College and Dyal Singh Library are today a mute testimony to the vision of this great man". The Library is a Charitable Public Trust.

Mission and Mandate

The Mission and Mandate of Dyal Singh Public Library is "Imparting knowledge and Dissemination of Information to general public from all sections of society without any discrimination and without any fee".

Daily visitors: Around 90 to 100

Daily consultation of books: Between 125-150

Working hours/days	9.30 AM to 5.30 PM 6 days / week
Closed on	Sundays and Gazetted Holidays

Library Clientele

Registered Library Members are 9000. The membership breakup in percentage is as follows:

Students	70 Percent
Professionals	18 Percent
Govt/Private officials	9 Percent
Businessmen	2 Percent
Retired Persons	1 Percent
Housewives	0.3 Percent

Subject Interest of Library Clientele

English Literature (Fiction)	100 Percent
Computer Science	62 Percent
Management	59 Percent
History	56 Percent
Science & Technology	19 Percent

Library Use

In yet another Survey conducted by Delhi Library Association in 2007, it was found that out of 25 readers present in the Library on the day of distribution of the Questionnaire, 40 percent of them were students and the other 60 percent were teachers, government officials, executives, engineers, medical professionals, journalists, etc. The readers were having qualifications as graduate, MBA, CA, MBBS, MD, MCA, BCA and so on.

Users had shown their interests in the subjects like economics, business management, accountancy, science, sociology, history, English literature, computer science, philosophy, general study, current affairs, engineering, education, public administration, etc.

Library Building

The Library is housed on the ground floor of the two-storey building of its own. Except for few rooms for Trust Officials and readers, the entire upper floor is rented to other offices and to the daily *Tribune* (newspaper). The total area of Library compound is 1.31 acres.

Floor Plan

Reading hall on ground floor opens to the view of first floor of the building with high ceiling. Stack rooms and reading hall is a unified one. Stack area is a mix of steel and wooden double faced unit racks of 7.5 feet and 6 feet of height respectively. There are 198 unit racks/ book shelves. Ninety units fixed on one side of entrance and 102 units on the other side stand organized into six blocks.

Other Facilities

- A Genset with automatic backup is there in standby to meet the load shedding situation.
- Water Cooler.
- One air conditioner (Samsung) in computer server room. The other AC is fixed in librarian's room.
- Wall mounted fans

Governing Body: Dyal Singh Library Trust Society

- President
- Honorary Secretary

- General Manager
- Administrator

Book Selection Committee

It comprises following members:

- President
- Honorary Secretary
- General Manager
- Any Trustee, and
- Librarian

Library Manpower

Manpower in position	=	7
Professionals	=	2
Semi Professional	=	1
Library Attendants	=	4

Budget

Main source of Revenue of Dyal Singh Public Library Trust is from the rent of the building. Roughly the earnings are distributed as below:

For staff	=	Rs. 5,00,000
For books	=	Rs. 3,00,000
For periodicals	=	Rs. 1,20,000
For binding	=	Rs. 60,000

Library Collection

Books = 40,000+

E-books: Encyclopedia Britannica on CD-ROM 2 CDs.

Audio-visual CDs, DVDs and Audio-visual Cassettes are a available in small numbers

Periodicals / Magazines

through subscription	=	100
complimentary basis	=	25-30
annual Report (ICRA)	=	1
newspapers (National)	=	21

Arrangement of Book Collection

Books have been organized on shelves in a classified order using *Dewey Decimal Classification* Scheme. Library is using e-Granthalaya open library software for management of its collection.

Computer H/W & Accessories available

- IBM Server X series with 2 GB RAM
- IBM computers P-4 = 11
- Laser Printer 1
- Scanner 1

Conventional Services

- Book loan/Issue and Return service. Books are issued for two weeks.
- Inter library Loan to DELNET members for Two weeks.
- Book reservation on demand from readers.
- Book Acquisition. Book selection is done through
  - — Books on Approval
  - — Books selection tools,
  - — On user demands
- Book processing: Books are technically processed using *Dewey Decimal Classification Scheme* 22nd edition, and Cutters Table. Cataloguing is done following AACR-II code.
- Periodicals acquisition: some 100 periodicals and magazine and 21 National daily Newspapers are procured and put on display.

- Documentation work/bibliography compilation is done on demand.
- Reference service is given in routine manner.
- Binding of books is got done on rate contract basis from outside firms in once two-three years.

Electronic Services

- Retro conversion of all English language books is done and digital catalogue is made available through OPAC placed in Reading Room.
- Issue and Return of books is done electronically for English books.
- Internet browsing and E-mail facility is given in limited manner.
- CD-ROM (Encyclopaedia Britannica) is searched on specific demand.

Training

- Orientation / Guidance is provided to new users
- Training in library use is given
- OPAC: Hands on training is given to new users
- Multimedia and Audio-visual services are provided on a limited scale.

21

Use of 24/7 Hours Reading Room Facility in Prof. S.S. Basavanal Library: A Study

Gururaj S. Hadagali
Assistant Professor,
Department of Library and Information Science,
Karnatak University, Dharwad – 580 003

Satishkumar Naikar
Librarian, Chetan Business School, Hubli, Karnataka

M.M. Bachalapur
Librarian, BLDEA Dr. P.G. Halakatti College of Engineering and Technology, Bijapur – 586 103

Satish V. Totar
Head, Library and Information Center, K.L.E. Dr. M.S. Sheshgiri College of Engineering and Technology, Udyambag, Belagavi – 590 008

ABSTRACT

The main aim of the present survey is to determine the use of 24/7 hours reading room by the P.G. students and research scholars. A questionnaire method was employed to elicit the opinion from the respondents. A total of 200 questionnaires were distributed to P. G. students, research scholars and outsiders, out of which 191 questionnaires were received with duly signed by the respondents. The response rate was 95.50 %. The outcomes of the study were: more than 107 respondents use 24/7 reading room to prepare for civil services exams; 123 respondents spend more than three hours in the reading room; more than 161 respondents found reading room very useful; and more than 69 respondents use wi-fi facility extended to readers in reading room.

INTRODUCTION

Library forms an essential part of the chain of human communication. Library as a social institution, works for greater enlightenment of the society and gradually creates a climate in which it can flourish. Library provides essential information for the individuals in every walk of life. Mere collection of information materials in library will not serve the purpose of any library. A reading room should be necessary wherein the users can read and take note of information. A well furnished reading room with all facilities is a good sign of a library. In some of the institutions / organizations a separate reading room facility is being provided where the user brings his / her favorite / text books to read. Such reading room will be kept open round the clock with necessary arrangements. The present is an attempt to determine the use of newly established 24/7 hours reading room facility in Karnatak University, Dharwad. The reason for this initiative was the growing demand for study zones at Karnatak University, Dharwad.

24/7 READING ROOM

The Karnatak University has Prof. S.S. Basavanal Library (central library) which is catering to the needs and requirements of its users. The Library was established along with the Karnatak University in 1950. At present, it has more than four lakhs volumes and more than 5,000 electronic journals. From June 1967, the Library has been designated as a Depository Center for the United Nations publications. The University has another library i.e. Green Library opposite to the administrative building spread across in more than two acres of land with wi-fi facility. Prof. S.S. Basavanal Library is kept open from 8 a.m. to

8 p.m. (Monday to Saturday). In addition to that the University Library has recently started 24/7 hours reading room / hall for the benefit of the students and research scholars. It was inaugurated on 13th July, 2014 by Sri. R.V. Deshapande, the then Minister for Higher Education, Govt. of Karnataka. The 24/7 reading hall was constructed under the financial assistance of University Grants Commission – University with Potential for Excellence (UGC-UPE project) programme. It was constructed besides the central library of Karnatak University and spread over 202 sq. meters. It has a seating capacity of 80 students.

OBJECTIVES OF THE STUDY

The main objective of the present survey is to study the use of 24/7 hours reading room facility extended by Prof. S.S. Basavanal Library of the users of Karnatak University, Dharwad.

The specific objectives of the study are to:

1. study the purpose of using the 24/7 hours reading room facility by the respondents;
2. find out the time spent by the respondents;
3. check whether there is an encouraging atmosphere in the 24/7 reading room;
4. know the usefulness of reading room;
5. determine the use of wi-fi facility extended in 24/7 reading room; and
6. study the purpose of using wi-fi facility.

METHODOLOGY

There are various established methods by which one can collect the relevant data for the study. For the present study the questionnaire method has been adopted. The questionnaire has been so designed that it could be answered within a short time, by eliminating descriptive type questions. A total of 200 questionnaires were distributed to the P.G. students, research scholars and outsiders (see table 1 for distribution of questionnaires). Out of which 191 questionnaires were received back with duly signed by the respondents resulting into response rate of 95.50 %. The data then collected were fed into MS-Excel for its frequency calculation and tabulations.

ANALYSIS AND INTERPRETATION

Distribution of Questionnaires

The table 1 presents the distribution of questionnaires among the respondents. A total of 200 questionnaires were distributed to P.G. students, research scholars and outsiders, out of which 191 questionnaires were received with a response rate of 95.50 %. The respondents include P.G. students and research scholars of Karnatak University, and outsiders. There are some students who are preparing for civil services examinations also making use of 24/7 reading room facility (with prior permission from the authorities).

Table 1. Distribution of Questionnaires

Sl. No.	*Types of users*	*No. of questionnaires distributed*	*No. of questionnaires received*	*Percentage (%)*
1	P.G. students	140	135	70.68
2	Research Scholars	20	17	08.91
3	Outsiders	40	39	20.41
	Total	200	191	100.00 %

Distribution of questionnaires based on Gender

Out of 191 respondents, the majority, i.e. 171 (91.1 %) are male and only 17 (8.9 %) are female. The study reveals that male respondents full use of 24/7 reading room facility compared to female respondents.

Table 2. Distribution of questionnaires based on Gender

Sl. No.	*Gender*	*No. of respondents*	*Percentage (%)*
1	Male	174	91.1
2	Female	17	8.9
	Total	191	100.00 %

Purpose of visiting 24/7 reading room

A question was raised to the respondents about the purposes for which they make use of the 24/7 reading room. The study reveals that majority, i.e. 107 (56.02 %) respondents visit for preparing civil services exams, followed by 101 (52.88 %) respondents visit because there is a pin drop silence in the reading room which creates congenial atmosphere for reading. Whereas, 90 (47.02 %) respondents use it for reading semester end exams. The other details are presented in table 3.

Table 3. Purpose of visiting 24/7 reading room

Sl. No.	*Purpose*	*No. of respondents (n=191)*	*Percentage (%)*
1	Reading for semester end exams	90	47.12
2	Preparing for Civil services exams	107	56.02
3	Reading Novels	39	20.42
4	Reading text books	88	46.07
5	Because of pin drop silence in the reading room	101	52.88

Time spent in the reading room

The table 4 depicts the time spent in a day in the reading room. The majority of respondents, i.e. 123 (64.40 %) spend more than three hours a day, followed by 28 (14.66 %) respondents spend three hours for reading purpose. The study reveals that the respondents are making use of reading room even in the late night, because one can use this reading room round the clock.

Table 4. Time spent in the reading room

Sl. No.	*Time spent*	*No. of respondents (n=191)*	*Percentage (%)*
1	One hour	13	06.81
2	Two hours	27	14.13
3	Three hours	28	14.66
4	More than three hours	123	64.40
	Total	191	100.00

Opinion about the atmosphere in the reading room

A question was posed to the respondents whether there is an encouraging atmosphere for reading or not. More than 176 (92.15 %) respondents are of the opinion that the reading room atmosphere is encouraging, since there is a pin drop silence, good ventilation, and with enough lighting arrangement.

Table 5. Opinion about the atmosphere in the reading room

Sl. No.	*Opinion*	*No. of respondents (n=191)*	*Percentage (%)*
1	Yes	176	92.15
2	No	15	7.85
	Total	191	100.00

Usefulness of 24/7 reading room for the study

The table 6 depicts the usefulness of 24/7 reading room for the study. The majority, i.e. 161 (84.29 %) respondents opine that it is more useful and 24 (12.57) are uncertain about the statement. It is evident from the study that the 24/7 reading room facility is one of its kinds in the neighboring institutions.

Table 6. Usefulness of 24/7 reading room for the study

Sl. No.	*Opinion*	*No. of respondents (n=191)*	*Percentage (%)*
1	More useful	161	84.29
2	Uncertain	24	12.57
3	Less useful	6	03.14
	Total	191	100.00

Use of Wi-Fi facility

The 24/7 reading room has wi-fi facility for users. A question was asked to the respondents for its use by them. The majority of the respondents, i.e. 122 (63.87 %) are not using wi-fi facility extended to them and at the same time some of the respondents are unaware of it. Only 69 (36.13 %) respondents are making use of the wi-fi facility.

Table 7. Use of Wi-Fi facility

Sl. No.	*Opinion*	*No. of respondents (n=191)*	*Percentage (%)*
1	Yes	69	36.13
2	No	122	63.87
	Total	191	100.00

Purpose of using Wi-Fi facility

The table 8 indicates that the purposes for which the wi-fi facility was used. The majority, i.e. 61 (88.4 %) respondents use wi-fi to access e-resources. Prof. S.S. Basavanal Library gives access to more than 5000 e-journals and more than 20 e-databases. Whereas, 33 (47.83 %) respondents use it for social networking sites and 26 (37.68 %) respondents use it to access email.

Table 8. Purpose of using wi-fi facility

Sl. No.	*Purpose of using wi-fi*	*No. of respondents (n=69)*	*Percentage (%)*
1	Access e-resources	61	88.40
2	Email	26	37.68
3	Use social networking sites	33	47.83
4	For entertainment	11	15.94

Fig.1. 24/7 hours reading room
***Source:* www.kud.ac.in**

CONCLUSION

Dharwad is well known for its cultural heritage which has produced international reputed musicians and a hub of higher education in this part of Karnataka. The Hubballi-Dharwad twin cities have three universities viz. Karnatak University, University of Agricultural Sciences, Dharwad and Karnataka State Law University along with reputed professional colleges catering to the needs of students of this part. The present study reflects the use of 24/7 reading room, a unique library facility for students in the nearby vicinity. In one of the interviews to NDTV, the prime minister of India, Shri Narendra Modi ji said that we will get information from Google but not knowledge. In the twenty first century the reading habit of users is declining due to internet and mobile technologies. The library has to motivate and find out new ways to install love for reading and make use of books. Karnatak University has made an attempt in this regard to provide such facilities through 24/7 reading room to encourage students and research scholars of Karnatak University, Dharwad.

REFERENCE

- Karnatak University, Dharwad. Accessed February 12, 2016, from http://www.kud.ac.in

22

Research Publication Trends Among College Librarians In North Maharashtra University, Jalgaon

Rahul B. Khandare
Librarian, Sardar Vallabhabhai Patel Arts & Science College, Ainpur, Tal. Raver, Dist. Jalgaon (M.S.)- 425507

Shashank S. Sonwane
Assistant Professor, Dept. of Library and Information Science, Dr. Babasaheb Ambedkar Marathwada University, Aurangabad (M.S.) – 431004

B. G. Mukhyadal
Librarian, Shri Vitthalrao Shankarrao Naik Arts, Commerce and Science College, Raver, Dist. Jalgaon -425506

ABSTRACT

The paper presents on research publication trends among library and information science professionals in North Maharashtra University, Jalgaon from 2008 to 2012. The study covers language preferred for research publication, research method, awareness about citation styles, impact factor, plagiarism/copyright software, publication trends among librarians etc.

Keywords : Publication Trends, College Librarian, Impact Factor, Research Method, Citation Style

INTRODUCTION

Research plays an important role in all round development of a country.The development of any country to a great extent depends upon how researchers, scientists, librarians and managers etc. play unique role in extraction, management, persuasion, transfer and generation of knowledge in it for human cause (Krishna, 2011).The Library and Information Science is theyoungest profession but fast developing, in the lastfew decades (Raju, 2008). The Library and Information Science professionals publishing a good number of books, articles, conference papers etc., during recent years. The growth of publications especially journals in LIS at national and international level has also increased (Sivakumaren, Jeyaprakash, Swaminathan&Karthikeyan, 2012). Recent days, the publications of articles and papers in digital forms have been increased tremendously and these resources are available in the open access domain also. The books published on library and information science discipline is very low when it is compared with other discipline. LIS professionals need to develop their attitudes to publish printed books as well as electronic books on various topics related to library and information science (Sudhier, 2013). The LIS professionals should be encouraged to publish articles in the electronics journals preferably in the Open Access Journals. It will increase the usage of articles and visibility of the authors will also be increased at global level.

RESEARCH PUBLICATION TREND

Research is common parlance refers to a search for knowledge. Research is an art of scientific investigation. Some people consider Research as a movement, a movement from the known to the unknown. It is actually a voyage of discovery. Research is thus, an original contribution to the existing stock of knowledge making for its advancement. It is the pursuit of truth with the help of study, observation, comparison and experiment. In short, the search for knowledge through objective and systematic method of finding solution to a problem is Research (Kothari, 2010).

Publication trend can be explain as 'the act or process of publishing matter in print or electronic form or an issue of printed or electronic matter, such as a book, journal or magazine, offered for distribution or sale and making it available to the public' (Free Dictionary, n.d.)

NORTH MAHARASHTRA UNIVERSITY, JALGAON

North Maharashtra University, established on 15th August, 1990, is one of the leading universities in India. Its jurisdiction includes three districts in North of Maharashtra state – Jalgaon, Dhule and Nandurbar with total of 229 colleges and institutes being affiliated to this university under 08 different faculties. Presently, there are 13 schools and 01 Institute on the campus imparting education through the blend of modern, applied, job oriented and conventional courses to more than 3000 students complimented with the state-of-the-art research facilities, supporting infrastructure and 04 Satellite campuses. The university is ranked at 40th among 620 universities in India by the reputed national weekly 'India Today' through a country-wide survey by Nelson Research and Consultancy Company (2013).The National Assessment and Accreditation Council (NAAC), Bangalore has bestowed prestigious 'A' grade (CGPA 3.11 on 4 point scale) at 3rd cycle re-accreditation of the university in 2015.

REVIEW OF LITERATURE

Previously many studies have been carried out in recent years on research productivity. Out of them few given below;

Sevukan and Sharma (2008) the study aims to

examine research output of Biotechnology faculties in some Indian Central Universities. They found that Banaras Hindu University is leading from the front with 42, 55% contribution. There is a trend towards collaborative research with two-authored papers being maximum followed by three-authored papers. R. Prasad is most productive author of JNU. The articles contributed by the Faculties appeared in journals published from 16 different countries with a maximum from the Netherlands followed by US. Only 0.32% articles were published from India.

Waghmare (2009) conducted a study on publication patterns of faculties of Languages in Marathwada Region. He reveals that Majority percentage of publication i.e. 45.12% publications were books and 42.79% publication of journals. The Professor's publication is 66.05% while a publication of Reader and Lecturers combine is 33.95%. 100% publications preferred by the faculties were publishing in India.

Sakharkar (2011) conducted study on research productivity in Language during 2005-2008. 111 Ph. D. thesis was produced during 2005 to 2008. The subject like Marathi (34 Ph. D.) is favourite Language among the Professionals. Among the 11 Languages department studied, Marathi language stand first position, followed by English with 30 and stand second position and Hindi with 13 and stand third position in the research productivity in the year 2005-2008. The study shows that these three departments have actively been engaged in guiding research projects and also higher number of guides available in these departments for the guidance.

Sivakumaren and et al. (2012) reveals that majority of Teachers 66.7%, 52% of Librarians and few Library Assistants (25%) have published more than five papers in the conference and seminars. 74.50% have preferred two authorship patterns for their publications. Teachers (88.9%), Librarians 51%, and Library Assistants

(25%) were interested to publish their publications with single authorship. Majority of respondents (82.5%) have preferred to publish articles in the printed journals and followed by 70.8% of respondents were interested to contribute papers in the conferences. Majority of the Teachers preferred to publish journal articles (88.9%) in the printed journals and papers (88.9%) in the conferences/seminars.

Sonwane, Adhe and Vaishnav (2012) reported that the Scientists of Dr. BabasahebAmbedkarMarathwada University, Aurangabad had published 2505 publications. The Professors productivity is 69% while productivity of Readers and Lecturers combine is 31%. It means that the productivity of professors is double than the Readers and Lecturers. Male professors have published 70.97% publications, followed by male Readers 20.42% and Lectures publications were very few (8.60%). However female professor have published 48.76%, female Lecturers have published 39.30% and Readers were at third position i.e., 11.94%.

Baskaran (2013) conducted study on research productivity of Alagappa University during 1999-2011. He highlight that Multi-authored papers are more in number 750 (96.64%) and single-authored papers 26 (3.35%) of the research publications of Alagappa University. South Korea rank first by producing 7.61% of collaborative papers out of total research output. Institutions-wise contribution of research output by Central Electrochemical Research Institute publications reveal first rank with 129 (16.62%) of papers. The subject-wise contribution of research publications by the researchers from Material Science shows more number of papers with 172 (22.26%) from the research output.

Kumbar and Gupta (2013) the study is based on research output of two universities i.e. Mysore University &Karnatak University. They found that both universities have published 2911 and 1615 papers during 2002-2011.

Both universities largest priority was assigned to physical sciences (with 56.96% and 42.41%). Mysore University has contributed more paper in terms of overall research output, research output across subjects, international collaboration share, institutional share in 10 broad subjects and average author productivity per paper. Mysore University has contributed comparatively larger share of international collaborative papers than Karnatak University. Both the universities have developed extensive national collaborating links, but mainly confined to academic institutions.

Sagar, Kademani and Bhanumurthy (2014) highlight the agriculture research publications in India during 1993-2012 based on the Web of Science database. A total of 22615 publications were published in Agriculture during 1993-2012. The highest total impact factor (1865.33) was in 2008. The highest average impact factor per publications (1.29) was in 2006. India had 1744 (7.71%) international collaborative publications with 104 countries in Agriculture. Indian Institutions had the highest number of collaborative publications with countries like the USA, Australia and Germany etc. Dairy & Animal Sciences accounts for the largest share 8713 (38.53%) of publications in the total Indian publications output in Agriculture. More than 60% of the publications were published in only eight key journals. Most of the publications in Agriculture are published in Indian and low impact factor journals.

Nwaogu and Ifijeh (2014) the study analyses the survey of the application of scientific methods to research among librarians in South East Nigeria. 27 (30.6%) of the respondents employed scientific methods to quantify and analyze data, 25 (28.4%) employed scientific methods to check for accuracy in search investigation. 78 (88.6%) of the respondents agreed that scientific methods of investigation are very effective in carrying out research while the remaining 10 (11.4%) disagreed. 13 (14.8%)

indicated lack of equipment and expertise as an obstacle to the use of scientific methods, 10 (11.4%) indicated time constraint, while the major constraint to the application of scientific methods to research in librarianship is inadequate fund as indicated by 58 (65.9%).

Bala and Kumari (2014) did a study on cumulative publication output of National Institute of Technology (NIT) consist of 8841 papers with an average number of papers per year as 884, witnessing an average annual growth rate of 38.45%, registering an impact of 2.14 citations per paper during 2001-2010. Out of 8841 citations, 66.41% are published as articles, 31.09% as conference papers, 1.55% as reviews etc. NIT Rourkela scored the first rank with its publication share of 12.83%. USA is the major collaborating partner with NIT's with 22.76% international collaborative publication share. Among the broad subject wise contribution of NIT's engineering sciences subjects together scored the maximum average citation impact per paper (3.6) during 2001-10.

Ismail, Ahmed and Subpouto (2015) investigated a study on Library and Information Science Research in the Khyber Pakhtunkhwa, Pakistan. They found that majority of LIS professional in Pakistan published books that other resources. Majority of the respondents writes on University library. Majority of the respondents were facing problem of Lack of financial support in the form of research fellowship/scholarship andLack of research journal in the field of LIS, Research unfriendly environment.

STATEMENT OF THE RESEARCH PROBLEM

The problem under investigation is "Research Publication trends among College Librarians in North Maharashtra University, Jalgaon". The study will evaluate the research publication trends among academic librarians which are affiliated to North Maharashtra University, Jalgaon.

OBJECTIVES OF THE STUDY

The objectives of the present studies are as follows:

- To find out language preferred for research publication
- To know research method used for publication
- To know awareness about citation styles, impact factor and plagiarism/copyright software among librarians
- To find out interested research area of librarians
- To identify communication channels used in research
- To recognize publication trend among librarians

SCOPE AND LIMITATIONS OF THE STUDY

Present study is limited to only 46 college librarians in Jalgaon district which are affiliated to North Maharashtra University; study is limited only to Arts, Commerce, and Science colleges during 2008-2012.

METHODOLOGY

Present study has done with the help of survey method. Survey research is distinguished by its reliance upon the selection of person from large and small population and the making of observation. So that inference can be applied to present population. A population is may be group of person, objects institution or other units that passes at least on common characteristics.

DATA ANALYSIS

The total numbers of Academic Libraries in North Maharashtra University, Jalgaon (NMU) are 46. Out of them 34 librarians have responded, 12 librarians have not responded.

Gender Wise Publication Trends

Respondents were asked about Gender. The response received presented in Table 1.

Table 1. Gender wise Publication Trends

Gender	*No. of Respondents*	*Percentage (%)*
Male	28	82.35
Female	06	17.65
Total	34	100

It can be observed from table 1 that majority 28 (82.35%) of the respondents were male and 06 (17.65%) of the respondents were females.

Purpose of Research

Respondents were asked about purpose of research. The responses received are presented in table no. 2 and figure no. 1.

Table 2. Purpose of Research

Purpose	*No. of Respondents*	*Percentage (%)*
To get promotion	30	88.24
To upgrade qualifications	12	35.29
To maintain social/professional status	10	29.41
To upgrade knowledge	15	44.12

Note : Multiple answers were permitted

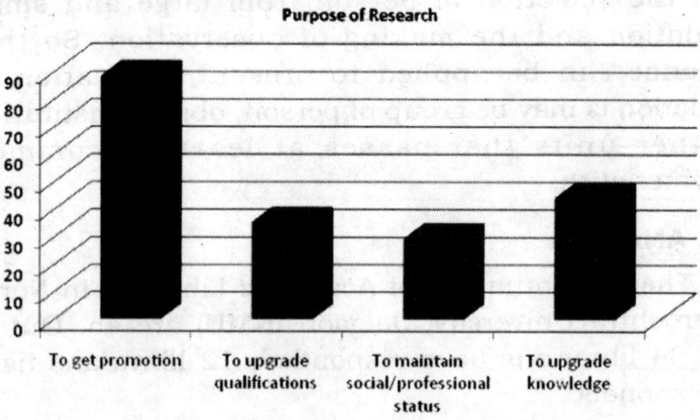

Fig. 1. Purpose of Research

It is depicted from the above table no. 2 and figure no. 1 that majority 30 (88.24%) of the respondents did research 'to get promotion' followed by 15 (44.12%) 'To upgrade knowledge', 12 (35.29%) 'To upgrade qualifications' and 10 (29.41%) did research 'To maintain social/professional status'.

Language Preferred for Research Publication

Respondents were asked about language preferred for research publication. The responses received are presented in table no. 3.

Table 3. Language Preferred for Research Publication

Language	*No. of Respondents*	*Percentage (%)*
English	18	52.94
Marathi	16	47.06
Hindi	-	-
Total	34	100

Table no. 3 shows that majority of the respondents i.e. 18 (52.94%) preferred English language for research publication. 16 (47.06%) of them write in Marathi language. Nobody used Hindi language for research publication.

Research Method used for Publication

Respondents were asked about research method used for publication. The responses received are presented in table no. 4.

Table 4. Research Method used for Publication

Method	*No. of Respondents*	*Percentage (%)*
Survey	13	38.24
Descriptive	10	29.41
Case Study	11	32.35
Total	34	100

Table no. 4 indicates that maximum 13 (38.24%) of the respondents prefer Survey method. Whereas 11 (32.35%) respondents were interested in Case study. 10 (29.41%) of the respondents used Descriptive method for research publication.

Awareness of Citation Styles Manual

Respondents were asked about awareness of citation styles manual. The responses received are presented in table no. 5 and figure no. 2.

Table 5. Awareness about citation styles manual

Awareness	*No. of Respondents*	*Percentage (%)*
Yes	32	94.12
No	02	05.88
Total	34	100

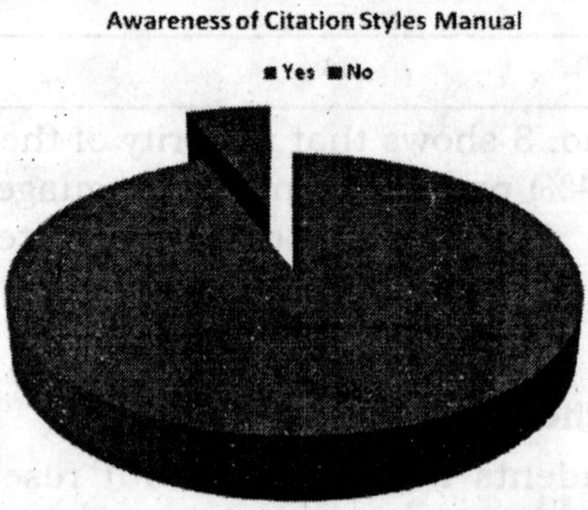

Fig. 2. Awareness of citation styles manual

From the table no. 5 and figure no. 2, it is clear that maximum respondent i.e. 32 (94.12%) were aware about various citations styles manual. Only 02 (05.88%) of the respondents were not aware about citation styles.

Number of Citations Used in Research Paper

Respondents were asked about number of citations used in research paper. The responses received are presented in table no. 6.

Table 6. Number of Citations used in research paper

Citations	*No. of Respondents*	*Percentage (%)*
1-10	19	55.88
10-20	08	23.53
20-30	05	14.71
More than 30	02	05.88
Total	34	100

It is evident from table no. 6 that majority 19 (55.88%) of the respondents used 1 to 10 citations in one research paper. 08 (23.53%) of them used 10 to 20 citations, 05 (14.71%) cite 20 to 30 references in research paper. Whereas 02 (05.88%) of the respondents used more than 30 citations in research paper.

Citation Style Used for the Research Paper

Respondents were asked about citation style used for the research paper. The responses received are presented in table no. 7 and figure no. 3.

Table 7. Citation style used for the research paper

Citation Style	*No. of Respondents*	*Percentage (%)*
APA	19	55.88
MLA	07	20.59
Chicago	04	11.76
Harvard	02	05.88
Not using any citation style	02	05.88
Total	34	100

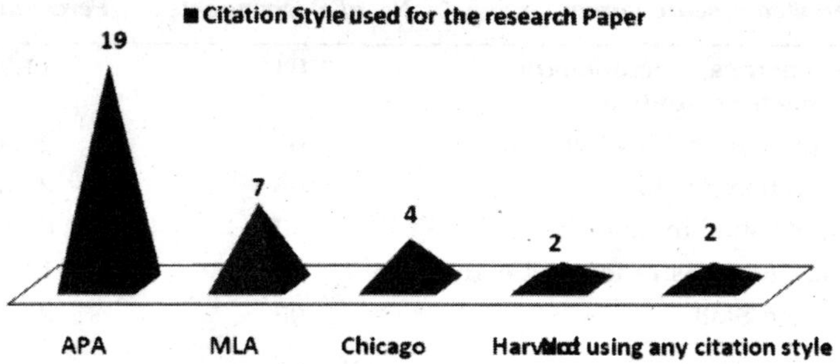

Fig. 3. Citation style used for the research paper

It is observed from table no. 7 and figure no. 3 that 21 (55.88%) of the respondents used American Psychological Association (APA) referencing style. 07 (20.59%) used MLA citation style, 04 (11.76%) used Chicago and 02 (05.88%) of the respondents prefer Harvard referencing style. 02 (05.88%) of the respondents not using any citation style.

Awareness about Plagiarism/Copyright Software

Respondents were asked about awareness about plagiarism/copyright software. The responses received are presented in table no. 8.

Table 8. Awareness about plagiarism/ copyright software

Awareness	*No. of Respondents*	*Percentage (%)*
Yes	15	44.12
No	19	55.88
Total	34	100

It is found from table no. 8 that majority 19 (55.88%) of the respondents were not aware about plagiarism/ copyright software. While 15 (44.12%) of them were aware about plagiarism/copyright software.

Interested Research Area

Respondents were asked about interested research area. The responses received are presented in table no. 9 and figure no. 4.

Table 9. Interested research area

Interested research area	*No. of Respondents*	*Percentage (%)*
Bibliometrics/Scientometrics/ Webometrics Studies	04	11.76
Information Seeking Behaviour	09	26.47
Information Needs	08	23.53
IT Application in Libraries	23	67.65
Library Administration and management	05	14.71
Librarian Skill	08	23.53

Library Automation/Digital Library	17	50.00
Library Services	12	35.29
Electronic Resources	13	38.24
Web 2.0	06	17.65
Consortia	04	11.76
As per requirement	08	23.53

Note : Multiple answers were permitted

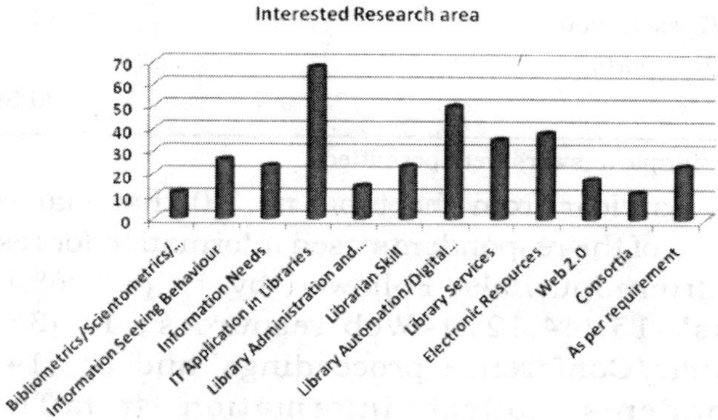

Fig. 4. Interested Research Area

It can be seen from the data presented in the table no. 9 and figure no. 4that 23 (67.65%) of the respondents interested in 'IT Application in Libraries' research area. Followed by 17 (50%) 'Library Automation/Digital Library', 09 (26.47%) 'Information Seeking Behaviour', 08 (23.53%) respondents has 'Information Needs' and 'Librarian Skill' interested area, respectively.

Communication Channels Used in Research Work

Respondents were asked about communication channels used in research work. The responses received are presented in table no. 10.

Table 10. Communication channels used in research work

Communication Channels	*No. of Respondents*	*Percentage (%)*
Journals (Periodicals)	23	67.65
Books	16	47.06
Seminar/Conference proceedings	12	35.29
Web resources	15	44.12
Theses/Dissertation	05	14.71
Research Reports	-	-
Any others	07	20.59

Note : Multiple answers were permitted

It is clear from the table no. 10 that majority 23 (67.65%) of the respondents used information for research work from Journals. Followed by 16 (47.06%) used 'Books', 15 (44.12%) 'Web resources', 12 (35.29%) 'Seminar/Conference proceedings' and 05 (14.71%) respondents collect information from'Theses/ Dissertation'. Nobody used research reports as a communication channel.

Publication Trends

Respondents were asked about publication preference/trends. The responses received are presented in table no. 11.

Table 11. Publication Trends

Publication Preference	*No. of Respondents*	*Percentage (%)*
Printed Journals	11	32.35
Conference Proceedings	24	70.59
Online Journals	06	17.65
Chapter in Edited Books	07	20.59
Edited Books	06	17.65
Textbooks	03	08.82
Reference Books	07	20.59

Note : Multiple answers were permitted

It can be seen from the data presented in the table no. 11,24 (70.59%) of the respondents published research work in Conference proceedings. 11 (32.35%) of the respondents publish articles in printed journals. 07 (20.59%) of them publish research as a 'Chapter in edited books' and 'reference books', respectively. 06 (17.65%) of them publish research work in 'online journals' and 'edited books', respectively. Only 03 (08.82%) of the respondents write/publish 'textbooks'.

Awareness about Impact Factor

Respondents were asked about awareness about impact factor. The responses received are presented in table no. 12.

Table 12. Awareness about Impact Factor

Awareness	*No. of Respondents*	*Percentage (%)*
Yes	22	64.71
No	12	35.29
Total	34	100

It is depicted from the above table no. 12 that22 (64.71%) of the respondents were aware about Impact factor and 12 (35.29%) of them were not aware about Impact factor.

MAJOR FINDINGS AND CONCLUSION

- It's found that majority 30 (88.24%) of the respondents did research 'to get promotion'.
- Majority of the respondents i.e. 18 (52.94%) preferred English language for research publication.
- Maximum 13 (38.24%) of the respondents prefer Survey method.
- It is clear from the study 32 (94.12%) respondents were aware about various citations styles manual.
- Majority 19 (55.88%) of the respondents used 1 to 10 citations in one research paper.

- It is depicted from the study 21 (55.88%) of the respondents used American Psychology Association (APA) referencing style.
- Majority 19 (55.88%) of the respondents were not aware about plagiarism/copyright software.
- Maximum 23 (67.65%) of the respondents interested in 'IT Application in Libraries' research area.
- Majority 23 (67.65%) of the respondents used information for research work from Journals.
- It is revealed that 24 (70.59%) of the respondents published research work in Conference proceedings.
- It is depicted that 22 (64.71%) of the respondents were aware about Impact factor.

REFERENCES

- Bala, Adarsh & Kumari, Santosh (2014). Research performance of national institutes of technology (NITS) of India during 2001-2010: a bibliometric analysis. In I.K. Ravichandrarao& A. Neelameghan (Eds.), *Scientometrics*(pp. 113-132). New Delhi, India: EssEss Publication.
- Baskaran, C. (2013). Research Growth Trend and Author Collaboration of Alagappa University in India during 1999-2011. *International Journal of Library and Information Studies*, *3*(1), 57-64.
- http://www.merriam-webster.com/dictionary/publication retrieved on 27 January 2016.
- http://www.thefreedictionary.com/publication retrieved on 27 January 2016.
- Ismail, Muhammad, Ahmad, Sajjad&Subpouto, Nisar (2015). Library and Information Science Researchin the Khyber Pakhtunkhwa, Pakistan. *Pakistan Journal of Library and Information Science, 46*(2), 25-33.
- Khandare, R.B. (2014). Research Productivity of Academic Librarians Affiliated to North Maharashtra University, Jalgaon: A Scientometrics Study (2008-2012). Minor Research Project submitted to University Grants Commission Western Regional Office, Pune.
- Kothari, C.R. (2010). *Research Methodology: Methods and*

Techniques. New Delhi: New age International Publishers.

- Krishna, K.M. (2011). Studies on doctoral theses in agricultural sciences of Rajasthan Agricultural University, Bikaner. *SRELS Journal of Information Management,48*(4), 459-464.
- Kumbar, B.D. &Gupta, B.M. (2013). A comparative study of Mysore University and Karnatak University in S&T: Research Output, Citation Impact and Collaboration during 2001-10. *SRELS Journal of Information Management, 50*(5), 573-590.
- *National Workshop on Natural Language Processing & Image Processing* [Brochure]. (2016). Jalgaon, India: North Maharashtra University.
- Nwaogu, Humphrey O. &Ifijeh, Goodluck I. (2014). Application of Scientific Methods in Library and Information Research: A Case Study of Librarians in South East Nigeria. *International Research: Journal of Library & Information Science, 4*(1), 45-54.
- Raju, P. Soma (2008). Research in Library and Information Science. *PEARL - A Journal of Library and Information Science, 2*(1), 3-9.
- Sagar, Anil, Kademani, B.S. &Bhanumurthy, K. (2014). Agriculture Research in India: A Scientometric Mapping of Publications. *DESIDOC Journal of Library & Information Technology, 34*(3), 206-222.
- Sakharkar, ShaliniMunindra (2011). Research Productivity of Doctoral Thesis Awarded By R. T. M. Nagpur University, Nagpur 2005-2008: A Study. *Library Progress (International), 31*(2), 235-250.
- Sevukan, R. & Sharma, Jaideep (2008). Bibliometric Analysis of Research Output of Biotechnology Faculties in Some Indian Central Universities. *DESIDOC Journal of Library & Information Technology, 28*(6), 11-20.
- Sivakumaren K.S., Jeyaprakash B., Swaminathan S. &Karthikeyan G. (2012). Publication pattern of library and information science professionals: a study. *International Journal of Information Dissemination andTechnology, 2*(3), 160-165.
- Sonwane, Shashank, Adhe, Govind&Vaishnav, AA (2012). Science Indicators of Scientists in Dr. Babasaheb Ambedkar Marathwada University, Aurangabad. Online retrieved from http://inflibnet.ac.in.

- Sudhier, K.G.P. (2013). Research publication trends among physicists of the Indian Institute of Science and the University of Kerala: A bibliometrics study. *International Journal of Information Dissemination andTechnology,3*(2), 99-106.
- Waghmare, S.S. (2009). Publication Patterns of Faculties of Languages in Marathwada Region (M.Phil. Dissertation). Dr. BabasahebAmbedkarMarathwada University Aurangabad, Maharashtra, India.
- Wani, Z.A., Hameed, O. &Iqbal, A. (2013). Research productivity of medicos at All India Institute of Medical Sciences (AIIMS). *International Journal of Information Dissemination and Technology, 3*(2), 107-113.

23

Scholarly Communication and Evaluation through Metrics: From Librametrics to Altmetrics

Prof. B Ramesh Babu

Professor (Retd), University of Madras, Chennai & Former Visiting Professor, Mahasarakham University, Thailand

INTRODUCTION

The Scholarly Communication is an important aspect of research process and it is an age old activity practiced by the academics since the advent of research activity. It is the process used by scholars to share the results of their research and an essential part of any scientific research, which has an important role in the social and economic development of our society. Scholarly communication can be defined as "the system through which research and other scholarly writings are created, evaluated for quality, disseminated to the scholarly community, and preserved for future use. The system includes both formal means of communication, such as publication in peer-reviewed journals, and informal channels, such as electronic listservs" *(ACRL, 2004)*. In a simple terms, it is the life-blood of the university's teaching and research mission and reflects the process of academics, scholars and researchers sharing and publishing their research findings so that they are available to the wider academic community (such as University academics) and beyond. Borgman (2000) describes scholarly communication as "the study of how scholars in any field (e.g. physical, biological, social and behavioural sciences, humanities and technology) use and disseminate information through formal and informal channels. The study of scholarly communication includes the growth of scholarly information, the relationships among research areas and disciplines, the information needs and uses of individual user groups, and the relationships among formal and informal methods of communication". The measurement and assessment of scholarly impact have been experiencing rapid changes over the past two decades, thanks to developments in how scholarship is communicated and advances in the tools and techniques that may be used to study scholarly communication.

METRICS STUDIES

Librarians and Information Science professionals have adopted a number of quantitative methods such as metric studies in the recent years to measure the literary output and evaluate library resources and services more objectively and effectively. The word 'Metrics' indicates the science of metre which means the measurement. It is derived from the Latin or Greek word *'metrics'* or *'metrikos'* meaning "measurement". Webster's Comprehensive Dictionary of English Language defined metrics as "the mathematical theory of measurement". The measurement involves counting artifacts to the production and use of information, and arriving conclusions from the counts. Metrics reveres to ways to quantitatively and objectively measure the scholarly significance of publications.

Metric studies are one of the primary areas of Information Science research in the recent years. The terms like 'Librametrics', 'Bibliometrics', 'Informetrics' and 'Scientometrics' have been used synonymously in order to study the growth of literature in a discipline and other aspects of literature quantitatively. Metric studies in Library and Information Science is typically used to measure scholarly communication; identify research trends and growth of knowledge; identify users of different subjects; estimate comprehensiveness of secondary periodicals; forecast past, present and future publishing trends; identify authorship and its trends in documents on various subjects; measure productivity of publishers, individual authors, organisations, country or that of an entire discipline (Kumar, 2003). Research contributions from statistical sciences, scientific visualization, network analysis, text mining, and information retrieval have provided tools and techniques to investigate metric phenomena and to assess scholarly impact in new ways.

The chronological development of metric studies is as follows:

Table 1. Chronological Development of Metric Studies

S. No	*Name of Metric Study*	*Year of origin*	*Originator*
1	Statistical Bibliography	1922	H W Hulmein
2	Librametry	1948	S R Ranganathan
3	Bibliometrics	1969	Alan Pritchard
4	Scientometrics	1969	Vassily V. Naimov & ZM Mulchenkoin
5	Informetrics	1979	Seigal Lackert & Otta Nacke
6	Webometrics	1997	T C Almind & P. Ingwersen
7	Altmetrics	2010	J. Priem, D. Taraborelli, P. Groth, & C. Neylon

LIBRAMETRICS

Quantitative method applied to library management and services have come to be known as Librametry. The term 'Librametry' was coined by Dr S R Ranganathan (1948) which was historically appeared first and perhaps seemed proper to streamline the services of librarianship, that denotes "Measurement of various library activities and services using mathematical and statistical techniques". Raising (1962) defined it as "The assembling and interpretation of statistics relating to books and periodicals....to demonstrate historical movements, to determine national and universal research, and to ascertain in many local situations the general use of books and journals". It is regarded as one of the classical definitions of bibliometrics. Merton and Garfield (1963) defined it as the "Field of inquiry given over to the quantitative analysis of science and scientific field".

In 1948, S R Ranganathan suggested, at the ASLIB Conference in Lamington Spa, that it was necessary for librarians to develop "Librametry" on the lines of biometry, econometry and psychometry, since "many of the matters connected with library work and services involve large numbers". Despite his attempts to define the scope of Librametry, the field did not develop until the early 1970s. Ranganathan, again in 1969 in a paper to the Annual Seminar of the Documentation Research and Training Centre (DRTC), Bangalore, illustrated with some examples of the application of statistics to library work and service.

He applied work study and operations Research Methodology in exhaustively analysing Library routines to arrive at daily, weekly and periodical groupings, and ended the analysis with a library Staff Formula. He suggested the use of Librametry for determining the optimum size of a service library, design of library building, size of reading rooms and so on. Even in classification and cataloguing there was scope for Librametry, such as, determining the most helpful facet sequence through statistical analysis of readers, queries, use of sampling technique in testing the accuracy of catalogue entries, finding out difference between cataloguers and making the rules more rigorous and so on. Librametry is not a mere theoretical statistical formulation, nor is it information retrieval problems emanating from automation. It is born out of the Use of Resources, User's habits, service aspects, Literature Analyses, surveys, Citation Studies, Grading of periodicals, Inter-Library Cooperation, professional satisfaction of Librarians and Information Scientists etc. In short, whatever is quantifiable in a Library and Information Centre, that yields results or formulae, can be termed as Librametry. Measurement of library activities and results of its services would from the core of Librametry. Essentially the method is an objective analysis that puts down quantitative phenomenon as data, measuring by a uniform norm, and examines the inter-relationships of the assembled data, drawing formulae of behaviour maxima- minima limits for the phenomena. In simple terms, Librametry is a measurement of various library activities and services using mathematical and statistical techniques.

BIBLIOMETRICS

The term 'Bibliometrics coined by Alan Pritchard in the year 1969. This term is mainly used to study 'the application of mathematics and statistical methods to books and other media of communication of all aspects of the literature of science and technology. Thereafter the word Bibliometrics had wide recognition by LIS professional and others. Bibliometrics is an academic discipline and much research is being carried out for a quantitative study of the various aspects of literature of a given subject. It is a branch of Information Science which analyses quantitatively the published information based on bibliographic data elements. It is the study and measurement of the patterns of all forms of published knowledge. It is coined to describe the studies dealing with the quantification of written communication. It analysis is the quantitative study of a subject growth by using bibliometric techniques. Many attempts have been made to define the term bibliometrics and its analogous terms since the use of the term 'statistical bibliography' The purpose of statistical bibliography is to "Shed lights on the process of written communication and of the nature and course of development of a discipline, by means of counting and analysis its various facets of written communication" (Hulme ,1923).

Sengupta (1990) viewed bibliometrics as the "Organisation, classification and quantitative evaluation of publication patterns of all macro and micro communications along with their authorship by mathematical and statistical calculus. Bibliometrics is a type of research method used in Library and Information Science. It is nothing but the application of mathematical and statistical methods to books and other printed media, process of written communication and of the nature and course of discipline. It is a tool to measure scientific research output, has seen major changes over the last five decades and has emerged as an established filed of research in library and information science. Researchers may use bibliometric methods of evaluation to determine the influence of a single writer, for example, or to describe the relationship between two or more writers or works.

Bibliometrics provides information about the structure of knowledge and the way it is communicated; measure the publication pattern of all forms of written communication; provides quantitative evaluation of publication patterns of all macro and micro subjects; indicates literature growth rate and pattern in macro and micro levels; provides evaluative measures to indicate individual countries output; indicates the citation pattern of literature and studies the use of documents.

Bibliometrics has become a standard tool of science policy and research management. All significant compilations of science indicators heavily rely on publication and citation statistics and more sophisticated bibliometric techniques.

Three laws became the cornerstones of bibliometrics. They are:

1. Lotka's law dealing with productivity of authors of scientific papers;
2. Zipf's law dealing with frequency occurrence of words in along text; and
3. Bradford's law about the scattering of articles.

SCIENTOMETRICS

Vassily Nalimov coined the term "Scientometrics" in the 1960s, this term has grown in popularity and is used to describe the study of Science: growth, structure, interrelationships and productivity. Scientometrics is defined as "the study of the measurement of scientific and technological progress". It is related to and has overlapped interests with bibliometrics, Scientometrics and Informetrics. It is an emerging thrust area of research in the field of Library and Information Science. It is a tool by which the state of science and technology can be observed through the traces of communication in the science technology system, most notably the published documents which comprise books, monographs, reports, theses, papers in serials and periodicals. It is referred to as a science of science; it is a distinct, recognized and well-established scholarly field with its own identity, history, theory and methodology. Scientometric analysis is being used very frequently for evaluating the research activities and impact from the macro level to the level of individual scientists as well as mapping a scientific discipline. It is a discipline which analyses scientific publications and citations appended to the papers to gain an understanding of the structure and growth of science at global level, performance of a country in a particular domain, performance of institutions, departments / divisions and scientific eminence of an individual scientist. It is considered as the study of the quantitative aspects of science as a discipline or economic activity. It is part of the sociology of science and has application to science policymaking. It involves quantitative studies of scientific activities, including among others, publication, and so overlaps bibliometrics to some extent. It is the quantitative study of scientific communication-challenges science and technology studies by demonstrating that organization knowledge production and control is amenable to measurement.

Scientometric indicators are important metrics to evaluate the quantity and quality of the scientific output. (Durieux and Gevenois 2010). These indicators provide numerical scales that are intended to quantitatively determine the value of scientific research and the scholarly publication in which that research is published. A set of commonly used scientometric indicators such as number of publications and citation rate is used to identify the comparative strengths and weakness of selected disciplines (Davarpanah 2010).

Haitun (1983) classified the scientometric methods as follows:

- Statistical method with measures
  - — Number of discoveries
  - — Number of journals
  - — Number of institutions
  - — Number of scientists
  - — Frequency of co-authorships etc.,
- Publication counting with a measure
  - — Number of research products (articles, monographs, patent descriptions, reports etc.,)
- Citation Index with a measure

— Number of citations

A more modern classification is by W. Glanzel (2003) who classifies Scientometrics and its methods into the following structural entities:

Dynamical scientometrics: handling with the construction of comprehensive models of growing of the scientific knowledge, the aging of the scientific information, the development of the citation processes, etc.;

Structural scientometrics : corresponding mainly with the problem "mapping of the cognitive structure of scientific knowledge", based on methods as cocitation, bibliographic coupling or coword analysis;

Evaluative scientometrics: with a subject the assessment in the sphere of scientific research, and for the purposes of the science policy;

Prognostic scientometrics : drawing visions about the development of the science processes in the future.

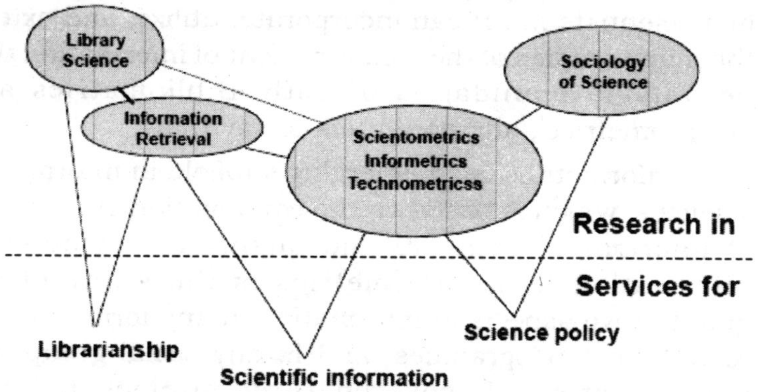

Fig. 1. Links of bibliometrics with related fields and application services (Glanzel, 2003).

The relationship as to how bibliometrics/ scientometrics is linked with related fields and application services are shown in Figure 1. According to Glanzel, present-day bibliometric research is aimed at the following three main target-groups that clearly determine topics and sub-areas of "contemporary bibliometrics" such as bibliometricians (Methodology), scientific disciplines (Scientific information) and science policy and management (science policy) and finally he has provided a pictorial representation of how bibliometrics/ scientometrics is linked with related fields and application services (Glanzel, 2003).

INFORMETRICS

In 1979, the term Informetrics was coined by Nacke which deals with the quantitative study of information. It is an emerging subfield in Information Science, which is based on the combination of advances of information retrieval and quantitative studies of information flow. The Informetrics is (Tague – Sutcliffe, 1992) "the study of the quantitative aspects of information in any form, not just records or bibliographies, and in any social group, not just scientists ..... It can incorporate, utilize, and extend the many studies of the measurement of information that lie outside boundaries of both 'Bibliometrics and Scientometrics', and continues to say that".

Informetrics is an emerging subfield in information sciences, which is based on the combination of advances of information retrieval and quantitative studies of information flow. Informetrics is the study of the quantitative aspects of information in any form, not just records or bibliographies, and in any social group, not just scientists. It covered three subject areas in Information Science in which such quantitative research takes place such as : Information users and information usage; Evaluation of information system; and Information itself. It deals with the electronic media and thus includes topics like statistical analysis of science text and hypertext systems, library circulations, information use measures in electronic libraries, models of information generation processes and quantitative aspects of information retrieval. The retrieval performance measures have been studied by information retrieval theorists in Information and Computer Sciences' for both theoretical and practical aspects. Thus, it can be said that the scope of 'Informetrics' is both practical and theoretical. However, the primary emphasis has been on the development of mathematical models, and a secondary emphasis on the derivation of measures for the diverse phenomena studies. The value of a model lies in its ability to summarize, in terms of a few parameters, the characteristics of many data sites: the overall shapes, concentration, scatter, and the way the data sets change over time, such models provide a basis for practical decision-making.

WEBOMETRICS

Since the mid-1990s the nature and properties of the World-Wide Web have been increasingly investigated by applying modern informetric methodologies. The term webometrics is a coinage from two modern English words, "web" and "metric". The word web is a short of World Wide Web. The Dictionary of Science defined web as: "a hypermedia system... that allows users to view and retrieve information from information from "documents" containing links'. On other hand, metrics has to do with counting or measurement. Webometrics is the new discipline that intends to apply Bibliometrics, Scientometrics, Informetrics and Cybermetric techniques to the process of scientific communication, which takes place on Internet in order to know and describe them from a quantitative point of view. Webometrics, the quantitative study of web related phenomena, originated in the realisation, that methods originally designed for bibliometric analysis of scientific journal article citation patterns, could be applied to the web with commercial search engines providing raw data.

Webometrics is the study of the quantitative aspects of the construction and use of information resources, structures and technologies on the Web drawing on bibliometric and informetric approaches (Björneborn & Ingwersen, 2004, p. 1217; Thelwall & Vaughan, 2004). This field mainly concerns the analysis of web pages as if they were documents.

Webometrics *also called cybermetrics* is a relatively new information discipline that aims to quantitatively measure web phenomena. By web phenomena it means the number of hyperlinks on a web site, their structure and patterns of use by web users, and their reciprocal links by other websites. Generally speaking, this data can be mined by search engine websites although several experts in webometrics recommend the use of *data cleansing* heuristics to ensure their reliability. The web and its linkages are not unlike library catalogues in their infinite variety of connections; however, as most librarians are well aware, there are some challenges in examining these connections, and elucidating impact metrics from them.

Studies of the Web have been named as "Webometrics" (Almind and Ingwersen, 1997). Webometrics, then, describes counting or measuring web resources in mathematical value. It defines the extent of web usage for research. Since the web allows documents to be linked together, the measurement of these links forms the fabric of Webometrics. It has been defined as web "measured on the basis of web characteristics or presence on the Internet by (NUC, 2006). Therefore webometrics is based on two indicators namely,

- Volume of published materials of institutions/ individual on the web, and
- The visibility and impact of the web pages measured by the citation (site citations or links they receive).

Bjorneborn (2004) defined Webometrics as "the

study of the quantitative aspects of the construction and use of information resources, structures and technologies on the World Wide Web drawing on Bibliometrics and Informetrics approaches". This definition covers the construction side and usage side of the web which embrace the four main areas of Webometrics study. They are:

a. Web page content analysis;
b. Web link structure analysis (e.g. Hyperlink, self link and External link);
c. Web usage analysis (e.g. exploiting log files for users searching and browsing behaviour) ;and
d. Web technology analysis (including search engine performance).

The Webometrics study interprets in a broad sense encompassing research from disciplines outside of Information Science such as Communication Studies, Statistical Physics and Computer Science etc. This study will concentrate on types of link analysis; link structures, Web Impact Factor etc. It also covers the other Webometric areas that Information Scientists have been involved with, including web log file analysis. In this text Webometircs is used to denote a heritage to Bibliometrics and Informetrics and to stress an Information Science perspective on web studies.

CYBERMETRICS

Cybermetrics is a both an Electronic-only Journal and a Virtual items to the study of the quantitative analysis of scholarly and scientific communications in the Internet. It provides open to world-wide researchers to publish and discuss their findings. Internet offers them new and increased capabilities to distribute their results to a greater audience. "Cybermetrics" is an electronic journal <http://www.cindoc.csic.es/cybermetrics/cybermetrics. html>, which has been founded by Isidro Aguillo.

CYBERMETRICS VIS – A – VIS WEBOMETRICS

Cybermetrics has been proposed for analysis of web documents before the term Webometrics. Cybermetrics is "the study of the quantitative aspects of the construction and use of information resources, structures and technologies on the whole internet, drawing on bibliometric and informetric approaches". Cybermetrics thus encompasses statistical studies of discussion groups, mailing lists and other computer mediated communication on the internet including the web. The breadth of coverage of Cybermetrics is limited and where as webometrics implies large overlaps with proliferating computer science based approaches in analysis of web contents, link structures and web usage and web technologies.

RELATIONSHIP BETWEEN VARIOUS METRICS

In Figure 2, the relationship among the various metrics is depicted clearly. Sizes of the overlapping ellipses are made for the sake of clarity only. If one looks at the relationship between Informetrics, Bibliometrics, Scientometrics, Cybermetrics and Webometrics, can observe that Webometrics associates with Bibliometrics and overlaps Scientometrics to an extent. Further it shows that the field of Informetrics embracing the overlapping fields of Bibliometrics and Scientometrics. In this context, the field of Webometrics may be seen as entirely encompassed by Bibliometrics, because web documents, whether text or multimedia, are recorded information stored on the web servers. Further, in the figure the field of Cybermetrics exceeds the boundaries of Bibliometrics, because some activities in cyberspace are normally not recorded, but communicated simultaneously as in chart rooms. One of the most visible outputs of Webometrics is the ranking of Educational Institutions based upon their web sites and online impact. The inclusion of Webometrics expands the field of Bibliometrics, as Webometrics inevitably will contribute with further methodological developments of specific approaches. As ideas rooted in Bibliometrics, Scientometrics and Informetrics have contributed to the emergence of Webometrics.

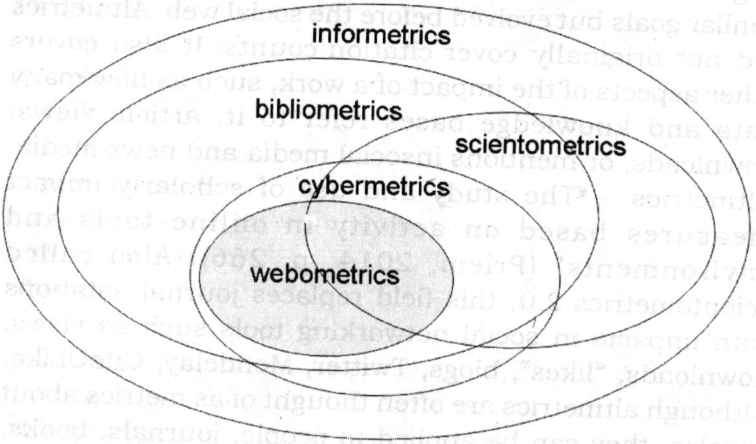

Fig. 2. Relationship between Informetrics, Bibliometrics, Scientometrics, Cybermetrics, and Webometrics

(Source: Thelwall, Vaughan and Bjorneborn, 2005)

ALTMETRICS

In scholarly and scientific publishing, Altmetrics are non-traditional metrics proposed as an alternative to more traditional citation impact metrics, such as impact factor and *h*-index. The field of altmetrics was created by a group of US and European researchers led by Jason Priem in to study the potential to develop indicators for aspects of the impact or uptake of academic articles through indicators extracted from the social web, using APIs (Priem & Hemminger, 2010; Priem, Taraborelli, Groth, & Neylon, 2010). Altmetrics are new metrics proposed as an alternative to the widely used journal impact factor and personal citation indices like the h-index, g-index or i-10 index.

The term altmetrics was proposed in 2010, as a generalization of article level metrics. Although altmetrics are often thought of as metrics about articles, they can be applied to people, journals, books, data sets, presentations, videos, source code repositories, web pages, etc. They are related to Webometrics, which had similar goals but evolved before the social web. Altmetrics did not originally cover citation counts. It also covers other aspects of the impact of a work, such as how many data and knowledge bases refer to it, article views, downloads, or mentions insocial media and news media. Altmetrics – "The study and use of scholarly impact measures based on activity in online tools and environments" (Priem, 2014, p. 266). Also called scientometrics 2.0, this field replaces journal citations with impacts in social networking tools such as views, downloads, "likes", blogs, Twitter, Mendelay, CiteULike. Although altmetrics are often thought of as metrics about articles, they can be applied to people, journals, books, data sets, presentations, videos, source code repositories, web pages, etc. Altmetrics does not cover just citation counts, but also other aspects of the impact of a work, such as how many data and knowledge bases refer to it, article views, download, or mentions in social media and news media. Altmetrics are a very broad group of metrics, capturing various parts of impact a paper or work can have. It demonstrates one aspect of the changing landscape of scholarly and academic production, dialogue and use.

Altmetrics had become possible because reference sharing sites, such as Mendeley, and social network sites like Twitter were being used by significant numbers of people to share research, creating a large public body of data about the use and sharing of academic articles. Moreover, the companies owing the social web sites often made data collection from them by computer programs possible by offering public API access. Given that academic articles are normally evaluated on a large scale by counting citations to them, two of the key promises of altmetrics were that they could reflect wider uses of articles than just those that led to citations (e.g., educational uses, and uses by practitioners) and that they could be collected much more quickly than could citations, so that altmetrics could be used as indicators for articles soon after publication even though citations might take a year to start to accumulate. This is particularly important for information retrieval since people are often most concerned with research that has been recently published (e.g., for horizon scanning).

APPLICATION / UTILITY OF METRIC STUDIES

Metric studies are mostly empirical in nature and they are mostly centered around presentation of facts and data. These studies have increasingly been used in the recent years and are useful to understand the evolution of literature or trends in a particular field or within a geographical area. Bibliometric research includes studies pertaining to scattering of articles over journals, growth of literature, obsolescence of documents, productivity and impact of research, distribution of scientific publications by country, by language, citation studies, and so on. Most of these studies are pertaining to countries, user groups, institutions, disciplines and documents. It has recently enlarged into informetrics. It covers all quantitative analysis of information transfer, irrespective of the media. Bibliometrics furnishes possible methods by which significant features of literature may be delineated and its working monitored. In fact, bibliometrics has grown out of the realisation that literature is growing and changing at a rate with which no librarian or information worker or a scientist equipped with traditional bibliographic methods and skills could keep abreast. The Bibliometric analysis has received adequate attention in the recent years and it has been widely applied to evaluate the research performance of the scientists and the growth of various disciplines of science. Further, bibliometrics could be used in the identification of emerging research areas.

Bibliometric and other metric techniques are now being used for a variety of purposes like determination of various scientific indicators, evaluation of scientific output, selection of journals for libraries and even forecasting potential Nobel Laureates. Bibliometrics is therefore the statistical distributions of the processes relating to information management in libraries and information centres based on any quantitative analysis of the characteristics and behaviour of documents, library staff and library users. In recent times, application of bibliometric techniques to various aspects of information centres is on the rise. These studies are useful for the efficient management of information sources and services.

Scientometric analysis can be used as a strategic tool to examine the impact and trends in various branches of knowledge. Scientometrics becomes a very perspective research field in the general studies of science, providing powerful and effective instruments for analyses and evaluations in the sphere of science as a significant accelerator of the economic growth and social prosperity. These studies can help libraries to understand their local community's journal usage patterns and to identify the most influential journals to subscribe in a particular subject area. The study of research output in the form of scientific papers and its citations have been increasingly applied to monitor scientific performance. These metrics methods have been gaining recognition and importance in the recent decades. The results of these studies are increasingly being applied to manage the library and information resources and services more effectively and efficiently. The popularity in the adaptation of metric techniques in various disciplines stimulated stupendous growth of literature on bibliometrics and its related areas. These techniques are now being vigorously pursued and with the result, it has been found that one-fourth of all the articles published in Library and Information Science Periodicals are on bibliometrics and its related topics. It has also been found that many of the Social Science periodicals are also carrying a large number of articles on these metric studies.

CONCLUSION

In the field of Library and Information Science, the applications of quantitative techniques are very popular today. Bibliometrics is just analogous to Ranganathan's 'Librametrics', , the Russian concept of 'Scientometrics', FID's 'Informetrics', Webometrics, Altmetrics and to some other well established sub-disciplines such as Econometrics, Psychometrics, Sociometrics, Biometrics, Technometrics, Chemometrics, Cliometrics, Eucametrics, Spintronics etc., where mathematical and statistical methods have been systematically applied to study and solve problems in their respective fields. As Kopelock (1978) points out, during the period 1969-1977 about 52 different terms have been used to describe bibliometrics. The variations of metrics ranging from Librametrics to Altmetrics are found to be very useful tools for evaluating the effectiveness and utilization of published literary output on any branch of knowledge. All metrics are categorized in three classes on the basis of respective time of inception, i.e. classical metrics, neo-classical metrics and modern metrics. The four metrics, i.e. librametrics, bibliometrics, scientometrics and informetrics are categorized under classical metrics. Cybermetrics is regarded as neo-classical metrics while remaining others evolved in 21st century are recognized as modern metrics... Continuous conceptual progress and necessary amendments in the ideas like altmetrics, article-level metrics, sociometrics etc., are going on to achieve new dimensions in the areas of performance measurement and impact analysis of research and scholarly communication (Dutta, 2014). In recent years these metric techniques present themselves as a key to objective evaluation of scholarly communication. The application of these quantitative measures to scientific research has highlighted the contributions of countries, institutions, journals and individual researchers. The usefulness of metrics for estimating impact is controversial, but the community shows a clear need, funders demand measurable on the impact of their spending. Like other metrics, Altmetrics are prone to self-citation, gaming, and other mechanisms to boost one's apparent impact. Additionally, it has been argued that the currently adopted metrics are suggestive of positive impact, while negative metrics are equally important. The metrics have changed and expanded the range of tasks investigated. This wide range of metric studies opens up new ways of understanding the scholarly communication process and the structure of science through citation. However, it should be kept in mind that the metrics are only one of the outcomes of tracking how research is used.

REFERENCES

- Almind, T.C and Ingwersen, Peter (1997). Informetrics analysis on the www: methodological approach to "Webometrics. *Journal of Documentation,* 53 (4): 404-426.
- Association of College and Research Libraries (2004). Principles and strategies for the reform of scholarly communication. Available at :http://www.ala.org/ala/acrl/acrlpubs/whitepapers/principlesstrategies.htm
- Bjorneborn, Lennart and Ingwersen, Peter (2001). Perspective of Webometrics. *Scientometrics,* 50 (1): 65-82.
- Bjorneborn, Lenned and Ingwersen, Peter (2004). Towards a basic framework for Webometrics. *Journal of the American Society for Information Science and Technology,* 55 (14): 1216-1227.
- Borgman, C.L. (2000). Digital libraries and continuum of scholarly communication. *Journal of Documentation, 56* (4): 412-430.
- Borgman, Christine L and Furner, Jonathan (2002). Scholarly Communication and Bibliometrics. *Annual Review*

of Information Science and Tecl nology, ed. By B. Cronin, Vol. 36.

- Bradford, S.C. (1934). Sources of Information on specific subjects, *Engineering,* 137: 85-86.
- Broadus, R.N. (1987). Definition of Bibliometrics, *Scientometrics,* 12: 373-398.
- Devarajan, G (Ed) (1997). Bibliometrics Studies; New Delhi: *Ess Ess Publications.*
- Davarpanah M R (2010). A scientometric model for the assessment of strength and weakness of scientific disciplines. *Library Review,* 59 (8): 596-605.
- Durieux V and Gevenois P A (2010). Bibliometric indicators : Quality measurements of scientific publication. *Radiology,* 255 (2): 342-351.
- Dutta, Bidyarthi (2014).*The Journey from Librametry to Altmetrics: a look back.,* In: Golden Jubilee Celebration of Department of Library and Information Science, Jadavpur University;, Jadavpur University, Kolkata, India, 8/8/14-10/8/14. [Conference paper] (Available at: http://eprints.rclis.org/23665/ accessed on 21 -1-2016)
- Fairthorne, R.A. (1969). Empirical hyperbolic distributions (Bradford. Zipf-Mandelbort) for bibliometric description and prediction. *Journal of Documentation.* 25: 319-343.
- Glanzel, W. (2003). *Bibliometrics as a research field: a course on theory and application of bibliometric indicators. Course handouts. Available at:* http://nsdl.niscair.res.in/bitstream/123456789/968/1/Bib_Module (accessed on 21-1-20160
- Haitun, S. (1983). Scientometrics: state and out - look . Nauka, Moscow, Quoted by Ludmila Ivancheva (2008). Scientometrics Today: A Methodological Overview. (Available at: http://www.collnet.de/Berlin-2008/Ivancheva WIS2008stm.pdf, accessed on 21 -1-2016)
- Hulme, E. (1923). Statistical bibliography in relation to the growth of modern civilization. London: Grafton, 1923.
- Ingwersen, Peter (2006). Webometrics: ten years of expansion. In *"Proceedings International Workshop on Webometrics, Informetrics and Scientometrics & Seventh COLLNET Meeting",* held at Nancy (France). May 10 - 12, 2006.

- Jeyshankar, R (2012). Webometrics: A New Dimension of Library and Information Science Research, edited by B Ramesh Babu. Chennai: Today Publishers.
- Jeyshankar, R. Ramesh Babu. B and Gopalakrishnan, S (2009). Conceptual Frame Work of Webometric Study: A Study, *KELPRO Bulletin.* 13(1): 41-48
- Kopelock, B. (1978). Bibliometrics: Access in the library literature, *Collection Management,* 2(3): 199-204.
- Kumar, P. S. G. (2003). *Research Methods and Statistical Techniques.* New Delhi: B R Publishing Corporation, p.470.
- Lotka, A.J. (1926). The frequency distribution of scientific productivity, *Journal of the Washington Academy of Sciences,* 16: 323.
- Merton, R.K. and Garfield, E.(1963). Foreword, *Little science, big science- and beyond,* by D J de Solla Price. New York: Columbia University Press.
- Mike, Thelwall (2008). Bibliometrics to Webometrics. *Journal of Information Science,* 34 (4): 605-621.
- Morales, M. (1985). Information and its Importance. *International Forum for Information and Documentation.* 10(2): 15-21.
- Nicholas, D. and Ritchie, M. (1978). Literature on Bibliometrics, London: Bingley. p .9-10.
- Potter, W.G. (1981). Introduction to Bibliometrics, *Library Trends,* 30:5-7
- Priem, J., & Hemminger, B. H. (2010). Scientometrics 2.0: New metrics of scholarly impact on the social Web. First Monday, 15(7). http://firstmonday.org/ojs/index.php/fm/article/view/2874
- Priem, J., Taraborelli, D., Groth, P., & Neylon, C. (2010). Altmetrics: A manifesto. altmetrics.org
- Pritchard, Alan. (1969). Statistical Bibliography or Bibliometrics, *Journal of Documentation,* 25(4): 348-349.
- Raising , L.M. (1962). Statistical Bibliography in the Health Sciences, *Bulletin of the Medical Library Association,* 50: 450-461.
- Rajan, T. N and Sen, B. K. (1986). An essay on informetrics: a study in growth and evelopment. *Annals of Library Science and Documentation,* 33(1-2): 1-12.

- Ramakrishnan, J and Parameswaran, R (2013). Bibliometrics : An overview. IN: In: *Libraries in the changing dimensions of digital technology,* Vol.2. Edited by B Ramesh Babu, *et al* , Delhi: B R Publishing Corporation, pp. 801-806
- Ramesh Babu, B (2015). Emerging Trends in the Scholarly Communication Systems in the Information Literate Society. IN: *Emerging trends in Scholarly communication in the Information Literate Society (NCETSC-2015) National Conference Proceedings,* conducted by Dravidian University, Kuppam, edited by S Sudarshan Rao *et al.* Hyderabad: Spectrum Publications, pp. 16-26
- Ranganathan, S.R. (1949). Librametry and its scope, *ASLIB Proceedings.* 1: 102.
- Rao, I K R and Neelameghan, A. (1993). From Librametry to Informetrics: an overview and Ranganathan's contributions. *Libri* , 12 (3): 242-53.
- Sengupta, I.N. (1990). Bibliometrics and its applications. In : *Information Science and Libraries.* Ed by Fushpa Dhyani. New Delhi: Atlantic.
- Sengupta, I.N. (1985). Bibliometrics: A bird's eye view, *IASLIC Bulletin,* 30: 167-174.
- Tague – Sutcliffe, J (1992). An Introduction to Informetrics. *Information Processing and Management,* 28 (1): 1-3.
- Thelwall, Mike, Vaughan, Liwen and Björneborn, Lennart (2005). Webometrics. *The Annual Review of Information Science and Technology,* 39 , Medford, NJ: Information Today Inc. for the American Society for Information Science.: 81-135.
- White H D and Mccain K W. (1989). Bibliometrics. In E. M E Williams (Ed), *Annual Review of Information Science and Technology.* Amsterdam, Netherlands: Information Today Inc. for American Society of Information Science, pp. 119-186
- Wilson, C. S. (2001), Informetrics. In: M. E. Williams, (Ed.), *Annual Review of Information Science and Technology, Vol.34,* Medford, NJ: Information Today Inc. for the American Society for Information Science, pp. 3-143
- Witting, Glenn R. (1978). Statistical Bibliography: A historical footnote, *Journal of Documentation,* 34: 240-241.

24

Social Networking in Libraries: Making Awareness Among the Library Professionals

Giriraj Halkar
Senior Technical Asstt.
National Documentation Centre
National Institute of Health & Family Welfare
Munirka, New Delhi -67

ABSTRACT

Social networking technologies enable individuals to simultaneously share information with any number of peers. Quantifying the causal effect of these mediums on the dissemination of information requires not only identification of who influences whom, but also of whether individuals would still propagate information in the absence of social signals about that information. The ability to disseminate and endorse one's work and research is an important of managing and communicating information. By disseminating information, an organization can reach members of its target audience and have a greater impact on policy and programming. The social networking site can serve as an invaluable tool in this effort to communicate the information across a wide audience. The purpose of the this paper is to explore social networking site (SNS), to work as an effective tool for imparting information or knowledge and prove helpful in making awareness among Library and Information Science (LIS) Professionals.

Keywords : Social network; Information dissemination, communication; Library professionals;

INTRODUCTION

Web 2.0 and its allied services have revolutionized the information services. Among them Social Networking has revolutionized the standard norms of interpersonal and social interaction. In modern Information world, Social Networking plays an important role in bonding and orchestrating different kinds of people and their allied activities. In the libraries also there are a number of social networking sites that provide impetus to the different facets of libraries.

Today libraries are using latest trends to make their services popular & user friendly especially in western countries. These trends are now also catching up with Indian library professionals. Everybody is now talking about Lib 2.0 applications. One of them is Social Networking (SN)!!

The last few years, libraries have been subject to significant force due to the information revolution. Information has to be properly composed, organized and disseminated for the user at right time in a right way. What, why, when and how to support information on user standpoint is continued to be a central debate for the library and information centre. Libraries around the world are facing vital challenges due to budget cuts, increased user base, the rapid growth of resources, rising costs, networking demands, competition of database vendors, and complexity in information requirements compelling the professionals to look up the open source technology available on the web. At the same situation require to promote and aware users for available sources, resources, services of library is very much important because library has always information authentication and due to non promotional way, users remain away from their require and authentic need of information in this global space.

Librarians are always maintaining good rapport with their users as well as other professional fellow beings. But doing the same with new resources provided by Information & Communication Technologies (ICT) is now termed as "Social Networking" where users especially college students are targeted as they gets fascinated by such applications. The basic aim is same as resource sharing.

Those who are not aware about SN may try following resources available on Internet. They also give insight how libraries can play role in social networking:

Today's global business marketplace requires a method of communication that is simultaneously fast, interconnected yet private, and easy to manage. Too, the faltering and unpredictable economy highlights the need for alternatives to in-person meetings and conferences with costly attributes. This is where an online social network can shine

DEFINING SOCIAL NETWORK

Social network is a broad term used to denote the blogs, user created videos and wikis. A social networking is an online served, platform or site that focuses on building and reflecting of social network or social relations among people who share interests and activities. Social networking often involves grouping specific individuals or organizations together. Social network provides a quick, low tech method to generate, maintain we based subject guides and act as communication tools to enable social interaction among LIS Professionals. Most social network services are web based and provide means for users to interact over the internet. They interact, share and exchange resources by social networks. It promotes free flow of information and sharing of resources beyond boundaries.

As defined by Wasserman et al (1994), "A *social network* consists of a finite set of actors and the relation or relations defined on them" (p 20) Any one individual can be part of multiple social networks, and the nature of these networks and the individual's connection to the networks can vary greatly For example, social networks are not necessarily rooted in traditional relation-ships, such as kinship or clan, but can develop out of geographic proximity, work relationships, or recreational activities Moreover, social networks can be described and analyzed in terms of their diverse characteristics (e g , how many people or organizations belong to a network, how well the members of the network know each other, and how equal their relationships are)

WHAT IS IT?

Even before the Internet, social networking existed. In a nutshell, social networking is when a person uses already existing contacts to meet new people as potential social or business links. Such links, in turn, will help expand future connections. Small and local businesses can even do this simply by attending community events or participating in trade shows.

Anything that gets the company name out there, or connects your company to helpful resources, is considered networking. Technology now makes this possible to do online, and not just face-to-face.

THE IMPORTANCE OF OUR SOCIAL NETWORKS

In the knowledge society, in addition to technical skills and access to information technologies, it is becoming increasingly important for people to have diversified and supportive social connections. Although resources and opportunities may be available, one may not necessarily be aware of their existence, or even have direct access to them. In those cases, knowing people from different backgrounds, grades of expertise, and social levels turns out to be essential. For instance, who among us has never required a letter of recommendation in order to get a job, or had to rely on somebody else's knowledge in order to find a specific doctor? Isn't it through word of mouth that many kids get to know about the Clubhouse? Social networking can help a business gain contacts, clients, and increased public awareness. Even entrepreneurs who run small businesses from their homes can take advantage of this resource to set up a global presence.

Keep in touch with staff, patrons, and more with these tools.

MySpace : It was launched in August 2003. If you want to go where the students are, one of the best places to find them is MySpace. Other libraries have taken advantage of this site's calendar and blog features to improve their presence. With a little help from your IT department, you can also include custom catalog search tools.

Facebook : Another social media site frequented by students, Facebook is librarian friendly. You'll find a group just for *librarian-centric Facebook apps*, a *JSTOR search*, and much more. Currently Facebook is the fifth most trafficked site on the internet worldwide and second most trafficked social media site on the world. It was first founded by Mark Zuckerberg in 2004.

Ning : Ning started development in October 2004 and launched its platform publicly in October 2005. Librarian can use this tool to get connected with students, library asoociations, and more. You can also use it to share information with many people at a time.

Blog : (an abbreviation for the term "Web log") are maintained sites with regular entries of commentary or news on various topics. Many blogs function as personal online diaries, but blogs also can focus on current events, history, travel, and politics. By creating a blog, you'll be able to disseminate information to lots of people at one time. Whether you're updating students on new collections, or just conversing with library staff, blogs are a powerful tool, especially when combined with *RSS*.

Meebo : Network and assist students on Meebo, no matter what IM client they use. You can even embed a chat screen on any webpage using this *tutorial*.

LinkedIn : This social networking site for professionals is a great way to get library patrons connected with the people that can help them find information. Whether that's you, faculty, authors, historians, or other sources, they can find them in your LinkedIn network.

Twitter : Use Twitter, a micro blogging application, to keep staff and patrons updated on daily activities, like frequently updated collections, or even just scheduling.

Tumblr : is a microblogging platform and social networking website founded by David Karp and since 2013 owned by Yahoo! The service allows users to post multimedia and other content to a short-form blog.

WhatsApp : Messenger is a cross-platform mobile messaging app which allows you to exchange messages without having to pay for SMS. *WhatsApp* Messenger is available for iPhone, BlackBerry, Android, Windows Phone and Nokia and yes, those phones can all message each other!

Pinterest is a social network that allows users to visually share, and discover new interests by posting (known as 'pinning' on *Pinterest*) images or videos to their own or others' boards (i.e. a collection of 'pins,' usually with a common theme) and browsing what other users have pinned.

Tencent QQ, popularly known as *QQ*, is an instant messaging software service developed by Chinese company Tencent Holdings Limited. *QQ* also offers a variety of services, including online social games, music, shopping, microblogging, movies, platform of games and group and voice chat.

Qzone (Chinese) is a social networking website, which was created by Tencent in 2005. It allows users to write blogs, keep diaries, send photos, listen to music, and watch videos.

WeChat (Chinese) is a mobile text and voice messaging communication service developed by Tencent in China, first released in January 2011. It is one of the largest standalone messaging apps by monthly active users.

Instagram is an online mobile photo-sharing, video-sharing, and social networking service that enables its users to take pictures and videos, and share them either publicly or privately on the app, as well as through a variety of other social networking platforms, such as Facebook, Twitter, Tumblr, and Flickr.

Baidu Tieba (Chinese) is the largest Chinese communication platform provided by the Chinese search engine company, *Baidu*. It is an online community bound tightly with internet search services, one of the main businesses of *Baidu*.

Viber is a mobile application that allows you to make phone calls and send text messages to all other *Viber* users for free! *Viber* is available over WiFi or 3G. Our sound quality is much better than a regular call. Once you and your friends install *Viber*, you can use it to talk and message as much as you want.

Sina Weibo (NASDAQ: WB) is a Chinese microblogging (*weibo*) website. Akin to a hybrid of Twitter and Facebook, it is one of the most popular sites in China, in use by well over 30% of Internet users, with a market penetration similar to the United States' Twitter.

Snapchat is a video messaging application created by Evan Spiegel, Bobby Murphy, and Reggie Brown Poster when they were students at Stanford University.

VK (originally *VKontakte*) is the largest European online social networking service. It is based in St. Petersburg. It is available in several languages, but is especially popular among Russian-speaking users. Like other social networks, VK allows users to message each other publicly or privately, to create groups, public pages and events, share and tag images, audio and video, and to play browser-based games.

YY (Chinese) is a major Chinese video-based social network with over 300 million users. It features a virtual currency which users can earn through activities such as karaoke or creating tutorial videos, then convert to real cash.

BlackBerry Messenger, also known as *BBM*, is a proprietary Internet-based instant messenger and videotelephony application included on BlackBerry devices that allows messaging and voice calls between BlackBerry, iOS, Windows Phone and Android users.

Skype is an application that provides video chat and voice call services. Users may exchange such digital documents as images, text, video and any others, and may transmit both text and video messages. Skype allows the creation of video conference calls. Skype is available for Microsoft Windows, Macintosh, or Linux, as well as Android, Blackberry, and both Apple and Windows smart phones and tablets.

DISTRIBUTION

These tools make it easy to share information from anywhere.

Flickr : This image distribution tool is a great way to share new image collections. You can create image sets with metadata, as well as take advantage of the many plugins available for Flickr users. Flickr users can also help gather missing information about images.

YouTube : Spread the word about library events,

share citizen journalism, and more on YouTube. You can see how other libraries are using YouTube by checking out the *youtubeandlibraries wiki.*

TeacherTube : TeacherTube, which is a YouTube for teachers, presents an excellent opportunity for instructor-librarian collaboration. Instructors can guide students to helpful library resources, and vice versa.

Second Life : On Second Life, you can create a virtual library with streamed media, discussions, classes, and more. For a good example of a Second Life library, visit the *murdochsecondlife wiki.*

Wikipedia : Wikipedia is an online encyclopedia updated by users. You can use this tool to share your knowledge by editing, or simply point library patrons in the right direction.

PBwiki : PBwiki is the world's largest provider of hosted business and educational wikis. It encourages collaboration from students, a way to showcase work, and offers a central gathering point for information. PBwiki offers controlled access, so you can give some editing privileges, while others can only read.

Footnote : On Footnote, you'll get access to original historical documents, and can update them with your own content and insights. You can even find personal anecdotes and experiences you won't find in reference books.

Community Walk : Community Walk offers a geographical way to interpret text and events. You can use it for instruction, such as showing someone where to find a book, or walk them through a historical and geographical timeline.

SlideShare : Encourage faculty, staff, and students to share their slideshow presentations for the greater community to access on SlideShare. It's a great way to disemminate information.

Digg : Digg is a great way to find useful content that you wouldn't come across in traditional ways. Find stories here, then share them with others using Digg's blog function.

StumbleUpon : Another way to find great content is with StumbleUpon. You can channel surf the Internet to find useful content, research tools, and more.

Daft Doggy : If you've found a particularly good resource, you can use DaftDoggy to create a website tour with instructions, pointing out useful references and items of note.

In general social networking services allow user to create a profile for themselves and can be broken down into two bread categories. Internal Social Networking (ISN) and External Social Networking (ESN) (MySpace, Facebook, Twitter and Bebo. Etc.). An ISN is a closed/ private community that consists of a group of people within a company, association, society, education provider and organization or even "invite only" group created by a user in a ESN. ESN's can be specialized communities or they can be large generic social networking sites.

Social networking sites typically have a section dedicated to comments by friends. On Friendster, this section called "Testimonials". On Facebook, this section is called "The Wall". In the beginning, this was a feature that encouraged people to write messages about the person in the profile. But over time, people started writing creative testimonials back, creating a form of conversions.

Some social networks have additional features, such as the ability to create groups that share common interests or affiliations, upload or stream live videos and hold discussions in forums.

BENEFITS OF SOCIAL NETWORKING SITES

There are a number of benefits associated with social networking. They are;

- Provides creators with a global list of contacts, and multi level contacts through the first level of contacts.
- Brings people together to communicate, learn and share
- Brings together people with similar interests
- Forms a platform to moot and regulate ideas
- Provides a flow of information dissemination
- Assists in creating online resources
- Accelerates the process of knowledge dissemination
- Cos-effective marketing tool

SOCIAL NETWORKING SITES IN THE LIBRARIES

Social networking helps librarian to share information with patrons and students in the easiest way for digital library environment. Librarian can use in three broad activities in library and information services. The major three are;

- Information communication
- Knowledge distribution
- Knowledge organization

Social Networking provides users with the ability to create a global list of contact details (either in a graphical or text-based format) of people with whom they have strong professional ties, co-workers, colleagues and people they do business with, who they trust enough to be associated with and even recommend to others. This contact list is different from other electronic directories in that the information is linked directly to the profiles created and maintained by the contact himself, allowing for automatic updates of changes to contact details, current activities, interest and specialist skills and expertise, in a searchable format. With Web 2.0, libraries are tweeting about resources, sharing research advice on blogs, posting pictures of events to Flickr, gaining fans on Facebook, and looking for new ways to make 2.0 works for their institution and users. Social networks are used by libraries as vehicles for outreach for promoting services, programs, and new resources, as well as for providing general information. Web 2.0 tools can also be used for reference services. Many libraries have developed applications for Facebook. The most common application is a search feature for library's catalog. Some libraries have created groups that Facebook users can join. Messages can be sent to all members in order to advertise library programs, services, or anything else the library feels is helpful and important.

Social Networks can be used for providing user centric service in social library environment. User attitude towards library is changing day by day. User wants most practical and speed information in e-learning age. But providing quick and easy retrieval information to user is a great challenge to library. Therefore library should find and search some new techniques for impacting valuable information to the user. The impact of SNS in libraries is growing day by day. Many libraries are using social networking platform to interact and reach out to their patrons of clients. It has also become a level playing ground for academics and students to interact on issues pertaining to course work. Students also use this platform to share information amongst themselves on any subject and topic. The use of these tools has been affirmed by Bell (2007), that Academic libraries do not only use social media for communication purposes, but had adapted their research strategies to this environment. Libraries with social networking wall. The walls are mostly used to;

- Announce programmes of the library
- Give students the opportunity to ask questions pertaining to the use of the library
- Teach basic search tools
- Paste new books on the wall to inform the University Community
- Send brief updates to patrons
- Ask a Librarian

There are lot of library related social networks are available on the Internet, now various libraries are using MySpace, Facebook, Ning etc. for user oriented services, suggestions, to form strong groups, marketing library services etc. Some of the libraries and LIS professionals which /who use social networking/web 2.0 technologies are listed in table-1. Apart from above there are several social networks available on the Internet in the field of Library science.

Table 1. Some of the Social Network worldwide

Name of Library/Network	*URL of Social Network*
Edmonton Public Library	*http://www.epl.ca/EPLFacebook.cfm*
University of Alberta	*http://www.library.ualberta.ca/*
Casa Grande Library	*http://www.twitter.com/cglibrary*
Georgina Public Library	*http://www.georgireads.blogspot.com*
Cambridge Libraries	*http://www2.cambridgelibraries.ca/blog*
Kendriya vidyalaya	*http://librarykvpattom.wordpress.com*
University of Oxford	*http://vereharmsworthlibrary.blogspot.com*
Eden Prairie Library	*http://www.youtube.com/watch?v=mi78YJ1CD4Y*
Denver Public Library	*http://podcast.denverlibrary.org/*
Cleveland PL on Twitter	*http://twitter.com/adalib*
YALSA	*http://twitter.com/yalsa*
Library 2.0	*http://library20.ning.com/*
Indian LIS professionals	*http://lislinks.ning.com/*
Library Junction	*http://libraryjunction.ning.com/*
Teacher Librarian Ning	*http://teacherlibrarian.ning.com/*
Roselle Public Library Network	*http://rosellelibrary.ning.com/*
ALA American Library Association	*http://alamembers.ning.com/*
Library Youth and Teens Services 2.0	*http://libraryyouth.ning.com/*
DepED Library Hub Community	*http://libraryhub.ning.com/*
Mashed Library	*http://mashedlibrary.ning.com/*
Power Libraries	*http://powerlibraries.ning.com/*
Law Libraries and Librarians	*http://lawlibraries.ning.com/*
Libraries of the future	*http://librariesofthefuture.ning.com/*
Help Desk For Library and Society	*http://lishelp.ning.com/*
ETTLIS 2010	*http://ettlis2010.ning.com/*

Leading social networks worldwide as of January 2016, ranked by number of active users (in millions)

This statistic provides information on the most popular networks worldwide as of January 2016, ranked by number of active accounts. Market leader Facebook was the first social network to surpass 1 billion registered accounts and currently sits at 1.55 billion monthly active users. Eighth-ranked photo-sharing app Instagram had over 400 million monthly active accounts. Meanwhile, blogging service Tumblr had more than 555 million active blog users on their site.

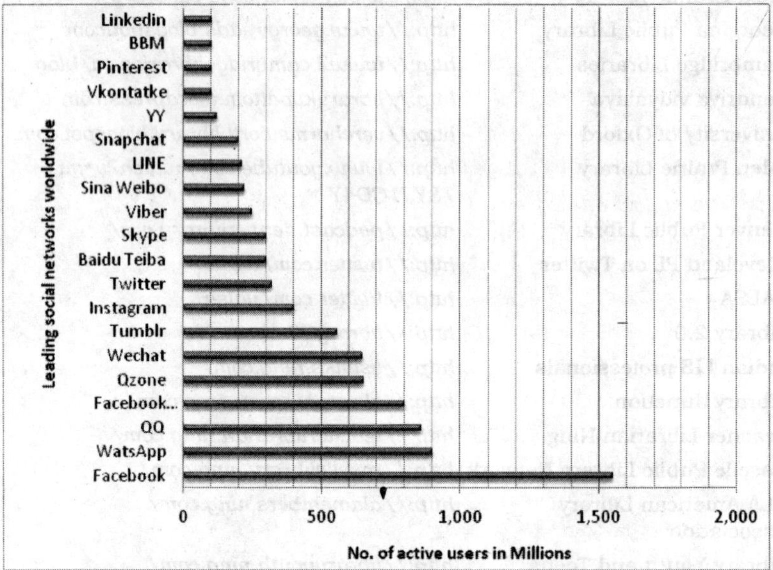

CONCLUSION

Social networking tools were being used by a number of libraries. The benefit of using these tools is perceived to outweigh the costs, which were reported to be minimal, if not none. Social networking tools were perceived to be helpful in promoting library services and interacting with students. Moreover, the tools were also reported to be helpful for internal staff communication. Social networking website provides great opportunities for library professionals to interact with their users as it places them in the digital social space of their users. Library professionals can get first hand information about the user through interacting with them. They can then understand the user and design services to meet the needs accordingly. Social networks are a great way to test your commitment to open communication.

REFERENCES

- www.flickr.com.
- www.diffdaff.com.
- www.facebook.com.
- www.myspace.com.
- www.bebo.com.
- www.orkut.com.
- www.zude.com (in Beta only; now closed).
- *www.linkedin.com.*
- Sahu Mahendra (2013). "Information Disseminating through using Networking sites among Library Professional in the Engineering Colleges of Odisha: A survey." International Journal of Digital Library Services, 3/1, 45-54.
- Praveen Noushia (2011), Use of Social Networking Site (Facebook) in marking awareness among the library and information science professionals of University Libraries of U P : case study . International Journal of Digital Library services, 1/1,9-17.
- social%20networking/%E2%80%A2%20Leading% 20global% 20social% 20networks%202016%20_ %20 Statistic.htm. accessed on 2/2/2016.

25

Social Networking Sites (SNS) and Library Services

P. Phani Bhargavi

Librarian , ViswaBharathi PG College of Engineering and Management, Nizampet, HYDERABAD

ABSTRACT

Defines social Networking Sites (SNS) and discusses their growing use particularly among young people. Elaborates their role in academic institutes and scholars. Enumerates the benefits of SNS. Describes some of the important SNS like Facebook, Twitter, LinkedIn, Friendster and Myspace. Concluded giving a bird's eye view of SNS as global phenomenon and trends of research in SNS.

INTRODUCTION

Although people have been using the internet to connect with others since the early 1980s, it is only in the last decade that social networking services have proliferated and their use has become a widespread practice – particularly amongst young people (Horizon.2009).

Social networking services can be defined as; Web-based services that allow individuals to (1) construct a public or semi-public profile within a bounded system. (2) articulate a list of other users with whom they share a connection, and (3) view and traverse their list of connections and those made by others within the system. The nature and nomenclature of these connections may vary from site to site (boyd&Ellison 2007).

While we use the term "social network site" to describe this phenomenon, the term "social networking sites" also appears in public discourse, and the two terms are often used interchangeably. We chose not to employ the term "networking" for two reasons: emphasis and scope. "Networking" emphasizes relationship initiation, often between strangers. While networking is possible in these sites, it is not the primary practice on many of them, nor is it what differentiates them from other forms of Computer-Mediated Communication (CMC).

What makes social network sites unique is not that they allow individuals to meet strangers, but rather that they enable users to articulate and make visible their social networks. This can result in connections between individuals that would not otherwise be made, but that is often not the goal, and these meetings are frequently between "latent ties" (Haythornthwaite,2005) who share some offline connection. On many of the large SNSs, participants are not necessarily "networking" or looking to meet new people; instead, they are primarily communicating with people who are already a part of their extended social network. To emphasize this articulated social network as a critical organizing feature of these sites, we label them "social network sites."

While SNSs having implemented a wide variety of technical features, there backbone consists of visible profiles that display an articulated list of frinds who are also users of the system. Profiles are unique pages where one can "type oneself into being" (Sunden, 2003, p. 3). After joining an SNS, an individual is asked to fill out forms containing a scries of questions. The profile is generated using the answers to these questions, which typically include descriptors such as age, location, interest and "about me" section. Most sides also encourage users to upload a profile photo. Some sites allow users to enhance their profiles by adding multimedia content or modifying their profiles look and feel. Others, such as facebook, allowusers to add modules ("applications") that enhance their profile.

VISIBILITY AND ACCESS

The visibility of a profile varies by site and according to the users discretion. By default, profiles on Friendster and Tribe.net are crawled by search engines, making them visible to anyone, regardless of whether or not the viewer has an account. Alternatively, LinkedIn controls what a viewer may see based on whether she or he has a paid account. Sites like MySpace allow users to choose whether they want their profile to be public or "friends only". Facebook takes a different approach – by default, users who are part of the same "network"can view each other's profiles, unless a profile owner has decided to deny permission to those in their network. Structural variations around visibility and access are one of the primary ways that SNSs differentiate themselves from each other.

RELATIONSHIPS

After joining a social network site, users are prompted to identify others in the system with whom they have a relationship. The label for these relationships differs depending on the site – popular terms include "Friends", "Contacts" and "Fans". Most SNSs require bi-directional confirmation for Friendship, but some do not. These one directional ties are sometimes labelled as "Fans"or "Followers", but many sites call these friends as well. The term "Friends" can be misleading, because the connection does not necessarily mean friendship in the everyday vernacular sense, and the reasons people connect varies (boyd, 2006a).

The public display of connections is a crucial component of SNSs. The Friends list contains links to each Friend's profile, enabling viewers to traverse the network graph by clicking through the Friends lists. On most sites, the list of Friends is visible to anyone who is permitted to view the profile, although there are exceptions. For instance, some MySpace users have hacked their profiles to hide the Friends display, and LinkedIn allows users to opt out of displaying their network.

Most SNSs also provide a mechanism for users to leave messages on their Friends' profiles. This feature typically involves leaving "comments," although sites employ various label for this feature. In addition SNSs often have a private messaging feature similar to webmail. While both private messages and comments are popular on most of the major SNSs, they are not universally available.

Not all social network sites began as such. QQ started as a Chinese instant messaging service, LunarStorm as community site, Cyworld as a Korean discussion forum tool and Skyrock (formerly Skyblog) was a French blogging service before adding SNS features.

Classmates.com, a directory of school affiliates launched in 1995, began supporting articulated list of friends SNSs became popular. Asian avenue, MiGente and BlackPlanet were early popular ethnic community sites with limited Friends functionality before re-launching in 2005-2006 with SNS features and structure.

Beyond profiles, Friends, comments, and private messaging, SNSs vary greatly in their features in user based. Some have photo-sharing or video-sharing capabilities; others have built-in blogging and instant messaging technology. There are mobile specific SNSs (e.g., Dodgeball), but some web-based SNSs also support limited mobile interactions (e.g., Facebook, MySpace, and Cyworld). Many SNSs target specific geographical regions or linguistic groups, although this does not determine site's constituency. Orkut, for example, was launched in the United States with an English-only interface, but Portuguese-speaking Brazilians quickly became the dominant user group (Kopytoff, 2004). Some sites are designed with specific ethnic religious, sexual orientation, political, or other identity driven categories in mind. There are even SNSs for Dogster and cats Catster, although their owners must manage their profiles

While SNSs are often designed widely accessible, many attract homogeneous population initially, so it is not uncommon to find groups using sites to segregate themselves by nationality, age, educational level or other factors that typically segment society (Hargittai, this issue), even if that was not the intention of the designers.

BENEFITS OF SOCIAL NETWORKING SERVICE USE

1. Media Literacy
2. Education
   (i) Formed
   (ii) Informed knowledge and skills
3. Creativity
4. Individual identity and self-expression
5. Strengthening Interpersonal Relationships
   (i) Developing New Interpersonal Relationships
   (ii) Convergence of Online and offline Spaces
6. Sense of Belonging and collective identity
7. Strengthening and Building communities
8. Civil Engagement and Political Participation
9. Wellbeing

Preibusch, Hoser, Curses and Berendt (2007) argued that the privacy options offered by SNSs do not provide users with the flexibility they need to handle conflicts Friends who have different conceptions of privacy; they suggest a framework for privacy in SNSs that they believe would help resolve these conflicts.

SNSs are also challenging legal conceptions of privacy. Hodge (2006) argued that the fourth amendment to the U.S Constitution and legal decisions concerning privacy are not equipped to address social network sites. For example, do police officers have the right to access the content posted to Facebook without a warrant? The legality of this hinges on users' expectation of privacy and whether or not Facebook profiles are considered public or private.

SOME IMPORTANT SOCIAL NETWORKING SITES (SNS)

Facebook

Use in Academic Libraries

Social networking sites have been at the forefront of discussion about the use of the web in libraries but there are several issues that might need to be considered (or reconsidered). Sekyere (2009 p. 26) argues that students use Facebook to escape, even for a short period of time, from their academic responsibilities, which is the opposite of what led academic libraries to exploit Facebook in the first place. Smith and Caruso (2010 p. 14) surveyed over 36,000 students and found that although more than 90% use social networking sites, only 30% of them use those sites for course-related purposes and 8% to communicate with course instructors. Fuchs (2009 p. 89) reports that university students consider the provision of information and news to be a minor advantage of social networking sites, with eight other purposes being valued more highly.

Reaction of users

Another aspect to consider when a library creates an account with a social network service, such as Facebook or MySpace, is the possibility that a portion of the targeted audience will reject the library's aim of finding new ways of communicating because they will think their privacy is, potentially, infringed, despite the fact they are users of that particular service (Connell, 2009) or simply because they do not want libraries as their "friends" (Breeding, 2007). Secker (2008) also reported students' concerns about libraries infiltrating their social spaces through Facebook. Xia (2009) investigated library related Facebook groups at two universities and found that it was hard for those groups to maintain a steady flow of posts and participation by the students.

Some studies

Scale (2008) studied the role of Facebook as a social search engine and concluded that it is mainly irrelevant, and Matthews (2006) had a response rate of only 3.2% when he reached out to his library audience through Facebook. Moreover, librarians who decide to use Facebook as a tool for marketing and promotion of library services should be aware of the fact that they might find themselves in an environment where the level of professionalism found in their libraries is difficult to maintain (Graham, et. al., 2007). Chu and Meulemans (2008) consider Facebook and MySpace to be good outreach tools for an academic library alongside other, older outreach tools.

Moreover, we should carefully consider if we should create applications and encourage our patrons to use them on some of the social networking sites, when it is now reported that user data are transmitted through various applications to advertising companies on the web (Steel and Fowler, 2010). Should we consider our list of "friends" as part of our services, when we know that it may be exploited for profit? (Stone, 2010). We might expect a commercial service to try to make a profit by selling user data. Problems can arise when institutions that users trust choose to lead users away from safe places and expose them to possible exploitation by third party services (Joint, 2010 p. 493). Fuchs (2009 p. 22) argues that the users of social networking sites are under constant state and economic surveillance.

TWITTER

As free Messaging Service

For many people, the word "twitter" brings to mind birds rather than humans. But information professionals know that Twitter (www.twitter.com) is a fast-growing, free messaging service for people, and it's one that libraries (and librarians) can make good use of—without spending much time or effort.

Twitter lets people send and receive short messages (called Tweets) via the web or via SMS using a mobile phone. Messages on Twitter are limited to a maximum of 140 characters, including spaces, and they're generally public. Because each message is just a sentence or two, a carefully crafted post can convey a good deal of information without taking a lot of time to read or write. In addition, because Twitter has millions of users, it's a good place to find and connect with people interested in your institution and your areas of expertise.

To automatically see what someone else is saying, you "follow" them. Those who regularly receive your posts are your "followers." You don't need to give each other permission to follow, and you can view Tweets without signing into Twitter, but you must sign in to follow someone.

Thanks to the brevity of messages on Twitter, people often refer to the medium as "microblogging." Like full-sized blogging, the pint-sized version is useful for exchanging many different kinds of information. Although Twitter users initially shared just personal updates ("Eating kale for lunch" or "Watching the Giants game on our new TV"), it's become common for people and organizations to Twitter about professional ideas and information too. Yes, organizations have now begun to use Twitter as a communications medium.

For example, a library could share all kinds of news that patrons want. Short messages can tell people about events such as readings, lectures, and book sales; newly available resources; or changes in the building hours. One message a day or one a week could share a tip on finding or accessing information online or in the building. Twitter posts can link to interesting news stories about literacy or about libraries. When appropriate, the posts can link to a library's own website and blog for more in-depth information.

LINKEDIN

Current Awareness

LinkedIn Today, offers current awareness on social media, technology development and many other aspects relevant to librarianship to help us keep engaged. There are also hugely valuable contributions from many 'thought leaders'. I would like to see more information-related stories but I think this depends on more librarians sharing within LinkedIn. *Below: a librarian shares content on LinkedIn.*

Social Networking With Our Users

Via status updates, also on the home page, we now have another way for us to socially network and share information with other librarians and more significantly with those people we are connected to outside of the profession. This has led me to a greater understanding and awareness of the faculty and students I support in particular. Twitter has yet to fully catch on with these communities so LinkedIn is filling an important gap.

Professional Development Record

We should all be keeping an eye on our professional development. The presence of this profile online is a great prompt for us to keep it up-to-date and this in turn means we will not have to climb such a horrendous mountain when we apply for next job by having to build a CV from scratch.

FRIENDSTER

Friendster launched in 2002 as a social complement to Ryze. It was designed to compete with Match.com, a profitable online dating site (Cohen, 2003). While most dating sites focused on introducing people to strangers with similar interests, Friendster was designed to help friends of friends meet, based on the assumption that friends of friends would make better romantic partners than would strangers (J. Abrams, personal communication, March 27, 2003). Friendster gained traction among three groups of early adopters who shaped the site—bloggers, attendees of the Burning Man arts festival, and gay men (boyd, 2004)—and grew to 300,000 users through word of mouth before traditional press coverage began in May 2003 (O'Shea, 2003).

As Friendster's popularity surged, the site encountered technical and social difficulties (boyd, 2006b). Friendster's servers and databases were ill equipped to handle its rapid growth, and the site faltered regularly, frustrating users who replaced email with Friendster. Because organic growth had been critical to creating a coherent community, the onslaught of new users who learned about the site from media coverage upset the cultural balance. Furthermore, exponential growth meant a collapse in social contexts: Users had to face their bosses and former classmates alongside their close friends. To complicate matters, Friendster began restricting the activities of its most passionate users.

The initial design of Friendster restricted users from viewing profiles of people who were more than four degrees away (friends of friends of friends of friends). In order to view additional profiles, users began adding acquaintances and interesting looking strangers to expand their reach. Some began massively collecting Friends, an activity that was implicitly encouraged through a "most popular" feature. The ultimate collectors were fake profiles representing iconic fictional characters: celebrities, concepts, and other such entities. These "Fakesters" outraged the company, who banished fake profiles and eliminated the "most popular" feature (boyd, in press b). While few people actually created Fakesters, many more enjoyed surfing Fakesters for entertainment or using functional Fakesters (e.g., "Brown University") to find people they knew.

MySpace

Few analysts or journalists noticed when MySpace launched in Santa Monica, California, hundreds of miles from Silicon Valley. MySpace was begun in 2003 to compete with sites like Friendster, Xanga, and AsianAvenue, according to co founder Tom Anderson (personal communication, August 2, 2007); the founders wanted to attract estranged Friendster users (T. Anderson, personal communication, February 2, 2006). After rumors emerged that Friendster would adopt a fee based system, users posted Friendster messages encouraging people to join alternate SNSs, including Tribe.net and MySpace (T. Anderson, personal communication, August 2, 2007).

Teenagers began joining MySpace en masse in 2004. Unlike older users, most teens were never on Friendster—some joined because they wanted to connect with their favorite bands; others were introduced to the site through older family members.

A Global Phenomenon

While MySpace attracted the majority of media attention in the U.S. and abroad, SNSs were proliferating and growing in popularity worldwide. Friendster gained traction in the Pacific Islands, Orkut became the premier SNS in Brazil before growing rapidly in India (Madhavan, 2007), Mixi attained widespread adoption in Japan, LunarStorm took off in Sweden, Dutch users embraced Hyves, Grono captured Poland, Hi5 was adopted in smaller countries in Latin America, South America, and Europe, and Bebo became very popular in the United Kingdom, New Zealand, and Australia. Additionally, previously popular communication and community services began implementing SNS features. The Chinese QQ instant messaging service instantly became the largest SNS worldwide when it added profiles and made friends visible (McLeod, 2006), while the forum tool Cyworld cornered the Korean market by introducing homepages and buddies (Ewers, 2006).

Blogging services with complete SNS features also became popular. In the U.S., blogging tools with SNS features, such as Xanga, LiveJournal, and Vox, attracted broad audiences. Skyrock reigns in France, and Windows Live Spaces dominates numerous markets worldwide, including in Mexico, Italy, and Spain. Although SNSs like QQ, Orkut, and Live Spaces are just as large as, if not larger than, MySpace, they receive little coverage in U.S. and English speaking media, making it difficult to track their trajectories.

RESEARCH TRENDS

In addition to the themes identified above, a growing body of scholarship addresses other aspects of SNSs, their users, and the practices they enable. For example, scholarship on the ways in which race and ethnicity (Byrne, in press; Gajjala, 2007), religion (Nyland & Near, 2007), gender (Geidner, Flook, & Bell, 2007; Hjorth& Kim, 2005), and sexuality connect to, are affected by, and are enacted in social network sites raise interesting questions about how identity is shaped within these sites. Fragoso (2006) examined the role of national identity in SNS use through an investigation into the "Brazilian invasion" of Orkut and the resulting culture clash between Brazilians and Americans on the site. Other scholars are beginning to do cross-cultural comparisons of SNS use—Hjorth and Yuji (in press) compare Japanese usage of Mixi and Korean usage of Cyworld, while Herring et al. (2007) examine the practices of users who bridge different languages on LiveJournal—but more work in this area is needed.

Scholars are documenting the implications of SNS use with respect to schools, universities, and libraries. For example, scholarship has examined how students feel about having professors on Facebook (Hewitt & Forte, 2006) and how faculty participation affects student-professor relations (Mazer, Murphy, & Simonds, 2007). Charnigo and Barnett-Ellis (2007) found that librarians are overwhelmingly aware of Facebook and are against proposed U.S. legislation that would ban minors from accessing SNSs at libraries, but that most see SNSs as outside the purview of librarianship. Finally, challenging the view that there is nothing educational about SNSs, Perkel (in press) analyzed copy/paste practices on MySpace as a form of literacy involving social and technical skills.

Future Research

The work described above and included in this special theme section contributes to an ongoing dialogue about the importance of social network sites, both for practitioners and researchers. Vast, uncharted waters still remain to be explored. Methodologically, SNS researchers' ability to make causal claims is limited by a lack of experimental or longitudinal studies. Although the situation is rapidly changing, scholars still have a limited understanding of who is and who is not using these sites, why, and for what purposes, especially outside the U.S. Such questions will require large-scale quantitative and qualitative research. Richer, ethnographic research on populations more difficult to access (including non-users) would further aid scholars' ability to understand the long-term implications of these tools. We hope that the work described here and included in this collection will help build a foundation for future investigations of these and other important issues surrounding social network sites

REFERENCES

- Acquisti, A., & Gross, R. (2006). Imaguned communities: Awareness, information sharing, and privacy on the Facebook. In P. Golle& G. Denezis (Eds.), *Proceedings of 5th Workshop on Privacy Enhancing Technologies* (pp. 36-58). Cambridge, UK: Robinson College.
- Adamic, L. A., Buyukkokten, O., & Adar, E. (2003). A social network caught in the web. *First Monday,* 8 (6). Retrieved July 30, 2007 from http://www.firstmonday.org/issues/issue8_6/adamic/index.html
- Backstrom, L., Huttenlocher, D., Klemberg, J., &Lan, X. (2006). Group formation in large social networks: Membership, growth, and evolution. *Proceedings of 12th International Conference on Knowledge Discovery in Data Mining (pp. 44-54). New York: ACM Press.*
- Gerolimos, M., K Konsta, R. (2011). Services for Academic Libraries in the New Era. D- LIB Magazine July/August 2011 Volume 17, Number 7/8.Retrieved March 21, 2016 from http://www.dlib.org/dlib/july11/gerolimos/07gerolimos.html
- Milstein, Sarah. (2013) Twitter for libraries (and Librarians). Retrieved March21, 2016 from http://www.infotoday.com/cilmag/may09/Milstein.shtml
- Priestner, Andy (2010). 8 reasons why LinkedIn is definitely for Librarians.Retrieved March 21, 2016 from https://libreaction.wordpress.com/2013/02/19/8-reasons-why-linkedin-is-definitely-for-librarians/

Source

- Excerted from. Boyd, DanandMand Ellison, Nicole B. Social Networking sites, Definition, History Scholorship.

26

Quality Management (TQM): Requisite for Libraries to Succeed and Survive in Digital Environment

J Lohia
Senior Documentation Officer
JNU, New Delhi - 110067

INTRODUCTION

TQM is an attitude and method for rapid improving the services and/or products offered to customers. New technologies and ICT have replaced national economic systems with a global economy. The organization irrespective of size and type that do not practice TQM can become globally non-competitive rather rapidly. This march towards noncompetitiveness can be avoided if library staff is helped to become TQM practitioners. Therefore, the potential benefits of TQM can be applied to libraries. TQM can help libraries provide better service to its primary customers. The continuous improvement focus of TQM is a fundamental way of fulfilling the accountability requirements common to library reform. Innovative and interactive techniques can be applied to improve the interest of library users. Therefore, the environment for learning is improved. Different techniques can be used for libraries are discussed in this paper. TQM, as its name implies, related to the monitoring of quality throughout the organization by everyone in that organization. This means that if problems are spotted during the production process or service, it is the responsibility of that person to solve the problem before it goes any further through the process. This way, problems should be identified before they ever get near the users but if they do, every effort is made to sort the problem out with the minimum of argument. To support the emphasis on quality, firms are also looking to get external verification for the standards that they are projecting to their customers. Various scholars have define total quality and explain how it can benefit performance and effectiveness, relating the basic principles to a library setting with particular emphasis on mission, measurement, charters, and customer needs.

WHAT IS QUALITY

Quality is often used synonymously with excellence. However, for proper quality management, defining quality and its measurement are essential. Quality has been defined variedly in different contexts. There is wide range of definitions or approaches to quality, describing the relative nature of the concept in the context of library management.

Some of the important terms involved in TQM are given below:

- Exceptional (high standards library services);
- Uniformity; (consistency in library services)
- Appropriateness for purpose (meeting stated purposes);
- Value for Time; and (Save the time of user: 4th law).
- Transformative (transformation of the library users).

"The term quality defies any definition which will be universally accepted. When it is linked to performance, quality implies evaluation for comparative purposes; 'measures' of quality involve norms and standards and judgments of quality are assisted through use of norm or criterion referenced indicators. Where measurement focuses on the student as a product of education, quality is seen as value- based' by the process of education. When the emphasis is management of quality, attention focuses on strategies for achieving or improving quality."

Quality inbuilt following approaches:

- Inspirational approach (Quality always exists)
- Service based approach (Library Products meeting high quality
- standards)
- User based approach (quality to meet user's requirements)
- Library-based approach
- Time-based approach.

CONCEPTS

The concept of TQM was developed by an American, W. Edwards Deming, after World War II for improving the production quality of goods and services. The concept was not taken seriously by Americans until the Japanese, who adopted it in 1950 to resurrect their postwar business and industry, used it to dominate world markets by 1980. By then most U.S. manufacturers had finally accepted that the nineteenth century assembly line factory model was outdated for the modern global economic markets. The concept of TQM is applicable to libraries. Many librarians believe that the concept of TQM provides guiding principles for needed library reform. TQM is the art of managing the whole to achieve excellence. The golden rule is a simple but effective way to explain it. TQM is defined as both a philosophy and a set of guiding principles that represent the foundations of a continuously improving organization. It is the application of qualitative methods and human resources to improve all the processes within an organization and exceed customer needs now and in the future. TQM integrates fundamental management techniques, existing improvements, and technical tools under a disciplined approach (Talukder and Ghosh, 2004).

OBJECTIVES

A library should focus on providing the best services possible, and be willing to change to serve its customers. To determine if changes need to be made, a librarian might ask: What are our target markets? What do the customers come in for? How can I look at the efficiency of my library?

How do we serve the current customers that exist today? First learn about the customer, and then solve the problems. The study of TQM of library and information systems and services becomes crucial. This paper intends to study the application of TQM to the provision of library and information services. The precise aims of the present study are to:

- To identify the concepts of excellence and TQM;
- To analysis the quality assertion in LIS;
- To recognize and study the relevance of TQM to LIS;
- To argue the standard for TQM in providing quality information service

TOTAL QUALITY MANAGEMENT

Basically, TQM is a business philosophy that seeks to encourage both individual and collective responsibility to quality at every stage of the production process from initial design and conception through to after sales service. Many businesses may not use the term TQM anymore but the philosophy is still very much part of most business thinking. It is seen as being a way in which a business can add value to its product and to gain competitive advantage over its rivals. The former may allow a business to charge a higher price for its product or service whilst the latter can be a key feature of its marketing programme. Total Quality Management takes an integrative approach for assuring quality in an organization. The four basic principles explain the nature of Total Quality Management. ReVelle, J.B. (2003) reveals that those of us who are confirmed members of the Total Quality Management (TQM) movement believe there are three major aspects of TQM and it is only when all three are employed together that we have a complete TQM effort. These components are: the cultural aspect, the technical aspect, and the managerial aspect.

QUALITY ASSURANCE STUDIES

The introduction to quality concepts also outlines Quality Assurance Standard ISO 9000, and the appendices feature criteria for information science, and a model mission statement and charter. Quality assurance studies were mostly restricted to special libraries and academic libraries.

Although quality assurance studies based on ISO 9000 and other accreditation schemes were conducted in libraries in UK, USA and Canada, such studies are rarely reported in Indian libraries and information systems. The quality assurance initiative in LIS has primarily come from the parent organization to which it provides services. However, in the later years, the quality assurance system has become as essential feature of LIS management. Quality studies in LIS are mostly isolated and are made on different aspects of library management, services, user- studies, etc. The evidence produced by the few TQM cases in the LIS sector indicates that TQM is a highly relevant management theory for information sector. The information products in LIS Sector can be Information Abstracts, Bibliographies, indexes, Current Awareness Bulletins, etc. These products should be produced according to set norms or criteria (like - following CCF; circulation before the information becomes obsolete). User-based approach lies on the idea that quality lies in the eyes of the beholder and that the customer or user is the ultimate quality judge.

ISO 8420 defines quality as: 'the totality of features and characteristics of a product, process of service that bear on its ability to satisfy stated or implied needs'. However, there are certain limitations to this approach.

The usefulness of user-based quality definition is dependent on how well the library user is informed about opportunities and limitations of a product or service offered. User satisfaction level may also vary in terms of value for money and value for information content received. In the value-based definition, quality is defined in terms of costs and prices. Thus, a quality product is one that provides conformance at an acceptable price or cost.

KEY COMPONENTS AND SUPPORTS

Following are four major component and supports of TQM for libraries to improve its images in the eye of library users are:

Synergistic Associations

According to this principle, a library must focus, first and foremost, on its services and users. In a TQM library, everyone is both a services provider and information supplier. This confusing concept emphasizes "the systematic nature of the work in which all are involved". In other words, teamwork and collaboration are very essential. Traditionally, library services have been prone to same for one and all. Now, this outdated practice no longer serves the library users because of specific needs. To survive in a world technological competence teamwork and collaboration result in high-quality benefits for the greatest number of library users. The very application of the TQM to library services emphasizes the synergistic relationship between the "library services" and "library users". The concept of synergy suggests that performance and library product is enhanced by pooling the talent and experience of library staff. In a library, library staff and library services are the same as of management front-line personnel and their production. The library product which is generally its services is responsible for the development of library user's capabilities, interests, and character. Viewed in this way, the librarians and the libraries are suppliers of effective learning tools, environments, and systems to the users who are the libraries primary customer. The library is responsible for providing long- term services welfare of users by literate them with new techniques and facilities available to them. Also, how to access quality services in their own work by maximizing opportunities for growth in every aspect of their studies.

Constant Development and Self Assessment

The TQM applied to libraries is the total dedication to continuous improvement, personally and collectively. Within a Total Quality library setting, administrators work collaboratively with their customers the library users. The foundations for this system were apprehension, intimidation, and an adversarial approach to problem-solving. Today it is in our best interest to encourage potential library users by dedicating ourselves to the constant development of their abilities to seek information. Total Quality is, very essentially, it is positive approach which works to users ultimate advantage. According to Deming, no human being should ever evaluate another human being. Therefore, TQM emphasizes self-evaluation as part of a continuous improvement process. In addition, this principle also laminates to the focusing on users' strengths, learning styles, and different types of intelligences.

Method of Continuing Process

Continuous improvement of all operations and activities is at the heart of TQM. Once it is recognized that library users' satisfaction can only be obtained by providing a high-quality product or services, continuous improvement of the quality of the product is seen as the only way to maintain a high level of users' satisfaction. TQM also recognizes that product quality is the result of processed services. As a result, there is a focus on continuous improvement of the library's processes. This will lead to an improvement in processed service. In turn this will lead to an improvement in product quality, and to an increase in users' satisfaction.

The users-driven approach helps to prevent errors and achieve defect free services. When problems do occur within the library services, they are generally discovered and resolved before they can get to the next library users. TQM as applied in libraries is the recognition of the organization as a system and the work done within the organization must be seen as an ongoing process. Total Quality speaks to working on the system, which must be examined to identify and eliminate the flawed processes that allow its users to fall short. Since systems are made up of processes, the improvements made in the quality of those processes largely determine the quality of the library services and product. In the new paradigm of scholarship, continual improvement of learning processes based on the performance of library services.

Direction or Leadership

TQM is a way of life for a library. It has to be introduced and led by top library management. This is a key point. Attempts to implement TQM often fail because top library management doesn't lead and get committed - instead it delegates and pays lip service. Commitment and Personal involvement is required from top library management in creating and deploying clear quality values and goals consistent with the objectives of the library, and in creating and deploying well defined systems, methods and performance measures for achieving those goals.

These systems and methods guide all quality activities and encourage users by all staff. The development and use of performance indicators is linked, directly or indirectly, to users' requirements and satisfaction, and to library management. The library staff must establish the context in which library users can best achieve their potential through the continuous improvement that results from library staff and users working together. Librarian who emphasizes content area library services and principle- centered services provide the leadership or direction, framework, and tools necessary for continuous improvement in the library process.

TQM IN LIBRARIES

Users-Driven Quality

TQM is "a system of continuous improvement employing participative management and centered on the needs of customers" (Jurow & Barnard, 1993). Key components of TQM are employee involvement and training, problem-solving teams, statistical methods, long-term goals and thinking, and recognition that the system, not people, produces inefficiencies.

According to Jurow & Barnard (1993) libraries can benefit from TQM in three ways:

- breaking down interdepartmental barriers;

- redefining the beneficiaries of library services as internal
- customers (staff) and external customers (patrons); reaching a state of continuous improvement

TQM has a user-first theory or orientation. The user, not internal activities and constraints, comes first. User's satisfaction is seen as the libraries highest priority. The library believes it will only be successful if users are satisfied. The TQM library is sensitive to users' requirements and responds rapidly to them. In the TQM context, 'being sensitive to users' requirements' goes beyond defect and error reduction, and merely meeting specifications or reducing users complaints. The concept of requirements is expanded to take in not only product and service attributes that meet basic requirements, but also those that enhance and differentiate them for competitive advantage. Each part of the library is involved in Total Quality, operating as users to some functions and as a supplier to others.

TQM IN LIS

Total quality management can helps libraries to identify, analyze and assess qualitative and quantitative data that is relevant to their library services. These tools can identify procedures, ideas, statistics, cause and effect concerns and other issues relevant to their organizations. Each of which can be examined and used to enhance the effectiveness, efficiency, standardization and overall quality of procedures, products or work environment, in accordance with ISO 9000 standards.

In India, the library of the Indian Institute of Management, Lucknow (IIML) has been conducting innovative continuing professional development programs for professionals engaged in the library and information sector for many years. More than 30 such programs are employed in the context of library and information systems and services, in areas such as:

- quality management;
- marketing;
- information technology applications;
- human relations; and
- communication

Feedback from the participants has continually been revealing that the programs were very well received, and at times had even surpassed expectations. As a result, significant positive developments have also been seen to have taken place in many of the participants' library and information systems as far as their collection development, collection organization, service design and delivery activities are concerned (Raina, 2005) According to Quality America, Inc. (ReVelle, 2003) the number of TQM tools is close to 100 and come in various forms, such as brainstorming, focus groups, check lists, charts and graphs, diagrams and other analysis tools.

In a different vein, manuals and standards are TQM as well, as they give direction and best practice guidelines to the library staff. TQM illustrate and aid in the incorporation of complex information such as:

- Identification of target library users
- Optimistic and pessimistic forces affecting the library services
- Evaluation of library users needs
- Completion analysis
- Adaptation for new and bright ideas
- Efficiency change in library
- Preparation of various statistics
- Library staff and work flow

LIS AND TQM: A RAPPORT

The practice of quality management in LIS existed since the evolution of the subject itself, but the terminology used for these varied widely. Performance indicators; performance evaluation; evaluation of reference sources using check-list of criteria; Evaluation of Information Retrieval systems using Precision and Recall rations; Cost-Benefit and cost effectiveness studies; user surveys electing opinions on library services - all these studies make part and parcel of quality studies using different mechanisms of assessment and methodologies. In early 1980s, numerous studies were made on automated data validation, error rates and patterns, authority control which belongs to quality control in online databases.

However, customer and employee satisfaction are seldom in focus. Quality, with regard to the products of industries, depends on raw materials, vendor components, and different skills of performance of employees and production processes, and equipment that shows different degrees of performance. Similarly, quality with regard to library and information science or with respect to the processing of information services in the library depends on:

- the collection of documents and their technical processing by
- applying certain techniques and methods;
- the skills of employees;
- equipment and processing;
- the span of time of service to be rendered; and
- The attributes of services which are to be rendered.

From the above, it is clear that while quality in respect of industries fulfills the ultimate goal of user satisfaction, the same may be adopted in library and information centers. Quality in library services is most effective in user-oriented services (Talukder and Ghosh, 2004).

ADVANTAGES OF TQM

According to the practical evidences, the TQM principles help the libraries in following clauses:

- Redefine the role, purpose and responsibilities of libraries.
- Improve library as a "way of life."
- Plan comprehensive leadership training for library users at all levels.
- Create staff development that addresses the attitudes and beliefs of library staff.
- Use research and practice-based information to guide both policy and practice.
- Design comprehensive users-development initiatives.

In order to achieve the above as opportunities to the library scenario, in addition to patience, participatory management among well-trained and educated partners is crucial to the success of TQM in libraries; everyone involved must understand and believe in principles. Some personnel who are committed to the principles can facilitate success with TQM. Their vision and skills in leadership, management, interpersonal communication, problem solving and creative cooperation are important qualities for successful implementation of TQM.

Sirkin (1993) suggests some ways a library might use the principles of TQM to enhance library services.

- Create service brochures and information kits
- Conduct a user survey about library services
- Improve signage
- Change hours of operation
- Provide a more convenient material return
- Simplify checkout of materials
- Use flexibility in staff assignments
- Cooperate with local government

- Ask vendors to give product demonstrations
- Give new staff a thorough orientation
- Create interdepartmental library advisory groups
- Improve the physical layout of the library
- Track complaints
- Develop an active outreach program
- Open satellite offices
- Publicize new or changed services
- Develop user and staff training materials
- Target services to specific groups
- Offer electronic document delivery
- Follow the mission statement
- Smile

Riggs (1992) sum up the remarkable principles of TQM as:

Manage by fact : make library decisions after careful analysis of data gathered with tools such as check sheets, histograms, and Pareto charts;

Eliminate rework: library work is often labor intensive— simplify it and make sure it is done properly the first time;

Respect people and ideas : staff are the library's most valuable resources, and they should be encouraged to point out problems without fear of management; and

Empower people : trust library staff to act responsibly and give them the appropriate authority to make decisions that can improve the quality of work they do. Finally, remember that TQM is not a "quick fix." It needs to be implemented gradually over a two- to three-year period.

OBSTACLES WHILE IMPLEMENTING TQM IN LIS

TQM implementation is not a success due to following reasons.

Organizational Obstacles : The first is organizational context, such as a rigid organizational culture that is inflexible and a highly bureaucratic organizational structure and authoritarian management style. That is, the failures of TQM implementations are due not to external factors but to the failure of management to establish a proper system for its implementation (Shin et al. 1998). This perspective argues that often managers are not fully aware, or perhaps ignore, what it takes to implement TQM successfully and achieve high performance.

Cultural Obstacles : The second is the cultural barrier, because TQM implementation involves a paradigm shift in management values and attitudes and it should fit the national culture of the firm if it is to be implemented successfully (Sohal et al. 1998). Research on the culture barrier argues that management values differ significantly across national cultures that management is culture- specific and that managerial practices, such as TQM, must be tailored to fit the local culture. TQM is about transforming an organization's culture, yet with the expectation of establishing a quality infrastructure and eliminating middle management positions through attrition. It is difficult to make a change in organizational structures as TQM requires institutions to restructure. Resistance to change and people's attitudes are primary hindrances to implementing TQM in libraries. The other barriers are the problems of finding the money and time for training while maintaining current services in the library.

Miller and Stearns (1994) listed the following barriers to the implementation of TQM in libraries:

- the view that this is just another management fad of the day; management's fear of the loss control;
- employee reluctance to recommend changes because of fear of management;

- the business and industrial background of TQM might not lend itself to the non-profit sector, including libraries TQM requires a long-term investment of time over several years as processes are analyzed and an organization's culture is changed - this can cause resistance; and
- other difficulties in these days of increasing financial and other pressures Other research has focused on individuals within an organization. For example, (Reger et al. 1994) suggest that each person's response to an idea involves the cognitive process of interpretation, attribution and inference. This means that managers who propose the idea for quality improvement are convinced that it works and assume that employees will think so too). Candido and Morns (2000) describe TQM failure as the expression of differing desires, wants, needs and feelings at individual levels within the organization. However, the underlying causes of failure in the implementation of TQM may go beyond individual beliefs, expectations, cognitive processes of interpretation, perceptions, feelings, and desires to more deeply rooted unconscious archetypical projections on the part of each individual in the organization.

SUGGESTIONS

A successful TQM environment requires a committed and well-trained library staff that participates fully in quality improvement activities of the library. Such participation is reinforced by reward and recognition systems which emphasize the achievement of quality objectives. Ongoing education and training of all library staff supports the drive for quality. Library staffs are encouraged to take more responsibility, communicate more effectively, act creatively, and innovate. As library users come forward for a particular activity or services they must be suitably rewarded, TQM links reward to customer satisfaction. Based on the above discussion and observations, following suggestion are made for the implementation of quality in libraries.

- Quality Assurance of Library and Information System should be part of the Quality Assurance of library TQM project;
- There is a need to develop standards / norms for assessing quality of information services to libraries;
- There is a need to evolve methodologies and mechanisms for improvement of quality Library services;
- More funds to be allocated for studying the quality of information services on project basis;
- Training of staff members in providing quality information services.

CONCLUSION

Successful TQM implementation requires a thorough understanding of critical success factors, barriers to achieving these factors, and managerial tools and techniques to overcome these barriers. Research in developed countries listed top management commitment to TQM, training for TQM throughout the library, customer focus and continuous improvement, and a focus on library staff involvement and empowerment as the key determinants of successful TQM implementation. TQM is focused on the understanding that libraries are systems with processes that have the purpose of serving library users. TQM calls for the integration of all library activities to achieve the goal of serving users. It seeks to impose standards, achieve efficiencies, define roles of individuals staff members within processes and the library as a whole, reduce errors and defects by applying statistical process control, and to employ teams to plan and execute processes more efficiently. It requires leaders who are willing to create a culture in which people define their roles in terms of quality outputs to customers. The outlook that the clientele bring to a library have a critical effect upon their awareness of quality. It is better to obtain a reputation for one or two factors which are important to clientele and to concentrate upon further developing those. Service delivery is like a hypothetical performance. If customers are to gain maximum benefit from a service, they must know how to use it. So, properly planned user education is a must for library services. Library support systems should reflect library users' priorities. It is important to find out which services can be automated without losing the personal touch. Getting feedback from the user is important to ascertain the quality of service. Potential users of library can be given a questionnaire to get feedback from them for improving service. The circulation desk staff is the front line staff who plays a critical role in library; first deal with inquiries/crises; manage the reader interface. The staff at public dealing must be carefully- appointed and be given periodic training to keep up-to- date. All library staff must receive training, including skill training; on the job guidance; retraining. Well-trained staff is the competitive weapon for better quality service in library. Teamwork plays a vital role in giving better quality service. People have to develop a culture and commitment towards quality service in library.

REFERENCES

1. Candido, C.J.F. and Morris, D.S. "Charting Service Quality Gaps", *Total Quality Management,* Vol. 11 No.4-6, p.463-72, 2000.
2. Carl, J.G. Quality Management Principles and Methods in Library and Information Science theory and Practice. In *Encyclopedia of Library and Information Science,* V56, pp.318-352,1995.
3. Jurow, S. and Barnard, S. B. Introduction: TQM Fundamentals and Overview of Contents. *"Journal of Library*

Administration,,"18(112). p.1-13, 1993. (EJ 469099)

4. Miller, R.G. and Stearns, B. "Quality Management for Today's Academic Library", *College & Research Libraries News,* Vol. 55 No.7, p.406-22, 1994.
5. Moghaddam, G.G. "Total Quality Management in Library and Information Sectors" *The Electronic Library,* Vol.26 No.6, p. 912-922, 2008.
6. Raina, R.L. "Innovative Continuing Professional Development Programs for LIS Professionals Conducted by the Library at IIM Lucknow: An Overview", 2005. available at : www.ifla.org/IV/ifla71/papers/042e-La- Raina.pdf.
7. Reger, R.K. and others. "Reframing the Organization: why implementing Total Quality is easier said than done", *Academy of Management Review,* Vol. 19 No. 3, p. 565-84,1994.
8. ReVelle, J.B. TQM Tools & Tool Kits. (Retrieved on November 6, 2009) http://www.qualityamerica.eom/knowledgecente/articles/revelletqmtools.htm
9. Riggs, D. E. TQM: Quality Improvement in New Clothes. "College & Research Libraries," 53(6), p. 481483, 1992. (EJ 454 720).
10. Shin, D., Kalinowski, J.G. and El-Enein, G.A. "Critical Implementation Issues in Total Quality Management", SAM Advanced Management Journal, Vol. 63, p.10-15,1998.
11. Sirkin, A. F. Customer Service: Another side of TQM. '*Journal of Library Administration,* "18(1/2). p.71-83, 1993. (EJ 469104)
12. Sohal, A.S., Samson, D. and Ramsay, L. "Requirement for Successful Implementation of Total Quality Management", International Journal of Technology Management, Vol. 16p.505-19, 1998.
13. Sohal, A.S., Samson, D. and Ramsay, L. "Requirement for Successful Implementation of Total Quality Management", *International Journal of Technology Management,* Vol.16,p.505-19, 1998.
14. Talukder, T. and Ghosh, S. "Total Quality Management and its Implication on Library Laws", *SRELS Journal of Information Management,* Vol. 41 No.3, p. 255-66, 2004.

27

Virtual Reference Service In IISC/IISER Libraries : User Awareness

Amol D. Khobragade
Librarian, Yashavantrao Chavan Institute of Science, Satara
Shalini R. Lihitkar
Assistant Professor, Department of Library and Information Science, RTM Nagpur University, Nagpur

ABSTRACT

The paper highlights on virtual reference service (VRS) in IISc/IISER academic libraries. It is a new face of reference service which is known as virtual reference service rendering through online that enables library patrons to ask reference questions through a library websites. It gives greater opportunities to user. Who can access services at home, in house, in office, or in a library.

Keywords : Virtual reference service, user awareness, IIsc, IISER, Academic libraries, India.

1. INTRODUCTION

The primary aim of the library is to offer a variety of services to its clientele to meet their specific information requirements. Several techniques such as classification, cataloguing, shelving lists, OPAC, open access to its readers and similar other types of services are all indirect form of assistance to users to find their document in the library.

The Reference service is one of the library's primary services besides acquisitions, classification, cataloguing and physical planning. This service provides personalized assistance to library users in accessing and using suitable information resources to meet the needs of reader.

In the present era of Information and Communication Technology, the concept of library and its services has totally taken a new face. The World Wide Web provides information at users fingertips. The gap between information and user is minimizing day by day.

In the libraries and information centers "Reference Service" is an important personalized service. Traditionally, it is a one-to-one service with user and reference librarian. The user is helped by the variety of sources available to meet the information needs.[7]But in the present era, the library and information profession is facing the challenges of so called 'electronic age' and being transformed by technology. So the advancement in information technology has brought out incredible changes in almost every aspect of information services.

2. VIRTUAL REFERENCE SERVICE

Technological developments have affected not only the format and sources of the information libraries use to provide reference service, but also where we provide reference service. Libraries and their resources have partially moved to the virtual world of the Internet. As a result, library patrons can access our resources from outside of the physical library. In an effort to reach patrons accessing the library via their computers, many libraries and library consortia are extending their reference service to include virtual reference. Technology now allows users to submit their queries to the library at any time from any place in the world. Virtual reference is responsive to patrons' need for convenient access to reference service[10].

Virtual reference, which allows users to connect easily with librarians online, is becoming highly popular. Librarians answer thousands of questions everyday over the Internet[4]. Although the service is maturing much more research is still needed. In particular, there is a need to gain a better understanding of the role of virtual reference in providing services to diverse and cross-cultural user groups[12]. This research gap is now becoming more important with the increase numbers of diverse and non-traditional students attending colleges and universities.

The provision of online reference services, specifically via e-mail, enable users who were uncomfortable approaching a librarian in person to submit anonymous questions to a virtual reference service[3]. Likewise, certain user groups do not come to the library due to physical disabilities, scheduling constraints, or geographical distance.These users too might find virtual reference to be more accessible for their needs as it provides services to users anytime, anyplace[2]. Users can send reference queries via e-mail whenever they have questions[13].

3. DEFINITION OF VIRTUAL REFERENCE SERVICE

Virtual Reference Service is also an Internet based reference service where a user can ask a question online, where the user and the librarian communicate in real time[1]. It uses computers and communication technology to provide reference service to users anytime and anywhere.

Virtual Reference Service is an online reference service that enables library patrons to ask reference questions through a library's website. The user may be at home, in office, at school, or in a library. Some Virtual Reference Services also place answers to frequently asked questions (FAQs), selected reference tools, and access to selected databases on the website[6]. The question answering service using Internet technology is the essential component, without which the use of the name "Virtual Reference" is misleading.

VRS is defined as the provision of real-time personal assistance to patrons via web- based interactive software. To meet the user at his or her "point of need" and to satisfy the patron's information need, the librarian can use a "Chat" component of the software to answer a fairly specific or simple question, possibly deliver slideshows, 'push' web sources to the patron, and provide online bibliographic instruction[11]. The "point of need" may happen when the library is closed, or when the user is unable to get to the library. This way, users can still be in contact with experienced reference librarians.

4. MODES OF VIRTUAL REFERENCE SERVICE:

The Virtual Reference Service can be broadly divided in to three categories these are as follows.

4.1. Asynchronous Transaction

The Asynchronous transaction involves a time delay between the question and answer[8]. Following are the examples of asynchronous transaction.

- E-mail based,
- Web-form or Ask a service,
- Virtual Reference Desk (VRD) service,
- Question Point,
- Online Pathfinders, etc.

4.2. Synchronous Transactions

The synchronous transaction, on the other hand takes place in 'real time' with an immediate response to the query[9], the examples of synchronous transaction are

- Chat-based services,
- Video Conferencing or web cam services,

- Digital Reference Robots,
- Real-time Reference services (Live Ref, 24/7 Ref), etc.

4.3. Collaborative Networks

Many libraries and organizations have recognized the benefits of providing Digital Reference Service through collaborative services. Some regional library consortia are offering member libraries the opportunity to share reference questions with each other using the internet and other technologies. The collaborative Digital Reference Service (CDRS)[5], operated by the library of congress, is an international network of libraries, consortia, museums, Ask a services that uses a help desk system to route questions to appropriate institutions based on member profile.

5. PROFILE OF IISC/IISERS

The Indian Institutes of Science Education and Research (IISERs) are a group of science education and research institutes in India. The institutes were created by the Government of India, through the Ministry of Human Resource Development (MHRD). One IISc and Five IISERs have been established across the country, namely IISc Bangalore in Karnataka, IISER Kolkata in West Bengal, IISER Pune in Maharashtra, IISER Mohali in Punjab, IISER Bhopal in Madhya Pradesh and IISER Thiruvananthapuram in Kerala.

6. DATA ANALYSIS

Table 6.1. Distribution of Questionnaires among the users of IIsc/IISER Libraries in India

Sr. No.	Name of the Institute	Questionnaire Distributed	Questionnaire Received
1	IIScBangalore	20	16 (80%)
2	IISERPune	20	18 (90%)
3	IISERKolkata	20	15 (75%)

Total		60 (100%)	49 (81.66%)

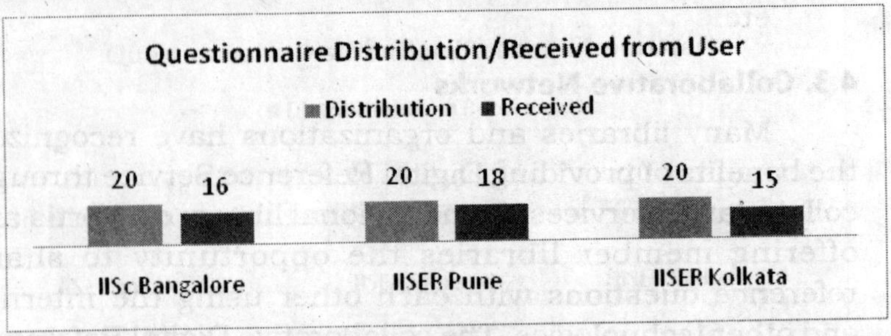

Graph No. 5.1

While analyzing the above table no. 6.1it is revealed that, A total of 60 questionnaires (20 questionnaire for each library were sent to 3 institutes) 49 (81.66%) received from IISc/IISER libraries.

Table 6.2. Analysis of Usability of Internet by Users

Sr. No.	*Name of Institutes*	*Frequency of Use of Internet* *Always*	*Frequently*	*Sometimes*	*Rarely*	*Total*
1	IIScB	7 (43.75%)	5 (31.25%)	3 (18.75%)	1 (6.25%)	16 (100%)
2	IISERP	9 (50%)	4 (22.22%)	4 (22.22%)	1 (5.55%)	18 (100%)
3	IISERK	6 (40%)	4 (26.66%)	3 (20%)	2 (13.33%)	15 (100%)
Total		22 (44.89%)	13 (26.53%)	10 (20.40%)	4 (8.16%)	49 (100%)

The Internet is a continually growing organism of information that is constantly morphing into new ways of communicating. From the above mentioned Table 6.2 the usability of Internet, there are 44.89%of users always using internet, 26.53% of users frequentlyusing the

Table 6.3. Analysis of the main purpose of Accessing the Internet

Sr. No.	Name of Institute	Total Number of Users	Main Purpose of Accessing the Internet					
			Communication	Education	Viewing current news	Business	Entertainment	Research
1	IIScB	16	13 (81.25%)	14 (87.50%)	11 (68.75%)	9 (56.25%)	11 (68.75%)	14 (87.50%)
2	IISERP	18	15 (83.33%)	16 (88.88%)	13 (72.22%)	11 (61.11%)	14 (77.77%)	16 (88.88%)
3	IISERK	15	11 (73.33%)	13 (86.66%)	11 (73.33%)	6 (40%)	10 (66.66%)	14 (93.33%)
Total		49 (100%)	39 (79.59%)	43 (87.75%)	35 (71.42%)	26 (53.06%)	35 (71.42%)	44 (89.79%)

internet, 20.40% of users sometimes using the internetand only 8.16% of users use the internet rarely.

Knowledge is not restricted to the printed media and the reader has also changed their habit for getting the required literature. Table 6.3 reveals that maximum 89.79% of users access internet for Research purpose, 87.75% of users use internet for Educationpurpose, 79.59% of users use the internet for Communication purpose, 71.42% of users use the internet for Entertainment and Viewing current news purpose and 53.06% of users accessing internet only business purpose.

Table 6.4. Analysis of Importance of Computer Literacy in the usage of Electronic Resources/ Services

Sr. No.	*Name of the Institute*	*Total No. of Students*	*User opinion about electronic resources/ services*				
			Strongly agree	*Agree*	*Somewhat agree*	*Disagree*	*Strongly disagree*
1	IIScB	16	6 (37.50%)	9 (56.25%)	1 (6.25%)	—	—
2	IISERP	18	8 (44.44%)	7 (38.88%)	2 (11.11%)	1 (5.55%)	—
3	IISERK	15	6 (40%)	5 (33.33%)	3 (20%)	1 (6.66%)	—
Total Percentages		49 (100%)	20 (40.81%)	21 (42.85%)	6 (12.24%)	2 (4.08%)	— —

Electronic resources are increasingly available on the internet or websites of the particular institutes thereby making it possible for students to access and use current and relevant literature for studies and research. Print medium is increasingly giving way to the electronic form of materials. Table 6.4 represents that 42.85% of users were agreed that computer literacy is importance in the usage of electronic resources, 40.81% of users are strongly agree that computer literacy is importance in the usage of electronic resources/ services, 12.24% of users somewhat agree for computer literacy is importance in the usage of electronic resources/ services and only 4.08% of users disagree for the above mentioned statement.

Table 6.5. Users Awareness about Virtual Reference Services

Sr. No.	Name of Institutes	Library offering VRS Yes	No	Total
1	IIScB	13 (81.25%)	3 (18.75%)	16
2	IISERP	16 (88.88%)	2 (11.11%)	18
3	IISERK	12 (80%)	3 (20%)	15
	Total	41 (83.67%)	8 (16.32%)	49 (100%)

The table 6.5 represents that, 83.67% of users are aware about their institutions library offering virtual reference services and only 16.32% of users are not aware about the institutions library offering VRS.

CONCLUSION

Traditionally an individual institution provides reference service in a physical location, that is, in a library. With the development of technology, especially Internet technology, libraries have developed virtual reference services (VRS) in order to provide efficient and effective reference services to the library users in and out of the library. Now technology allows users to submit their queries to the library at any time from any place in the world.

REFERENCES

- Bhatia, Neeru.,& Vohra, R. (2007). Trends in Reference and Information Services in the Electronic era: A case study of A C Joshi Library, Panjab University, Chandigarh' *5th International CALIBER -2007, Panjab University, Chandigarh.* Available on *http://ir.inflibnet.ac.in/bitstream/1944/1437/1/617-630.pdf*(Last access on 23/09/2012)
- Bushallow-Wilbur, L., DeVinney, G., & Whitcomb, F. (1996). Electronic mail reference service: A study. *Reference Quarterly*,35(3), 359"371.

- Coffman, S. (2003). Going live: Starting and running a virtual reference service. *Chicago: American Library Association.*
- Coffman, S., &Arret, L. (2004). To chat or not to chat: Taking yet another look at virtual reference. *The Searcher*, 12(8), 49"56.
- Diane, Nester Kresh (2000) The Collaborative Digital Reference Service (CDRS). *D-Lib Magazine*, Available on *http://www.dlib.org/dlib/june00 /kresh/06kresh.html* (Last access on 24/1/2013).
- Lihitkar, Shalini R. (2010). Establishing a Virtual Reference Service. *DESIDOC Journal of Library & Information Technology*, 31(1), 31-34.
- Maharana, B., & Panda, K.C. (2005). Virtual Reference Service in Academic Libraries: a Case Study of the Libraries of IIMs and IITs in India. Available on *http://eprints.rclis.org/copyright/*(Last access on 24/06/2011)
- *Ibid* pp. 4.
- *Ibid* pp. 4.
- RUSA. Guidelines for Implementing and Maintaining Virtual Reference Services. available on *http://www.ala.org/rusa/resources/ guidelines /virtrefguidelines* (Last access on 12/10/2013)
- Sawant, Sarika. (2012). Virtual Reference Services. Available on *http://liscompendium.wordpress.com/article/virtual-reference-services-3u4xbpvtd97y2-1/* (Last access on 24/11/2012).
- Shachaf, P., Hara, N., Meho, L., Kwon, N., Li, B., Sakai, Y., &Lankes, D. (2005). Cross-cultural analysis of virtual reference. [electronic version]. *Proceedings of the 68th Annual Meeting of the Society for Information Science and Technology*, vol. 42.
- Stacy-Bates, K. (2003). E-mail reference responses from academic ARL libraries: An unobtrusive study. *Reference and User Services Quarterly*, 43(1), 59"70.

28

Web Based Library And Information Services

Sandeep S. Pradhan
Librarian, N.S. Science & Art's College,
Bhadrawati, Dist. Chandrapur (MS)

ABSTRACT

In today's world information transfer through web plays a significant role in the utilization of its resources. Technological developments have affected not only the formats and sources of the information, but also how and where to provide library services. Libraries and their resources have partially moved to the virtual world of the Internet. The use of Internet has increased the efficiency of the library and informational professionals altered the nature of library and information related work, and have provided users with an opportunity to access information sources without entering a library at all. The paper analyzes details studies regarding the services provided through web for information user and application of the web services. It gives brief idea about the emerging web tools and technology, its importance in the library and information dissemination.

Keywords : Information Services, Web Based Services, Internet, Database, ICT

INTRODUCTION

In recent years Internet has emerged as the most important and powerful medium for storage and retrieval of information. There is a tremendous growth in the number and variety of information resources available on the Internet and it made a great impact on information. At beginning library was just a store house of books and other document. A large number of different services came into the picture during the middle of the 20th century due to the innovation and use of computer the mode of library services changed dramatically. After long time library started document delivery service and circulation came into picture.

A web technology (Internet) has emerged as the largest repository of knowledge and information containing billions of documents, a major part of which is available free of cost. It means that the library has access to more reference tools that are more up to date and cheaper. Finding particular information in an electronic web reference tool is also very convenient and fast. Search engines now provide tremendous power to search and select Internet information effectively and in a user friendly manner.

In today's world information transfer through web plays a significant role in the utilization of its resources. Technological developments have affected not only the formats and sources of the information, but also how and where to provide library services. Libraries and their resources have partially moved to the virtual world of the web (Internet). As a result, library users can access the resources from outside the physical library. Technology now allows users to submit their queries to the library at any time from any place in the world. Web Based Services, Digital Library Services, Internet Library Services and Electronic Library Services are terms with similar meanings.

WHAT IS WEB?

WEB is "World wide web, internet". WEB is popularly used as the synonymous term of World Wide Web or

Internet. The Web, or World Wide Web, is basically a system of Internet servers that support specially formatted documents. The documents are formatted in a markup language called HTML (HyperText Markup Language) that supports links to other documents, as well as graphics, audio, and video files.

The web is a client or server system used to access all kinds of information to anyone on the net. The information can be in the form of regular text, hypertext, pictures, sounds, Usenet newsgroups and other types of data. To access this information, use a client program called browser. Within the web, the information is stored in pages. Each page can hold not only information but links to other pages. In each page a particular word or sequence of words highlighted item and the other information related to that words in some other pages. This means that there is a link between the highlighted item and the other information, the service is called hypertext. Keeping in mind today's tremendous increase in information and changing users behavior we can say that web is an ideal media for providing library information services.

There are some common facilities we can enjoy form web.

- Hypertext document with Text, Pictures, Sound and Animation facilities
- Information sharing for any number of users at any time.
- Provides a distributed information system
- Exchange of electronic mail and other data files in a wide area environment.
- On-line real time interaction with other network users.
- Participation in electronic media mailing lists and conferences.

- Access to data stored on remote computers.
- Access to wide selection of public domain and shareware software.

LIBRARY SERVICES

Library services refer to facilities, which are provided by a library for the use of books and dissemination of information for the need and meet the users' requirement. The well known existing library services are cataloguing, classification, circulation services, reservation, renewal, new arrivals, current contents, current awareness service, selective dissemination of information, indexing and abstracting, reference service, document delivery, inter library loan, externally purchased database, CD-ROM databases, access to other library catalogues, access to online databases, internally published newsletter, reports and journals, bibliographic services, and so on. All these services have changed its mode to an extent with web environment.

RESOURCES AVAILABLE ON THE WEB OF LIBRARIAN'S INTEREST

Following resources are available for Library and Information professionals for providing various type of information.

- E-journals
- E-books
- Standards
- Preprints
- Library catalogue
- Bibliographical tools
- Share wares
- News Papers
- Dictionary
- Magazine

- Encyclopaedias
- Database
- Directories
- Films
- Technical Reports
- Audio
- Patents
- Video
- Companies, Institutions, Organization, Associations etc.

WEB BASED LIBRARY SERVICES

Web-based Library Services means, library services provided using Internet as medium and library website as a gateway with the help of integrate library management system. Today almost every important information is available in electronic web format on online, providing convenience of use, storage, timeliness and currency of information. Web storage and compression technologies have made it possible to store large amount of data and information on web media, eliminating requirement for large space for holding. Library networks offer much potential and new capabilities for sharing information among different library and information centers at local, regional, national and international levels and eliminate the size, distance, and language barriers among users through resource sharing.

GENERAL SERVICES OFFERED BY WEB

Following are the very common and general services offer by the web.

- List Serve
- Document Delivery
- Commercial Resources
- Bulletin Board

- Abstract and Indexing
- E-Books
- E-Journals
- E-mail Facilities
- Surfing Facilities.
- Subject Database
- Research Databases
- Community Information
- Government Resources
- Library Catalog
- Shopping and other commercial transactions
- Electronic Publications

WEB BASED LIBRARY SERVICES FOR USER

Database Access

A database is a collection of information that is organized so that it can easily be accessed, managed, and updated. In one view, databases can be classified according to types of content: bibliographic, full-text, numeric, and images. Several publishers today offer web-based, intranet solutions for providing local access to their databases. Large R&D libraries can take advantage of these developments and provide desktop access to key database and electronic publications to their users.

Apart from the externally purchased databases, libraries have their own collection of CD-ROM databases mounted on their CD server/tower. Online database vender such as Lexis-Nexis, Dialog, ERIC are delivering their database over internet. So a library which subscribes to these databases can now easily access them over Web.

Bibliographic and Cataloguing Service

This service can also be prepared from different databases available on the Web. . Library of Congress

Catalog is a very popular online service LC which are on the Web, can be easily accessed through telnet services, which help the researchers.

Bulletin Board Service

A bulletin board system, or BBS, is a computer server running custom software that allows users to connect to the system using a terminal program. Once logged in, the user can perform functions such as uploading and downloading software and data, reading news and bulletins, and exchanging messages with other users through email, public message boards, and sometimes via direct chatting.

A bulletin board is a public discussion area where people can post message without sending them to anyone's e-mail address that can be viewed by anyone who enters the area.

CAS

The purpose of a current-awareness service is to inform the users about new acquisitions in their libraries. Used display boards and shelves to draw attention to recent additions, and many libraries produce complete or selective lists for circulation to patrons. Some libraries have adopted a practice of selective dissemination of information.

A library can provide this service through e-mail, which is easiest and common procedure. Otherwise a library can refer or link directly to some location to their WebPages.

E-SDI : Link to remote information

Selective dissemination of information ("SDI") was originally a phrase related to library and information science. SDI refers to tools and resources used to keep a user informed of new resources on specified topics. Electronic SDI service was formulated to deliver current information of interest to faculty members on their desktop. Thus this service not only function as a Current Awareness Tool, but also influenced the acquisition of information sources as well as usage of other library services like document delivery, resource sharing and acquiring reprints. For promoting E-SDI services on the web, library should create a link from the existing library environment (i.e. E-SDI page is accessed by clicking the SDI siblink from the information service link of library main page) and the different task followed provide the services can be traced by hyper-navigating the active link.

Electronic Journals

Electronic journals form a large part of the collection of a library for providing web based services. Today many journals are available electronically - some are full text and some contain only bibliographic information with abstract. Major advantage of electronic journals is that they are constantly updated and easy to access but disadvantage is that breaching of copyright law is very easy. They are available as bitmaps, PostScript, PDF, ASCII, SGML and HTML. Library services may be delivering to users on CD-Rom, through email or through web. Some international societies and associations have developed their own digital libraries through which users can get access to all their publications. Services are available to the members of society or associations through subscription.

E-mail delivery

Email, short for "electronic mail," is one of the most widely used features of the Internet, along with the web. It allows you to send and receive messages to and from anyone with an email address; anywhere in the world. That e-mail is not at all web based library service. It is a web based excellent media and most probably most popular media and library professionals can use this web medium for various purposes specially for delivering some web based services. It is the easiest and convenient method to access the web sources is e-mail.

Portals

Portals are either commercial or free web facilities that offer information services to a specific audience. The facilities include web search to communication to email to news etc. There are three kinds of portals; Consumer (or horizontal), Vertical and Enterprise.

- Consumer portals are aimed at consumer audiences and offer free email, games, chat etc. Examples are Yahoo!, MSN and AOL.
- Vertical portals, target a specified audience, such as a particular industry, and offer many of the consumer portal features. Example includes VerticalNet.
- Enterprise portals on the other hand are similar to consumer portals, but they are offered only to corporations or similar organizations. Examples include Epicentric and Corporate Yahoo! These portals can be best understood as electronic pathfinders for users, pulling together in one place in a web site selected links to subjects or interest-oriented resources located on the WW W.

Frequently Asked Questions (FAQ)

FAQ stands for Frequently Asked Questions. A compilation of Frequently Asked Questions and their answer is referred to as a FAQ list or FAQ article. FAQs are compilations of information which are the result of certain questions constantly being asked hence the name FAQ. There are thousands of FAQs on the World Wide Web. AskERIC is an Internet question answering services run buy the ERIC Clearinghouse on Information and Technology at Syracuse University, NewYork.

ILL (Inter-Library Loan) and Document Delivery Services

Resource sharing using web tools through Inter-library loan is a necessity for the libraries. Access to the catalogue of partner libraries is crucial to inter-library lending. Union catalogues, standardization and machine readable catalogues are aimed at promoting resource sharing. Librarians can now access catalogues of thousands of libraries across the world using Internet. Libraries use document delivery services from other libraries and commercial organizations for copies of research papers etc using web tools. Web tehnoogy has made the document delivery services very simple and reliable. From searching the holdings to ordering and delivery have been benefited by the use of ICT. A large number of libraries now host their up to date holdings on their website and can be searched on internet.

Internet Subject Gateways

A subject gateway is a web site that provides searchable and brows able access to online resources focused around a specific subject. Subject based Information Gateways are subject entrances (clearing houses) to quality assessed Internet resources. This can be contrasted with gateways where resources are arranged according to where they are physically placed or "geographically" according to what type of resource they are. A number of libraries in Europe are involved in the development of internet subject gateways services that aim to help users find high quality resources of internet subject gateways offer an alternative to the Internet search engines and Web directories.

News Clipping Service

News clip service is one of the CAS provided in many libraries in print/ photocopy form. To provide this service, news items from selected news papers are first marked and then the clippings are pasted on a white sheet. These filed clippings are then circulated among the users. The risk of misfiled and unreturned documents is virtually eliminated in an electronic format. The format may be Text or PDF (Portable Document Format). The image may represented as GIF (Graphic Interchange Format) or JEPG (Joint Photographic Experts Group). All the document should be copied to the server root and the executable to the CGI-BIN directory. A homepage for news clips service has been created and through which access to the news clips has been achieved.

Ask-A-Librarian

Ask-A-Librarian services are Internet-based question and answer service that connects users with individuals who possess specialized subject knowledge and skill in conducting precision searches. Most "Ask-a-Librarians" services have a web-based question submission form or an e-mail address or both. Users are invited to submit their queries by using web forms or through e-mail. Once a query is read by a service, it is assigned to an individual expert for answering. An expert responds to the query with factual information and or a list of information resources. The response is either sent to the user's e-mail account or is posted on the web so that the user can access it after a certain period of time.

NewsGroup

They are on-line discussion groups on many topics of varied interest. A program called newsreader is required to view and post message in newsgroups. Unlike mail lists and chats, newsgroups allow readers to choose the topics to discuss. They can be of immense help to professionals and scientists. Special libraries must encourage users to participate in newsgroups thereby enhancing the organizational knowledge base. The library staff can post messages in the appropriate newsgroup and discuss library –related problems, adoption of new techniques in libraries, etc.

Newsletter services

It is very good service to the users, listing available Internet services, sites, new addition, publications, useful like Conference, Workshops, Training and Fellowship programs. A catalog of Internet base information sources is useful assets for all R&D libraries if given at regular intervals through e-mail or they can host it in their website.

OPAC

An online public access catalog (often abbreviated as OPAC or simply library catalog) is an online database of materials held by a library or group of libraries. Users search a library catalog principally to locate books and other material available at a library. OPACs are the gateways to information in libraries and provide facilities to browse search and locate information. OPACs were developed to meet the needs of users in two different ways (1) it meant access to library housekeeping operations especially circulation and (2) to give the library users direct access to the machine-readable bibliographic records.

WebPAC

Web OPAC can give different types of link: on the one hand there are links, which identify related records within the catalogues (link reports or cross searches as well as bibliographic hierarchies). On the other hand there are those which refer to external resources, i.e. full text links, links to companies or scientific societies, and links to publishers.

- It offers libraries the opportunities to have access to various resources on the web.
- It allows users to interact with documents stored on computers all over the world.
- Makes easier to access catalogue data in the form of bibliographic records.

- Sometime has the ability to search the OPACs of other libraries
- Powerful tool that links all the electronic resources for easy access.
- Providing access to large catalogue banks of actual information.
- Referred as 'Web Cats' and as well a type of 'Information Gateway'

Patent Information Services

Many patent issuing authorities now have made their complete full text patent records online. For example United States patent documents can be searched and downloaded free of cost from (www.uspto.gov/patft/index.html). Some of the commercial organizations such as Derwent also provide downloading of full text patent from either an online database vendor (e.g. Dialog, STN) or directly from their site to the subscribers.

Reference Services

The reference service in a library is often defined as direct personal assistance given to its reader for finding information. It is the branch of library services, which includes personal assistance given to in their search for information on various subject areas, irrespective of size and collection of the library.

Whereas much of traditional library networking has focused on information access within and between the physical boundaries of libraries and research institutions, web based reference services owe their increasing popularity amongst librarians to the increasing need to extend the reference desk beyond the library's walls. The goal is to meet the demand for easy 24 hours access to electronic reference sources from any place.

Audiovisual Services

Audiovisual materials are important sources of

information, education and entertainment. Many libraries particularly media libraries and large academic and public libraries hold audio visual material such as music, films, pictures and photographs etc. Old media of LP records and tape slide have long been replaced with audio and video tape. The new multimedia of audio CD, Video CD (VCD), and Digital Video Disks (DVD) have advantage of higher storage capacity, random access and longer life than audio and video tapes and cassettes. Multimedia documents can now be played on standard PCs, stand-alone or networked and also access through interne.

Usenet

The Usenet is a global electronic bulletin board, of sorts, in which millions of people exchange public information on every conceivable topic. Also called "Netnews", it consists of thousands of newsgroups covering a vast range of topics. The Usenet newsfeed can be read by a variety of newsreader software programs. Unlike messages received via e-mail, the Usenet newsgroup messages are not stored on your computer unless you specifically save each one.

Uncover

UnCover is an online periodical article delivery service and a current awareness alerting service. It indexed nearly 18000 English language periodicals in its database and is still growing. Over eight million articles are available through a simple online order system. Five thousand citations are added daily. It is very helpful to the people who need up-to-the minute information, delivered quickly. Articles located in the UnCover database can be sent via fax machine within 24-48 hours. Searching the UnCover database is absolutely free.

UnCover access—via telnet: database.carl.org

Webcasting

Webcasting which is another example of Push Technology is defined as the "Pre-Arranged updating of news, weather or other selected information on an Internet user's desktop through periodic and generally unobtrusive over the WWW". In other words, push technology or webcasting is a method of information delivery across the web that pushes information to the screens of user's computer. Presently most of the webcasters concentrate on news delivery.

Whiteboard-(White Board Environment)

In a whiteboard environment, there can be many users connected to discuss on a topic and it is different from the newsgroup in the sense that the computer screen serves as a whiteboard and the user can draw figure using the mouse and post message/ explanation in the comment box that appears simultaneously with the whiteboard for other users to view. It is multi-user Java chat and drawing program and so the systems that are connected must be enabled to download Java applets.

ListServe

Listserv discussion lists are topic oriented forums distributed by e-mail, dealing with a wide variety of topics, many of which are academic in nature. Once you've subscribed to a listserv discussion list, messages from other subscribers are automatically sent to your electronic mailbox. To subscribe to a listserv discussion group we have to send an e-mail message to a computer thousands of miles away. The listserv program handles subscription information and distributes messages to and from subscribers. There are varieties of listserv programs but they all work essentially the same way.

Course Material

A large number of web based course ware and teaching aids are being developed to facilitate flexible open learning by many universities and commercial organizations. Many academic institutions have adopted such course material for their curricula. Libraries can provide access to course material to the learners and teacher and thus contribute to open learning. This can be done by providing links to the courseware sites through subject gateways or provide local access after downloading the material.

Virtual Library

The concept of VL emerged simultaneously with electronic library and digital library. This emergence is perhaps because all the information uses are at present through networked libraries at the desktop. Virtual Library is another kind of Digital Library which provides portal to information that is available electronically elsewhere. This is referred so to emphasize that the Library does not itself hold content. VL, Electronic Library, Digital Library, Online Library, Networked Library, etc. have been used to describe the library as it exists in the networked environment, which is quite virtual (i.e. practical) without the physical existence of books or journals on the shelves

ADVANTAGES OF WEB BASED SERVICES

- To save the precious time of the user
- Availability of less number of library staff to carry out the library works and services
- Less dependence upon the library staff for getting the required information
- Direct access to latest information - for user where every they are located
- Instant and elaborate information requirements for R&D activities
- Information for decision making in MIS
- Always up-to-date information

- Multiple accesses of information with multiple user to same resources at the same time
- Preservation and conservation of information for a long time
- High potential of information storage
- Round the clock availability, at any time, 24 hours a day and 365 days of the year
- Multifold increase of the cost of books and journals
- Availability of information in different places and also in different formats

SCOPE OF WEB BASED SERVICES FOR LIBRARIES

Inter-library loan : can be provided by sending the information though e-mails using the network facilities.

Acquisition : On-line ordering and acquisition related activities can be carried out though e-mail Centralization and computerized on-line public access cataloguing service can be provided by networking system.

Networking : with union catalogues of various items of information is a boon as it avoids duplication in holding to the extent possible.

Information Sharing : Library networks offer much potential and new capabilities for sharing information among different library and information centers at local, regional, national and international levels and eliminate the size, distance, and language barriers among users through resource sharing.

Reference service : can be enhanced by e-mail and internet though LAN and WAN.

CD-ROM and multimedia service : can be provided effectively though web networks.

Database Service : research abstract and index database service can be provided effectively though networks.

Current Awareness service and SDI : may be given though networking systems and the users may retrieve information of their interest in a fraction of second from online database.

Speed : speed of data communication though networks are very high and one can obtain information within few seconds from any part of the world sitting anywhere.

Global information dissemination and retrival : The internet is a major tool providing access to vast quantities of information and it lets to communicate, share resource and share data with people around the world.

SOME ISSUES WITH WEB

The main issues of web are—

- A huge volume of information is generated every minute
- No order or rules are imposed on the generation, distribution , access and use of this information;
- No fully comprehensive record of the different documents is available at the moment;
- No classification and description framework for storing and retrieving documents
- Therefore documents of all kind of format type of information (electronic journal, tourist information, marketing services, commercial sales, library catalog) and subject can be found.

CHALLENGES WITH WEB

- The librarian should take one more step further instead of just providing access to the internet.
- Should take the responsibility of evaluating the web resource for providing the effective service.
- The librarian should have depth knowledge about the different web tools and resources

- The librarian should create a web directory for providing the services.
- Should take the users training and orientation program about internet and the search option.

CONCLUSION

Library services are the heart of any kind of library. Due to the advancement in web communication and networking technologies and the adaptation of web and Intranet Technologies in organizational networks has given the Library and Information Centers an opportunity to improve the information services to the Patrons in more effective way. Now a day's Web based library services is a trend. Libraries are taking full advantages of internet and web facilities. They are remarkable changing their mode of provision of services. Users also very happy by getting the library services through web. They can save their time and harassment from not getting the information. This new mode of service is highly effective in special libraries rather than academic libraries. Presently many libraries will enable to provide web based service it will popular and if the library and information center is being a professional about their services then in near future it can become a money making mode for libraries which help to improve library and information centers. Also Library and Information Professionals need to adopt the latest technological tools in order to provide efficient information services through web.

REFERENCES

- Bhatnagar, A. (2005). WEB-BASED LIBRARY SERVICES. *3rd Convention PLANNER -2005* (pp. pp. 426-435). Silchar: Assam Univ., Silchar.
- *Bulletin board system.* (n.d.). Retrieved January 25, 2015, from https://en.wikipedia.org/wiki/Bulletin_board_system
- Gokhale, P. A., & Chandra, S. (2009). *Web 2.0 and E-Learning: The Indian Perspective. DESIDOC Journal of Library & Information Technology* , pp. 5-13.

- Hatua, S. R. (n.d.). *Web Based Library and Information Services*. Retrieved January 25, 2015, from http://shatua.tripod.com/DRTCseminar.html
- Madhusudhan, D. M., & Nagabhushanam, D. V. (2012). USE OF WEB-BASED LIBRARY SERVICES IN SELECT UNIVERSITY LIBRARIES IN INDIA: A STUDY. *International Journal of Library and Information Studies* , pp. 1-20.
- *Online public access catalog.* (n.d.). Retrieved January 25, 2016, from https://en.wikipedia.org/wiki/Online_public_access_ catalog
- Seena, S., & Pillai Sudhier, K. (2014). Impact of Web 2.0 Technology Applications in Kerala University Library:Library Professionals' Perspective. *DESIDOC Journal of Library & Information Technology, , pp. 419-425.*
- *Selective dissemination of information.* (n.d.). Retrieved January 26, 2016, from https://en.wikipedia.org/wiki/Selective_ dissemination_of_information
- *Web - World Wide Web.* (n.d.). Retrieved January 25, 2015, from http://www.webopedia.com/TERM/W/World_Wide_Web. html

29

Changing Mode of Libraries Towards Web-Based Services

Rajwant Kaur
Assistant Librarians, Bhai Gurdas Library
Guru Nanak Dev University, Amritsar-143005

Balkar Singh
Assistant Librarians, Bhai Gurdas Library
Guru Nanak Dev University, Amritsar-143005

ABSTRACT

The recent advancements in IT have changed the face of libraries . This change has effected each and every aspect of the library. The role of traditional librarian has emerged as revolutionary librarian by providing electronic media and web services .

The present paper is an effort to highlight the conceptual terms of web services. It throws light on the resources required for providing web based services. How the web based services are effecting the users has also been discussed. The status of web based services in Indian libraries and the initiatives taken by Indian Library Consortia have also been studied. Advantages and disadvantages of printed and web based services constitute a part of this paper

Key words : Web Based Library Services, Web Resources, Indian Libraries.

INTRODUCTION

Due to technological revolution, there is a vast change between the traditional library services and web based library services. The user's demands and expectations are increasing day by day, which librarians need to take care to provide services very effectively and efficiently. "Accurate Service to Accurate User at a Accurate Time" is the need of the hour. In such a situation, web based servicse come to rescue as there are many services and tools which are very simple to use from user's point of view. Such tools give technological edge which assure satisfaction of users.

CONCEPTUAL MEANING : WEB BASED LIBRARY SERVICES

Web Based Information Services, Digital Library Services, Internet Library Services and Electronic Library Services are the services with similar meanings. Due to tremendous growth and continuous development of technology, traditional online services have been transformed into Internet based online services which use Web-based technologies.

The provision of these services is not confined by the traditional opening hours but can be offered on 24-hours, 7 days- a week basis known as 24/7. Face to face encounter is not possible. More than one user can use electronic/web service at a time.

Advantages and disadvantages of Web resources are show in the Table :

Print Form	*Electronic Form*
Advantages	
1. Format is tested and standardized	Format is in the early stages of development
2. Easy for users to use	Require some training for users to use
3. No special equipment needed	Special equipment (Hardware, software printers etc.) is required
4. Easy to locate if shelved properly	Access is currently unreliable (URL problems, Internet connection problems etc.

5. Use is limited only to copyright laws	Use is limited by copyright laws and licensing agreements
6. Archiving is effective and permanent	Archiving is "up in the air"
Disadvantages	
1. Operating costs are considerable (ordering, cataloguing and binding)	Operating costs are minimal, no cataloguing, binding etc.
2. Requires shelving	No shelving required
3. Often mutilated, stolen or miss helved	Cannot be mutilated, stolen or miss helved
4. Require extensive storage space	Saves considerable storage space
5. Allows only one user at a time	Allows for multiple users with simultaneous access
6. Slow delivery via "snail Mail"	Immediate receipt of issue
7. Issues can be easily lost in the mail or missing	No more missing problem
8. Slow publication	Fast publication

Web based services are established due to the following reasons:-

- Ensuring the needs of users and the accessible information sources are suitably matched at all times.
- Delivering the information sources to the user in a timely appropriate fashion.
- Ensuring the information provided is high quality, accurate and appropriate
- Assisting the user in interpreting the materials , if necessary
- Promoting user awareness of new services and information sources as they develop.
- Providing users with individualised guidance and support as they build their information search and application skills.

"RESOURCES FOR WEB BASED LIBRARY SERVICES"

1. OPAC's : Online Public Access Catalogues form an important part of many digital and hybrid library collections . It allows users to search for the bibliographic records contained within library collections . Now a days, some OPACs also provide access to electronic resources and databases in addition to the traditional bibliographic records

2. GATEWAYS : A gateway is defined as a facility that allows easier access to network based resources in a given subject area . Gateways provide a simple search facility and a much enhanced service through a resource database and indexes, which can be searched through a web based interface. Information provided by gateways is catalogued by hand. Gateways cover a wide range of subjects, through some areas such as music and religious studies, currently lack subject gateways. Some well known gateways are as follows:

- Internet Public Library (IPL)
- Bulletin Board for Libraries(BUBL)
- National Information Services and Systems(NISS)

3. PORTALS : In the library sense, Portals may be defined as an amalgamation of services to the users where the amalgamation is achieved through seamless integration of existing services by using binding agents , such as customization and authentication services, search protocols such as Z 39.50, loan protocols such as ISO 1061 and e-commerce.

Portals are either commercial or free web facilities that offer information services to a specific audience. The result is a personalized service which allows individual to access the rich content of both print based and electronic systems. The facilities include web search to communication to email to news, etc.

There are three kind of Portals ;

1. **Consumer (or Horizontal) Portals :** Yahoo, MSN and AOL are consumer Portals aimed at consumer audiences and offer free email, games, chat, etc.

2. **Vertical Portals :** Vertical Net is a Vertical Portal which targets a specific audience , such as a particular industry and offer many of the consumer Portal features

3. **Enterprise Portals :** Epicentric and Corporate Yahoo are enterprise Portals which are similar to consumer Portals. These Portals can be best understood or electronic pathfinders for users, pulling together in one place in website selected links subjects or interest oriented resources on www.

4. Subject PORTALS : Specific Web Search Engines in specific subjects are known as Subject Portal in which evaluation of the material covered in subject portals is a major task.

Two prime UK subject portals are Social Science Information Gateway (SOSIG) which covers social science resources and Organizing Medical Networked Information (OMNI) which covers medical resources. Subject portal sites can be very helpful. While using the subject portals users should always bear in mind the main important contents of the subject.

WEB BASED LIBRARY SERVICES

1. Virtual Library Tours

Web sites of libraries provide virtual library guide to the physical facilities including collections , services and infrastructure available in the library . The combination of library maps and floor plans, library departments and photographic views are used for the tour. VLT (Virtual Library Tours) are also using new technologies such as QuickTime movies are being used to replace image maps on main campus websites.

2. ASK-A-Librarian

ASK-A-Librarian services are Internet-based

question and answer services that connect user with individuals experts who possess specialized subject knowledge and skill in conducting precision searches. Most 'ASK-A-Librarian' services have a web–based question submission form or an email address or both . Users are invited to submit their queries by using web pages, web forms or through email. Once a query is read by a service , it is assigned to an individual expert for answering. An expert responds to the query with factual information and or a list of information resources .

The response is either sent to the user's email account or is posted on the web so that the user can access it after certain period of time. Many services have informative websites that include archives of questions, answers and set of FAQs (Frequently Asked Questions). USsers are usually encouraged to browse archives and FAQs before submitting a question in case sufficient information already exists.

3. Real Time Services

A new and exciting method of digital reference service in which libraries are attempting to provide more and more is live reference information to users

These are real-time interactive reference services in which the users can talk to a real, live reference librarian at any time, from anywhere in the world .

User and librarian can interact using chat technologies and unlike with email reference, the librarian can perform a reference interview by asking the users to elaborate or clarify if needed before proceeding to the answer the question. The librarian can perform Internet searches and push websites on to the user's browser and can receive immediate feedback from the user as to whether their question have been answered to their satisfaction.

4. Bulletin Boards

Bulletin Board is an electronic communication forum that hosts posted messages and articles connected to a common subject or theme or interest. It allows users to call in and either leaves or retrieves messages. The messages may be directed to all users of the Bulletin Board or only to a particular user, but all messages can be read by all users

Several libraries are using Bulletin Boards for their web based library services . The Bulletin Board System is also used as an interactive interface to invite suggestions on activities and services of a library. It can also be used as an interface to distribute library services

5. Web-Based User Education

Web guides and teaching tools are found everywhere on web because they are easily updated, accessed and printed on demand. The Web-Based User Education provides a high degree of interactivity and flexibility to the users.

The library websites can be used Web-Based User Education for imparting training to users in teaching the basic library skills along with glossary of library terms, using library OPAC, locating books, magazines, bibliographical data and library materials, understanding how to navigate the libraries websites and how to select the most relevant database, instructions for searching CD ROM and guidance in locating web based databases and other electronic resources and instructions on subject searching training, using Boolean Operators and searching internet resources through search engines

6. Web-Based services:Indian Scenario

Sincere efforts to accomplish web-based services to users by the Indian libraries are in practice. Many Indian libraries in India were weak for the access of e-resources due to various reasons particularly funds and infrastructure. The growth during eighties, the institutions like *CSIR, ISRO, DRDO, DAE, ICAR, SIRNET, NICNET, NISSAT, INFLIBNET, MHRD, and IMM* libraries are actively working continuously to improve the present situation. Annually, they spend a huge amount of money towards the web-based services like e-journals, e-databases and library acquisition.

Initiatives	*For Accessing*
Indian Institute of Management	Bibliographic Databases
CSIR Laboratories	Science Direct
FORSA	Astronomy and Astrophysics Journals
UGC-INFONET	Full Text and Databases like BIOSIS, CAS and INDEST

Indian library consortia are providing very remarkable services to users by investing big amount of money. Digital library infrastructure serves to access more number of e-journals, e-books and e-resources.

CONCLUSION

Web-Based Resources are in a stage of development. Librarians in present information era are active to adopt new techniques to develop new web services. These resources/services are volatile that are moving one side to other or may be moved all together from web. Web-based library services are becoming more sophisticated and wide spread throughout the world. Librarians are working actively to transfer their traditional services into web based services. Librarians are ready to face the challenge to develop "Library Without Wall", from paper to electronic delivery, from physical presence to virtual presence. Librarians are playing a leader role in providing better "Web Based Library Services" to techno savvy users of information.

REFERENCES

- Chopra, H.S. (Ed). *Librarianship in digital era.Proceeding of the Conference held on January 20-21, 2012.* Amritsar, Guru

Nanak Dev University.

- Griffiths, J.R. (2005) Student searching behaviour and the web :use of academic resources and google. *Library Trends*, 65(6) : 525-537
- LeComte,M (2004) *Computers in libraries.* San Diego, Academic Press :332-34.
- Padgett, D. (2000) *Information technology and libraries.* New York, University Press.
- Rao, Nageswara . (2009) Role of librarian in internet and World Wide Web environment. *Information science*, 4(1) :25-34.
- Singh, Pankaj Kumar (2014) *Library and information technology.* New Delhi, Discovery Publishing House: 143-44.
- Sukla, Shiva (2008) *Information technology:Bridge to the wired virtually.* New Delhi, ELBS :185-86.

30

Web 2.0, 3.0, Cloud Computing

Sunil H. Urkudkar

Head of Library, Arts & Science College, Pulgaon

INTRODUCTION

Web 2.0

Web 2.0 capabilities were present in the days of Web 1.0 but implemented differently. For example, a Web 1.0 site may have had a guestbook page to publish visitor comments, instead of a comment section at the end of each page. Server performance and bandwidth considerations meant that having along comments thread on each page could potentially slow down the site.The term Web 2.0 did not resurface until 2002. These authors focus on the concepts currently associated with the term where, as Scott Dietzen puts it, "the Web becomes a universal, standards-based integration platform". In 2004, the term began its rise in popularity when O'Reilly Media and Media Live hosted the first Web 2.0 conference. In their opening remarks, John Battelle and Tim O'Reilly outlined their definition of the "Web as Platform", where software applications are built upon the Web as opposed to upon the desktop. The unique aspect of this migration, they argued, is that "customers are building your business for you" They argued that the activities of users generating content (in the form of ideas, text, videos, or pictures) could be "harnessed" to create value. O'Reilly and Battelle contrasted Web 2.0 with what they called "Web 1.0". They associated this term with the business models of Netscape and the Encyclopedia Britannica Online. For example,

Netscape framed "the web as platform" in terms of the old software paradigm: their flagship product was the web browser, a desktop application, and their strategy was to use their dominance in the browser market to establish a market for high-priced server products. Control over standards for displaying content and applications in the browser would, in theory, give Netscape the kind of market power enjoyed by Microsoft in the PC market. Much like the "horseless carriage" framed the automobile as an extension of the familiar; Netscape promoted a "WebTop" to replace the desktop, and planned to populate that WebTop with information updates and applets pushed to the WebTop by information providers who would purchase Netscape servers· It's a story about community and collaboration on a scale never seen before. It's about the cosmic compendium of knowledge Wikipedia and the million-channel people network YouTube and the online metropolis MySpace. It's about the many wresting power from the few and helping one another for nothing and how that will not only change the world but also change the way the world changes.

Characteristics

- Static pages instead of dynamic HTML
- Content served from the server's file system instead of a RDBMS.
- Pages built using Server Side Includes or CGI

instead of a web application written in a dynamic programming language such as PHP or Ruby.

- The use of HTML 3.2-era elements such as frames and tables to position and align elements on a page. These were often used in combination with spacer GIFs.
- Proprietary HTML extensions, such as the blink and marquee tags, introduced during the first browser war.
- Online guestbook.

The key Features of Web 2.0

1. *Folksonomy* - free classification of information; allows users to collectively classify and find information
2. *Rich User Experience* - dynamic content; responsive to user input
3. *User Participation* - information flows two ways between site owner and site user by means of evaluation, review, and commenting. Site users add content for others to see
4. *Software as a service* -Web 2.0 sites developed APIs to allow automated usage, such as by an app or mash up

Technologies

To allow users to continue to interact with the page, communications such as data requests going to the server are separated from data coming back to the page (asynchronously). Otherwise, the user would have to routinely wait for the data to come back before they can do anything else on that page, just as a user has to wait for a page to complete the reload. This also increases overall performance of the site, as the sending of requests can complete quicker independent of blocking and queuing required to send data back to the client.

The data fetched by an Ajax request is typically formatted in XML or JSON (JavaScript Object Notation) format; two widely used structured data formats. Since both of these formats are natively understood by JavaScript, a programmer can easily use them to transmit structured data in their Web application. When this data is received via Ajax, the JavaScript program then uses the Document Object Model (DOM) to dynamically update the Web page based on the new data, allowing for a rapid and interactive user experience. In short, using these techniques, Web designers can make their pages function like desktop applications. For example, Google Docs uses this technique to create a Web-based word processor.

CONCEPTS

Web 2.0 can be described in three parts

Rich Internet application (RIA) : defines the experience brought from desktop to browser whether it is from a graphical point of view or usability point of view.

Web-oriented architecture (WOA) : defines how Web 2.0 applications expose their functionality so that other applications can leverage and integrate the functionality providing a set of much richer applications. Examples are feeds, RSS, Web Services, mash-ups.

Social Web : defines how Web 2.0 tends to interact much more with the end user and make the end-user an integral part.

Usage

A third important part of Web 2.0 is the Social web. The social Web consists of a number of online tools and platforms where people share their perspectives, opinions, thoughts and experiences. Web 2.0 applications tend to interact much more with the end user. As such, the end user is not only a user of the application but also a participant by:

- Podcasting Blogging Tagging Curating with RSS Social bookmarking Social networking
- Web content voting

The popularity of the term Web 2.0, along with the increasing use of blogs, wikis, and social networking technologies, has led many in academia and business to append a flurry of 2.0's to existing concepts and fields of study, including Library 2.0, Social Work 2.0, Enterprise 2.0, PR 2.0, Classroom 2.0, Publishing 2.0, Medicine 2.0, Telco 2.0, Travel 2.0, Government 2.0, and even Porn 2.0. Many of these 2.0s refer to Web 2.0 technologies as the source of the new version in their respective disciplines and areas. For example, in the Talis white paper "Library 2.0: The Challenge of Disruptive Innovation", Paul Miller argues

WEB-BASED APPLICATIONS AND DESKTOPS

Ajax has prompted the development of Web sites that mimic desktop applications, such as word processing, the spreadsheet, and slide-show presentation. WYSIWYG wiki and blogging sites replicate many features of PC authoring applications. Several browser-based services have emerged, including EyeOS and YouOS.(No longer active.) Although named operating systems, many of these services are application platforms. They mimic the user experience of desktop operating-systems, offering features and applications similar to a PC environment, and are able to run within any modern browser. However, these so-called "operating systems" do not directly control the hardware on the client's computer.

Numerous web-based application services appeared during the dot-com bubble of 1997–2001 and then vanished, having failed to gain a critical mass of customers.

DISTRIBUTION OF MEDIA

XML and RSS

Many regard syndication of site content as a Web 2.0 feature. Syndication uses standardized protocols to permit end-users to make use of a site's data in another context (such as another Web site, a browser plug in, or a separate desktop application). Protocols permitting syndication include RSS (really simple syndication, also known as Web syndication), RDF (as in RSS 1.1), and Atom, all of which are XML-based formats. Observers have started to refer to these technologies as Web feeds.

Criticism

Critics of the term claim that "Web 2.0" does not represent a new version of the World Wide Web at all, but merely continues to use so-called "Web 1.0" technologies and concepts.[5] First, techniques such as Ajax do not replace underlying protocols like HTTP, but add an additional layer of abstraction on top of them. Second, many of the ideas of Web 2.0 were already featured in implementations on networked systems well before the term "Web 2.0" emerged. Amazon.com, for instance, has allowed users to write reviews and consumer guides since its launch in 1995, in a form of self-publishing. Amazon also opened its API to outside developers in 2002. Previous developments also came from research in computer-supported collaborative learning and computer supported cooperative work (CSCW) and from established products like Lotus Notes and Lotus Domino, all phenomena that preceded Web 2.0.

WEB 3.0 THE THIRD GENERATION WEB IS COMING

Introduction

The Web is entering a new phase of evolution. There has been much debate recently about what to call this new phase. Some would prefer to not name it all, while others suggest continuing to call it "Web 2.0". However, this new phase of evolution has quite a different focus from what Web 2.0 has come to mean.

John Markoff of the *New York Times* recently suggested naming this third-generation of the Web, "Web 3.0". This suggestion has led to quite a bit of debate within the industry. Those who are attached to the Web 2.0 moniker have reacted by claiming that such a term is not warranted while others have responded positively to the term, noting that there is indeed a characteristic difference between the coming new stage of the Web and what Web 2.0 has come to represent.

The term Web 2.0 was never clearly defined and even today if one asks ten people what it means one will likely get ten different definitions. However, most people in the Web industry would agree that Web 2.0 focuses on several major themes, including AJAX, social networking, folksonomies, lightweight collaboration, social bookmarking, and media sharing. While the innovations and practices of Web 2.0 will continue to develop, they are not the final step in the evolution of the Web.In fact, there is a lot more in store for the Web. We are starting to witness the convergence of several growing technology trends that are outside the scope of what Web 2.0 has come to mean. These trends have been gestating for a decade and will soon reach a tipping point. At this juncture the third-generation of the Web will start.

More Intelligent Web

The threshold to the third-generation Web will be crossed in 2007. At this juncture the focus of innovation will start shift back from front-end improvements towards back-end infrastructure level upgrades to the Web. This cycle will continue for five to ten years, and will result in making the Web more connected, more open, and more intelligent. It will transform the Web from a network of separately siloed applications and content repositories to a more seamless and interoperable whole.

TIMELINE AND DEFINITION

Web 1.0. Web 1.0 was the first generation of the Web. During this phase the focus was primarily on building the Web, making it accessible, and commercializing it for the first time. Key areas of interest centered on protocols such as HTTP, open standard markup languages such as HTML and XML, Internet access through ISPs, the first Web browsers, Web development platforms and tools, Web-centric software languages such as Java and Javascript, the creation of Web sites, the commercialization of the Web and Web business models, and the growth of key portals on the Web.

Web 2.0. According to the Wikipedia, "Web 2.0, a phrase coined by O'Reilly Media in 2004, refers to a supposed second generation of Internet-based services — such as social networking sites, wikis, communication tools, and folksonomies — that emphasize online collaboration and sharing among users."

Web 3.0. Using the same pattern as the above Wikipedia definition, Web 3.0 could be defined as: "Web 3.0, a phrase coined by John Markoff of the New York Times in 2006, refers to a supposed third generation of

Internet-based services that collectively comprise what might be called 'the intelligent Web' — such as those using semantic web, microformats, natural language search, data-mining, machine learning, recommendation agents, and artificial intelligence technologies — which emphasize machine-facilitated understanding of information in order to provide a more productive and intuitive user experience."

NETWORK COMPUTING

- Software-as-a-service business models
- Web services interoperability
- Distributed computing (P2P, grid computing, hosted "cloud computing" server farms such as Amazon S3)

OPEN TECHNOLOGIES

- Open APIs and protocols
- Open data formats
- Open-source software platforms
- Open data (Creative Commons, Open Data License, etc.)

OPEN IDENTITY

- Open identity (OpenID)
- Open reputation
- Portable identity and personal data (for example, the ability to port your user account and search history from one service to another)
- Distributed databases — or what I call "The World Wide Database" (wide-area distributed database interoperability enabled by Semantic Web technologies)
- Intelligent applications (natural language processing, machine learning, machine reasoning, autonomous agents)

CONCLUSION

Web 3.0 will be more connected, open, and intelligent, with semantic Web technologies, distributed databases, natural language processing, machine learning, machine reasoning, and autonomous agents.

CLOUD COMPUTING

Introduction

Cloud computing, also known as 'on-demand computing', is a kind of Internet-based computing, where shared resources, data and information are provided to computers and other devices on-demand. It is a model for enabling ubiquitous, on-demand access to a shared pool of configurable computing resources. Cloud computing and storage solutions provide users and enterprises with various capabilities to store and process their data in third-party data centers. It relies on sharing of resources to achieve coherence and economies of scale, similar to a utility (like the electricity grid) over a network. At the foundation of cloud computing is the broader concept of converged infrastructure and shared services. Cloud computing is a model for enabling ubiquitous, convenient, on-demand network access to a shared pool of configurable computing resources (e.g., networks, servers, storage, applications and services) that can be rapidly provisioned and released with minimal management effort.

Origin of the term

The origin of the term *cloud computing* is unclear. The word "cloud" is commonly used in science to describe a large agglomeration of objects that visually appear from a distance as a cloud and describes any set of things whose details are not inspected further in a given context. Another explanation is that the old programs that drew network schematics surrounded the icons for servers with a circle, and a cluster of servers in a network diagram had several overlapping circles, which resembled a cloud. In analogy to above usage the word *cloud* was used as a metaphor for the Internet and a standardized cloud-like shape was used to denote a network on telephony schematics and later to depict the Internet in computer network diagrams. With this simplification, the implication is that the specifics of how the end points of a network are connected are not relevant for the purposes of understanding the diagram. The cloud symbol was used to represent networks of computing equipment in the original ARPANET by as early as 1977, and the CSNET by 1981 both predecessors to the Internet itself.

Similar concepts

Cloud computing is the result of the evolution and adoption of existing technologies and paradigms. The goal of cloud computing is to allow users to take beneût from all of these technologies, without the need for deep knowledge about or expertise with each one of them. The cloud aims to cut costs, and helps the users focus on their core business instead of being impeded by IT obstacles.

The main enabling technology for cloud computing is virtualization. Virtualization software separates a physical computing device into one or more "virtual" devices, each of which can be easily used and managed to perform computing tasks. With operating system–level virtualization essentially creating a scalable system of multiple independent computing devices, idle computing resources can be allocated and used more efficiently. Virtualization provides the agility required to speed up IT operations, and reduces cost by increasing infrastructure utilization. Autonomic computing automates the process through which the user can provision resources on-demand. By minimizing user involvement, automation speeds up the process, reduces labor costs and reduces the possibility of human errors.

Characteristics Cloud computing exhibits the following key characteristics:

- **Agility** improves with users' ability to re-provision technological infrastructure resources.
- **Device and location independence** enable users to access systems using a web browser regardless of their location or what device they use (e.g., PC, mobile phone). As infrastructure is off-site (typically provided by a third-party) and accessed via the Internet, users can connect from anywhere
- **Maintenance** of cloud computing applications is easier, because they do not need to be installed on each user's computer and can be accessed from different places.
- **Performance** is monitored and consistent and loosely coupled architectures are constructed using web services as the system interface.

CLOUD COMPUTING TYPES

Private cloud

Private cloud is cloud infrastructure operated solely for a single organization, whether managed internally or by a third-party, and hosted either internally or externally. Undertaking a private cloud project requires a significant level and degree of engagement to virtualize the business environment, and requires the organization to reevaluate decisions about existing resources. When done right, it can improve business, but every step in the project raises security issues that must be addressed to prevent serious vulnerabilities. Self-run data centers are generally capital intensive.

Public cloud

A cloud is called a "public cloud" when the services are rendered over a network that is open for public use. Public cloud services may be free. Technically there may be little or no difference between public and private cloud architecture, however, security consideration may be substantially different for services (applications, storage, and other resources) that are made available by a service provider for a public audience and when communication is effected over a non-trusted network.

Hybrid cloud

Hybrid cloud is a composition of two or more clouds (private, community or public) that remain distinct entities but are bound together, offering the benefits of multiple deployment models. Hybrid cloud can also mean the ability to connect collocation, managed and/or dedicated services with cloud resources.

Community cloud

Community cloud shares infrastructure between several organizations from a specific community with common concerns (security, compliance, jurisdiction, etc.), whether managed internally or by a third-party, and either hosted internally or externally. The costs are spread over fewer users than a public cloud (but more than a private cloud), so only some of the cost savings potential of cloud computing are realized.

Distributed cloud

A cloud computing platform can be assembled from a distributed set of machines in different locations, connected to a single network or hub service. It is possible to distinguish between two types of distributed clouds: public-resource computing and volunteer cloud.

Multi-cloud

Multicloud is the use of multiple cloud computing services in a single heterogeneous architecture to reduce reliance on single vendors, increase flexibility through choice, militate against disasters, etc. It differs from hybrid cloud in that it refers to multiple cloud services, rather than multiple deployment modes (public, private, and legacy).

SECURITY AND PRIVACY

Cloud computing poses privacy concerns because the service provider can access the data that is in the cloud at any time. It could accidentally or deliberately alter or even delete information. Many cloud providers can share information with third parties if necessary for purposes of law and order even without a warrant. That is permitted in their privacy policies which users have to agree to before they start using cloud services. Solutions to privacy include policy and legislation as well as end users' choices for how data is store. Users can encrypt data that is processed or stored within the cloud to prevent unauthorized access.

THE FUTURE

Cloud computing is therefore still as much a research topic, as it is a market offering.[103] What is clear through the evolution of Cloud Computing services is that the CTO is a major driving force behind Cloud adoption.[104] The major Cloud technology developers continue to invest billions a year in Cloud R&D; for example: in 2011 Microsoft committed 90% of its $9.6bn R&D budget to Cloud.[105] Centaur Partners also predict that SaaS revenue will be growing from 13.5B in 2011 to $32.8B in 2016.[106] Additionally, more industries are turning to cloud technology as an efficient way to improve quality services due to its capabilities to reduce overhead costs, downtime, and automate infrastructure deployment.

REFERENCES

- Electronic Resources in Legal Profession By Thanuskadi S.
- World Wide Web By Tom Alexander & Joe Mathews
- Internet & Web Designing By Tom Alexander
- Computer Internets and Web Designing By Manohar Singh

- Information Access in Digital Libraries By Kailash C. Das
- An Introduction to Library Network By R. L. Sehgal
- Digital Library Automation By Dr. Harshal Nirma
- Qualities and Excellence of Academic Libraries By Dr. Namita Khot

31

Alphabets, Writing Materials and their Preservation: A Historical Perspective

Sukhdev Singh
Assistant Professor, Deptt. of Lib. & Info. Sci.
Bhag Singh Khalsa College for Women
Abohar (Punjab)

ABSTRACT

Since the dawn of civilisation human beings have communicated through gestures, symbols, sounds, words and written media like clay tablets, papyrus, parchment and palm leaves, etc. The beginning of the 15th century heralded the use of printed books and journals and of late through electronic media. Preservation of written records is apparently just as old as written records themselves. The problem of preservation of rare documents, manuscripts and old records has continued since human being acquired the knowledge of writing. It is through the human effort of preservation that frontiers of human knowledge and human civilisation have been extended. This paper highlights the evolution of alphabets, genesis of writing materials and their preservation in different centuries. Preservation techniques being employed to keep the endangered documents in good health have also been discussed in this paper. Roles of international, national and state levels agencies in preservation and conservation of rare documents have also been mentioned at the last of paper.

Keywords/Descriptors: Alphabets, Clay Tablets, Parchment, Palm

Leaf, Papyrus, Manuscripts, Preservation, Conservation, IFLA, NAI, NMM, PDL.

On leaf of palm, on sedge-wrought roll;
On plastic clay and leather scroll,
Man wrote his thoughts;
The ages passed, and lo!
The press was found at last!

— Whittier, J.G.

1. INTRODUCTION

There was a period in the history of man when writing was not known and communication was only through speech which has been a vehicle of transmitting ideas from the dawn of human culture. Man evolved the technique of oral communication by the use of sounds that conveyed a message to the other person. Knowledge was transmitted from generation to generation only through hearing and speaking.

From the beginning of human civilisation especially with the invention of alphabets man was in search of a firm surface on which he could record his ideas and experiences of the world for posterity. Pre-historic rock carving and scratching on bone and antlers, ostraka, painted hides, carved amulets, notched sticks, runic calendars, clog almanacs, bronze plaques and many other artifacts on which man since earliest times has left a story in pictures, phonetic symbols, carved letters or writing. Paper was invented in China in 105 A.D. by T'Sai Lun. Now-a-days paper is the most prominent support material which is used extensively for writing, printing, currency notes and for packing material.

2. THE ORIGIN OF ALPHABETS

Nigerians used to believe that the first writers were monkeys. Ancient Chinese people credited a sacred turtle. The Mayans and Assyrians attributed the sons of their respective creator Gods. Certain Arab traditions maintained the first writer to have been no less a person than Mohammad. Stories explaining the origins of writing vary as widely as the cultures that produce them. But every human society that has crossed the threshold to literacy has assigned writing a status worthy of myth.

A more prosaic account for the origin of writing might take us to the city of Uruk, in the ancient kingdom of Sumer. By about 5000 BC, a growing population was coalescing into the first human settlement to resemble a city. The people of Uruk, who had mastered a few basic agricultural techniques started settling in a growing population centre with flourishing trade and ever increasing specialised classes of farmers, workers, builders, merchants, and a ruling class of elite citizens. It was the first boomtown of world.

The sheer concentration of skilled people resulted in large scale technological innovations. During this period, ancient Sumerians invented the wheel, sailing ships, moulded bricks, metals, and architectural breakthroughs like vaults and domes. They were the first people to divide the day into hours. Amid such a prolific period of innovation, the typical Sumerians might have scarcely noticed the curious little etchings that merchants were beginning to make on clay tablets while they tried to keep track of their accounts. The booming commercial trade in Uruck created an unprecedented volume of transactions: as merchants to keep up with an expanding commercial economy, they needed to develop better systems for keeping track of their accounts. V. Gordon Childe writes that the first forms of writing emerged not for magical and liturgical purposes but for practical business and administrations.

Samuel Johnson once remarked that no man but a fool ever wrote except for money. Indeed, if it was not for money, we might have no writing at all. Much as we like to think of writing as the fruit of high culture, all literature originates from all commercial transactions: sales receipts.

Writing appears to have emerged with little fanfare, arising as a practical innovation to take advantage of two prior techniques: drawing and counting. The earliest tabulating devices were notched bones dated to 35, 000 to 20, 000 BC- the earliest known representations of numbers. By the ninth century BC, clay token had emerged as unit of basic currency-appearing almost simultaneously in Mesopotamia, Iran, Sudan, Palestine, and Syria. The first written notations were called *bullae* (token). Shaped like disks, cones, spheres, tetrahedrons, ovoids, cylinders, triangles, or animal heads, each token represented some form of commercial transaction: records of purchases, debts, or contractual obligations. The oldest specimens yet discovered date back as far as 3500 BC. By 3000 BC the earliest examples of what we would recognise as "writing" emerged when merchants began transcribing the contents of *bullae* on to clay tablets.

As written tablets took hold as a commercial technology, a new class of professional scribes emerged. These early knowledge workers facilitated trade by serving as trusted third parties who could record transactions between two or more parties. A typical written receipt might read something like this: "offer Gentleman B the enclosed message from Gentleman A". After kneading wet clay into a cylinder or tablet, the scribe would record the details of the transaction by scraping marks into the surface using a wedge-shaped stylus. Both parties would put their marks on the tablets. The scribe would place his own seal, and the contract would be baked into the permanent record. Because clay dried quickly, the scribe had to work fast; this was no medium for poetry. Once the tablet was baked, the scribe would then carefully place it on a shelf or put it in a basket, with labels affixed to facilitate future search and retrieval.

On the basis of aforesaid text, it may be said that commerce is the mother of writing as writing invariably emerged at first to support practical business and administrations.

3. EVOLUTION OF WRITING

History of recording thoughts and ideas has undergone many changes. Earliest men have used four methods to record their discoveries and views about the universe. These are:

1. Pictograms
2. Word signs and symbols
3. Syllabic signs
4. Alphabets

Above list does not impose a firm pecking order, with the alphabets at the climax point. The stages in succeeding order are:

- Pictographic
- Ideographic, and
- Phonetic

A pictograph is a picture or a pictorial symbol used for a word or phrase. Examples of pictograms as a primitive communicative device, employed by the American Indians may be seen in caves in France. They convey a message by means of series of drawings. The second stage used graphic symbols that stand for ideas, emotions as well as to represent objects. Picture writing or pictography was the earliest form of writing used by the man. In pictography, symbols look like the things that they represent. However as the civilisation became more complex, the scribes had to begin depicting things that could not lend themselves to be presented in the form of pictures such as ideas, emotions, actions, etc. The result was the development of ideograph.

The most famous scripts of the ancient world

including Cuneiform, Egyptian hieroglyphics and Mayan and Aztec scripts were ideographic in origin, although they became partly phonetic as the individual signs represented syllables or vowels, the smallest elements of the words that can be isolated or spoken.

3.1. Indian scenario

Writing in India is mainly divided into two periods separated from each other by about two thousand years. The first period involves the early Indus Valley Civilisations of the third millennium BC. There are strong evidences of written communication in Indus Valley but these symbols have not yet been deciphered, and therefore, it is difficult to assume that they are alphabets. The second period involves the beginning of Indic writing proper in the fifth century BC, although the earlier documents, the *Ashokan* inscriptions-belong to the third century BC.

4. WRITING MATERIALS AND THEIR NATURE

With the gradual advancement of the art of writing, various forms of writing surfaces came into existence. Among them notched bones, clay tokens/tablets, stones, metals, leaves, barks, animal skins, and cloth were the earliest and prominent forms of writings. Their usage and form change from time to time depending upon the availability as well as nature and purpose. Prior to the invention of paper the most important writing materials were papyrus, parchment and vellum. All writing materials may be divided into two categories Inorganic, and Organic

Stones, metals, and ceramics are of inorganic nature while organic materials are wood, paper, textiles, leather, ivory, bone, feathers, and other objects derived from living beings and plants. Inorganic material is less prone to natural decay than organic material and therefore preservation of organic objects needs greater care. This does not mean however that inorganic objects are totally immune to deterioration. They also decay but at a slower rate than objects of organic materials.

4.1. History of paper

Although paper was discovered in China in About 103 AD, they kept it a very well guarded secret and paper making was not known in other countries till very late. It was eventually being made in Samarkand in the 8th century AD almost accidently. In 751 AD some Chinese were taken prisoner during the battle that was fought at Samarkand on the banks of Tharas River. It appears that amongst the Chinese prisoners there were several who knew paper-making. From them the art of paper-making was learnt by the people of Samarkand, from there the technique spread to the other neighbouring countries and cities like Baghdad, Damascus, Egypt, etc. Europeans learnt the method of paper-making almost 500 years after it was known in Samarkand.

It is difficult to point out the exact period when paper became known in India but it is widely believed that it happened in 10th or the 11th century. Before that the main writing materials in India were *bhojapatra* and palm leaf. Mellmut Lehmann Haupt says that with the invention of paper in China in about 103 AD and printing later in the 15th century, the book was born.

Writing materials have metamorphosed from the prehistoric drawings and paintings on the walls of the caves, clay tablets, stone, wood, metal, pottery, leaves, barks, leather, etc. to paper and now trendy e-documents. This journey now has a stage where paper of yester-years has altogether changed and improved to a great extent in quality. Paper is the ruling writing material and has come to stay forever now. It has invaded all walks of human life to an extent that no activity is possible without paper. Inspite of the numerous electronic writing materials, paper has proved to be the best writing material.

5. PRESERVATION OF WRITING MATERIALS IN ANCIENT TIME

Preservation of written records is apparently just as old as written records themselves. The problem of preservation of rare documents, manuscripts and old records continued since human being acquired the knowledge of writing. Deterioration of writing materials is not new phenomenon.

The early Mesopotamians were bothered about book worms which bored tunnels through soft clay writing tablets before they were hardened in the sun and even nibbled the surface of the baked tablets, defacing the markings. These clay tablets were easily chipped and broken by rough handling. They were preserved by storing them in covered jars. Then the jars were organised in a systematic order with labels affixed with straw.

Sargon I, founder of the Semitic Empire in Chaldea, established a well organised library of clay tablets which existed until the fall of Nineveh (an ancient city situated on the eastern bank of the river Tigris) when it was destroyed by burning.

In ancient China, prior to the invention of paper, wood was the most prominent material of writing. Narrow slips of wood were used for all kinds of records. Elsewhere in the East, custodians soon learned to preserve fragile palm leaf records by fastening strips of wood to each side of the bundles of palm.

Early Egyptians because of lack of clay in the Nile Valley used papyrus to manufacture a paper-like material. Superior to clay for writing, papyrus was less durable. To make it more convenient, the papyrus sheets were glued into long strips which were then rolled on wooden cylinders and wrapped in skins or cloth.

The library of Rameses II (1200 B.C.) undoubtedly contained records made of all the library materials available to the Pharaohs (rulers) at that time: clay from other lands, papyrus, palm leaves, wooden pallets, bark, linen, skins and stone. Parchment did not come into use until much later, about 200 B.C. With the exception of stone, all were vulnerable. Clay to worms; papyrus to insects, moisture and desiccation; bark, wood and palm leaves to termites; skin and linen to rot and to the cockroaches, silverfish, beetles and mud wasps that infested hot, dry land. For protection against vermin, dirt and dampness, Egyptians, Greeks and Romans stored their tightly wrapped scrolls in cylindrical boxes of wood and ivory.

Later, in the Alexandrian Library and in others in Greece and Rome, parchment and vellum had become common writing materials. The conservation problem eased somewhat because of the greater durability of lime-treated skins.

As more and more documents were created, the problems of storage increased. Even under ideal conditions, scrolls were not easy to handle or shelve and in excessively moist or dry areas. There were serious conservation problems. A dry tightly rolled parchment crumbles when unwound. Excessively moist parchment cockles badly, defacing any writing on it. Therefore it was only natural that those concerned with the making and keeping of records should investigate alternatives to the scroll and the codex form began to emerge.

Movement of people and goods in the middle age facilitated migration of the enemies of books. Book worms and fungi thrived in the entire temperate climate bordering the Mediterranean and were not unknown even in the colder countries to the North. A thirteenth century manuscript "Remedium contra Vermes Librarum" was widely circulated among the librarians.

In 993 AD, Saburibn-Ardashir's (942-1025) librarian in Bagdad used chemical to control termites. At a very early date the Chinese were using "*huangneih*" an extract from the seeds of the cork tree to ward off insects and Chinese law required that this extract be an ingredient in all paper manufactured in the kingdom. Cedar oil was widely used as insect repellent and for extra protection, volumes smeared with cedar oil were stored in tightly covered jars. Other earlier insecticides and protective devices were alum, chests of cypress wood, clay daubing, camphor, pepper, cloves and clove oil, oil of eucalyptus, musk and red myrrh. Most of them were of little value, but the fact is that early librarians were acutely aware of the importance of conservation and made intelligent efforts in this direction to ward off the book enemies.

As early as the fourth century AD, in the first organised Christian monastic community the concern for books was so great that its founder, Saint Pachomius (292-348) made book preservation one of the cardinal rules of his organisation (Ibid).

During the middle ages, there was a continuous but very gradual improvement in book making and in quality of materials. By the end of the middle age, the European book was essentially a sewn volume of parchment pages, protected by wooden boards. These wooden boards were replaced by paper boards in sixteenth century.

During seventeenth century, books had paper sides with leather spines. In the 18th century the use of decorated paper for interior and exterior designing became firmly established. It was during this time that trend towards cost cutting of books by the use of cheap materials and poor workmanship began. It was necessity to bring books within the reach of ordinary persons.

In the beginning of industrial revolution the most significant event was the evolution of codex book form. With the adoption of the codex and its simplification of handling and storage, the general trend in conservation was for the better.

With the great increase in the number of books subsequent to the invention of printing, there was a corresponding increase in the problems of caring them. Librarians and collectors were well aware of the disastrous effects of dampness and the importance of regular cleaning, frequent airing and drying by limited exposure to sunlight. In the eighteenth century learned societies and universities were offering prizes for practical solutions to the insect problems. Around 1774 ch'orine was discovered for bleaching paper. The residual chlorine bleaching compounds were not washed out of the finished product and as such book pages became acidic and brittle.

By the late nineteenth century the problems for book deterioration, with the exception of acid in paper and leather, had been identified but it was not until well into the twentieth century that truly effective preventive and curative measures began to appear.

5.1. Preservation scenario in ancient India

Manuscripts containing knowledge accumulated through ages in various subjects such as philosophy, sciences, medicine, literature, arts and the pluralistic faith systems of India are rich historical records. They portray the wisdom and experience of great thinkers and philosophers. In fact the entire account of history is still not explored or partially explored in manuscripts.

In India, the tradition of manuscript preparation, preservation and copying continued in full swing till the end of 19th century. The downward trend started from the beginning of the 20th century when printed books began gaining popularity. After Independence, the old traditions and conventions ceased to be practiced and it took a very long time to adopt new practices to preserve manuscripts. It is basically because of this vacuum in this transition period after independence that nearly half of the manuscript wealth in the country vanished away.

As the popularity of printed books started

increasing, people started taking keen interest in collecting and preserving of manuscripts in India. Some famous scholars and institutions built up and strengthened their collections with the result large repositories of manuscripts emerged which played a significant role in preservation and access to manuscripts in India.

Jains have been vastly credited for preserving manuscripts in India and they compiled the earliest known catalogue of manuscripts under the title *Brihattipanika,* as early as 1383 by an anonymous Jain saint. The original manuscript of this catalogue is still present in the *Shaninatha Bhandara.*

Jains used cloth of fine quality for preserving as well as respecting the religious works. Jain knowledge repositories used boxes made of either wood, cardboard, leather or ivory for keeping the precious collections. In order to protect the collection from moisture and worms, the exterior of the boxes was polished and the manuscripts were placed inside them and the boxes were wrapped in cloth. *Jain Granth Bhandars* a book by Kasliwal, describes that due to excessive insecurity manuscript repositories were established in Jaisalmer and chambers for safe keeping of the manuscripts were made in the basement of the Jain temples. In the event of attack, the manuscripts were shifted to these underground chambers. Such chambers can still be found in the Jain temples of Sanganer, Ajmer, Dunni, Jaisalmer, Delhi and various other temples where idols of religious deities as well as Granthas are still kept. The great name of the monastic Kavindracharya of Varanasi (Kashi) comes next. He built up a rich collection of manuscripts and compiled the subject-wise classified catalogue of 2192 manuscripts from 1628 to 1688.

Collecting manuscripts from different religions, traditions and comparing them for the purpose of writing commentaries were not unknown in ancient and medieval

India. Since the late medieval period, the emperors of Delhi and rulers of different states of India took keen interest in collecting and preserving manuscripts.

Manuscripts stands known as "*Sampada or Sampadi*" were used to hold the manuscripts while in use. These stands were introduced by Mughals. Folded stands of the yesteryears are still in use in Indian homes and temples to hold religious books like Ramayana and Sakhis (stories related to Sikh Gurus) while reading. Rich people used to get these stands made of sandalwood and beautified them with carved designs and colours.

Tippu Sultan of Mysore was among the independent rulers who built up a library of oriental manuscripts in Arabic, Persian and Hindustani languages. Local rulers under the rule of the East India Company and the British Royal Government, collected manuscripts and built up libraries. Noble rulers of Travancore, Cochin and Mysore are great names in this field. Kings of Bikaner and Jodhpur are also known to have collected manuscripts which have been documented after a very long time. The contribution of the Dogra rulers of Jammu and Kashmir in this field is also praiseworthy.

The British rulers, responsible for their efforts in spreading education and patronizing Indian traditional knowledge systems, drew their attention towards the Indian literary heritage embodied in the manuscripts. Since the establishment of the Asiatic Society in Calcutta, preservation and documentation of manuscripts began. Many government collections appeared in Calcutta, Varanasi, Pune and Madras.

Sincere efforts for survey and search for manuscripts were undertaken by Indian and European scholars in various regions of the country in 19th and 20th century. Such surveys and searches were conducted in Bengal, western, central, and northern regions.

6. PRESERVATION OF RARE RECORDS IN MODERN TIMES

In modern times various institutes, organisations, universities, archives, museums, and voluntary bodies, trusts, temples and individuals have been involved at international, national and state levels in preserving rich archival records. They have established conservation wings to undertake preventive and curative conservation treatment procedures to ancient original manuscripts and other rare documents. They are digitising rare records to make them available online. A few of them are: International Federation of Library Associations and Institutions (IFLA), National Archives of India (NAI), National Mission for Manuscripts (NMM) and Punjab Digital Library. Their vital roles in preservation and conservation of rare records have been mentioned below:

6.1. International Federation of Library Associations and Institutions (IFLA)

Founded in Edinburg (Scotland) on 30th September 1927, IFLA is the leading international body representing the interest of library and information services and their users. It is the global voice of the library and information profession. The Federation is also doing commendable work in the field of preservation and conservation of rich archival documents.

6.1.1. Activities and Groups

The most important work in IFLA happens in the various groups that make up the organisation. They are all filled with enthusiastic and dedicated people who gather materials and work to further the profession. Among the activities, programmes, sections, centres and divisions of IFLA, a few are related with preservation and conservation of rare records. They are:

6.1.1.1. Strategic Programme on Preservation and Conservation (PAC)

Created in Nairobi in 1984, the Programme focuses on issues of preservation and conservation of rare records and promotes worldwide cooperation for the preservation of manuscripts and library materials.

6.1.1.2. Preservation and Conservation Section

The Section is concerned with the preservation of the world's documentary heritage. It provides an international forum for all types of libraries to exchange, develop and disseminate knowledge and experience dealing with theories, policies and practices for the preservation of all recorded knowledge regardless the storage of medium. The section maintains a close working relationship with the IFLA PAC Strategic Programme.

6.1.1.3. Rare Book and Special Collection Section

The Section provides a platform for discussion and exchange of information regarding preservation, description and use of rare book, manuscript and special collections.

Except these activities, to preserve the manuscripts and rare documents of the world IFLA has established a number of Preservation and Conservation (PAC) Centres in different countries. Among them prominent are:

- New Preservation and Conservation (PAC) Centre for Tropical Climates and Pest Control (Sri Lanka);
- New Preservation and Conservation (PAC) Centre for Arabic speaking countries (Qatar);
- New Preservation and Conservation (PAC) Centre for Francophone Africa and oral traditions (Cameroon).

6.2. National Archives of India (NAI)

NAI is the premier national agency containing prized and precious archival records. As per the mandate of

Public Record Act of 1993 and Public Record Rules of 1997, NAI is the custodian of all non-current records of the Union Government of India and its predecessor bodies as also the former British Residencies in the erstwhile Indian princely states. It holds the records embodying rare and invaluable content. It may be said that it is a place where researchers and administrators have a peep into the past of India with the help of social, cultural, political, economical and historical documentary heritage.

The NAI owes its genesis to the Imperial Records Department which came into existence in March 1891 at Calcutta (Kolkata). After the transfer of capital from Calcutta to New Delhi in 1911, it shifted to its present site in 1926. Imperial Records Department was re-christened as National Archives of India on 30th August 1947. Today it is referred to as the Delhi's most intellectual destination and is an attached office of the Ministry of Culture, Government of India. It has a regional office at Bhopal and three record centres at Pondichery, Bhubaneswar and jaipur.

6.2.1. Mission

The Archive strives hard to help in spreading a sense of national pride in our documentary cultural heritage and ensuring its preservation for the future generation. The broad objectives of NAI are:

- To encourage scientific management, maintenance and conservation of records;
- To build up closer relations between archivists, archival institutions and archival profession in India and overseas;
- To encourage access to available holdings;
- To develop professionalism and a scientific temperament among curators, custodians and users;
- To ensure proper and appropriate care and use of documentary heritage.

6.2.2. Facilities

To fulfil the aforesaid objectives and to facilitate the work of research scholars, the NAI has a well equipped air-conditioned research room and the Conservation Research Laboratory. To make available the holdings, guides, press lists, subject lists, catalogues, etc. are provided so that information seekers may find their desired records at ease. The Archive provides the following facilities:

- Reprographic services on payment basis;
- Conservation techniques, research and guidance;
- Professional guidance in restoration and repair of documents;
- Advice on records management.

In nutshell, it may be said that being national agency NAI serves as the custodian of rare records and is sincerely dedicated to the welfare and development of archives and archival profession.

6.3. National Mission for Manuscripts (NMM)

To preserve manuscript treasure, the National Mission for Manuscripts was inaugurated on 7th February 2003 by honourable former Prime Minister and noted writer Atal Bihari Vajapayee. It was under the Tenth Five Year Plan that a sweeping initiative was announced. The Ministry of Tourism and Culture, Government of India established it with Indira Gandhi National Centre for the Arts (IGNCA) as its nodal agency. Its aim is to collect and preserve the manuscripts available in any nook and corners of the country so as to preserve the lone copies of manuscripts available in *deras*, *mathas*, individuals, temples, etc. It is doing a yeoman's job in collecting, digitising and preparing a national electronic database (*Kriti Sampada*) of all the manuscripts available in the country.

6.3.1. Objectives

The major objectives of the Mission are:

- To survey, document and catalogue Indian manuscripts in India and abroad;
- To compile a national database of manuscripts;
- To facilitate conservation and preservation of manuscripts through training, awareness and financial support;
- To provide ready access to the manuscripts through digitisation and publication;
- To promote scholarship and research in the study of Indian languages and Manuscriptology;
- To set up a National Manuscript Library.

To accomplish these objectives, the Mission functions through different types of centres established throughout the country. These are Manuscript Conservation Centres (MCCs), Manuscript Resource Centres (MRCs), Manuscript Partner Centres (MPCs), and Manuscript Conservation Partner Centres.

6.4. Punjab Digital Library (PDL)

Punjab Digital Library (PDL) project was initiated in the year 2003 at Chandigarh. It was started as a stepping stone with its motto *"Revealing the invisible heritage of Punjab"*. It was established with a mission to locate, preserve, document and digitise the lost or disappearing heritage of manuscripts and other rare records of Punjab region. To promote lifelong learning and open access, the PDL is doing marvellous job in digitisation of valuable records such as manuscripts, rare documents, books, magazines, photographs, newspapers, etc. It also provides other services like data mining, sharing, uploading, preservation, exhibitions and training programmes on digitisation.

Started as a non-profit and non-governmental

organisation in 2003-04 with a meagre budget of 10,000 and staff strength of only two people, it digitised only 5000 pages per month but gradually the capacity escalated to 25,000 pages per month in the very next year 2005-06. It did not accept any financial assistance from any outside agency but the increasing operational costs forced the PDL to accept donation from 2007 onwards and from that year the productivity was raised to 5000 pages per a single day.

The digitised collection of manuscripts at PDL dates back to 15th century on various subjects containing theology, history, philosophy, religion, language and literature, etc. in different scripts and languages with a thrust on Gurmukhi. Thousands of manuscripts have been digitised so far it includes 1000 sacred scriptures of Guru Granth Sahib and among them the oldest one is of 1653. Besides Gurmukhi, manuscripts in Sharda, Devnagri, Urdu, Sanskrit and Persian scripts and languages have also been digitised. A complete metadata is available with PDL for each of the digitised manuscript containing title, year, description, keyword, script, language, author, custodian, status, pages.

7. CONCLUSION

Manuscripts and other rare documents have always preserved the documentary and cultural heritage of our ancestors and these special documents are the prized possessions of every nation. These are the basic historical evidences and have great research value. Thus these valuable records are required to be preserved and conserved for posterity. It is through the human effort of preservation that frontiers of human knowledge and human civilizations have been extended. The successful preservation of history is the bedrock of current human information, knowledge and civilization.

REFERENCES

- Agrawal, O.P. & Barkeshli, Mandana (1997). *Conservation of books, manuscripts and paper documents.* Lucknow: Indian Council of Conservation Institute.
- Agrawal, O.P. (1993). *Preservation of art objects and library materials.* New Delhi: National Book Trust.
- Chakaraborti, M.L. (1975). *Bibliography in theory and practice.* Calcutta: The World Press Private Limited.
- Diringer, David (1972). Alphabet. In *Encyclopedia Americana.* New York: Americana Corporation, Vol. 1, p. 168.
- Gupta, K.K. (2010). *Rare support materials for manuscripts and their conservation.* New Delhi: National Mission for Manuscripts.
- Haupt, Mellmut Lehmann (1972). Book. In *Encyclopedia Americana.* New York: Americana Corporation, Vol. 4, p. 220.
- Mukherjee, B.B. (1973). *Preservation of library materials, archives and documents.* Calcutta: The World Press Private Ltd.
- Narang, Asha (2006). *Care and preservation of library documents in universities, archives and colleges of Punjab, Haryana and Chandigarh.* (Ph.D thesis). Amritsar: Guru Nanak Dev University.
- Rattan, Pardeep (2013). Role of Punjab Digital Library in digitizing manuscripts: A case study. *Library Philosophy and Practice* (e-journal).
- Sukhdev Singh (2015). Preservation and conservation of manuscripts and rare documents in National Archives of India and National Mission for Manuscripts: Problems and prospects. (Ph.D Thesis). Amritsar: Guru Nanak Dev University.
- Wright, Alex (2007). *Glut: Mastering information through the ages.* Washington, D.C.: Joseph Henry Press.
- www.home-school.com/ Articles/WholeLangGloss.html
- www.ifla.org
- www.namami.org
- www.nationalarchives.nic.in